Observability Engineering with Cilium

Observability Magic in the Cloud-Native Journey with Hubble and Tetragon

Dr. Mehdi Ghane

Apress®

Observability Engineering with Cilium: Observability Magic in the Cloud-Native Journey with Hubble and Tetragon

Dr. Mehdi Ghane
Frankfurt, Germany

ISBN-13 (pbk): 979-8-8688-1257-6 ISBN-13 (electronic): 979-8-8688-1258-3
https://doi.org/10.1007/979-8-8688-1258-3

Managing Director, Apress Media LLC: Welmoed Spahr
Acquisitions Editors: James Robinson-Prior, Divya Modi
Editorial Assistant: Jacob Shmulewitz

Cover designed by eStudioCalamar

Cover image by Gerd Altmann from Pixabay

Distributed to the book trade worldwide by Springer Science+Business Media New York, 1 New York Plaza, New York, NY 10004. Phone 1-800-SPRINGER, fax (201) 348-4505, e-mail orders-ny@springer-sbm.com, or visit www.springeronline.com. Apress Media, LLC is a Delaware LLC and the sole member (owner) is Springer Science + Business Media Finance Inc (SSBM Finance Inc). SSBM Finance Inc is a **Delaware** corporation.

For information on translations, please e-mail booktranslations@springernature.com; for reprint, paperback, or audio rights, please e-mail bookpermissions@springernature.com.

Apress titles may be purchased in bulk for academic, corporate, or promotional use. eBook versions and licenses are also available for most titles. For more information, reference our Print and eBook Bulk Sales web page at http://www.apress.com/bulk-sales.

Any source code or other supplementary material referenced by the author in this book is available to readers on GitHub. For more detailed information, please visit https://www.apress.com/gp/services/source-code.

If disposing of this product, please recycle the paper

To Tara

Table of Contents

About the Author

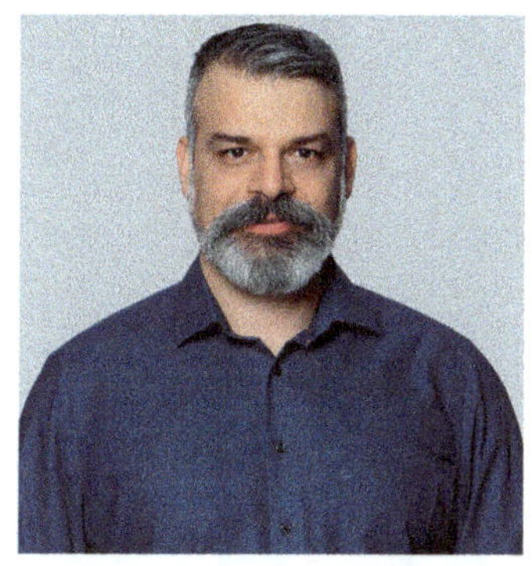

Dr. Mehdi Ghane A cloud-native and DataCenter delivery director with a focus on FinOps, value engineering, operation coaching, and modern delivery practices. Over the years, Mehdi has contributed to both DataCenter and cloud landscapes, specializing in cloud-native delivery with an emphasis on observability, scalability, and hybrid cloud infrastructure.

He is passionate regarding mentoring at the intersection of sociotechnical and socioeconomic systems, helping teams navigate complex challenges and deliver meaningful outcomes. Mehdi holds a PhD in DataCenter Energy Engineering and serves as Professor of Engineering Mathematics and Scientific Computing in state universities. His academic work includes authoring textbooks, publishing research papers, and conducting workshops on topics such as DataCenter consolidation, reliability engineering, and computational science.

Based in Frankfurt, Mehdi has held various roles, including CIO, Design Manager, Technology Architect, Engineering Manager, and Principal SRE. He has had the privilege of contributing to hyperscalers, capital markets and financial institutions, and other mission-critical infrastructure operations and DataCenter projects including AI-Native Base of Design. For more information, visit his LinkedIn page `https://www.linkedin.com/in/mehdighane/`.

About the Technical Reviewer

Shivakumar R. Goniwada is a renowned author, inventor, and technology leader with more than 26 years of experience in architecting cutting-edge cloud-native, data analytics, and event-driven systems. He currently holds a position as Chief Enterprise Architect at Accenture, where he leads a team of highly skilled technology enterprise and cloud architects. Throughout his career, Shivakumar has successfully led numerous complex projects across various industries and geographical locations. His expertise has earned him ten software patents in areas such as cloud computing, polyglot architecture, software engineering, and IoT. He is a sought-after speaker at global conferences and has made significant contributions to the field through his publications. Shivakumar holds a degree in Engineering and has earned certifications in Google Professional, AWS, and data science. He has also completed an Executive MBA at the prestigious MIT Sloan School of Management. His notable books include *Cloud-Native Architecture and Design*, *Introduction to Datafication*, and *Introduction to One Digital Identity*, all published by Apress.

Introduction

This book was born out of high demand of the cloud-native microservice platform and frustration with Kubernetes networking issues and incomplete resources that failed to address the modern world challenges of observability. With *Observability Engineering with Cilium,* I aim to fill that gap, providing you with a strategic preceptive and technical toolkit that goes beyond what vendor manuals or AI assistants can offer. Whether you're troubleshooting your production Kubernetes cluster or leading a global team through digital transformation in the financial sector, this book is your companion for mastering the complex, exciting, and ever-changing world of cloud-native observability.

Welcome to a journey of discovery, innovation, and excellence. Are you ready to unlock the full potential of Kubernetes and cloud service providers and elevate your engineering service capabilities? Let's dive in!

In today's fast-paced world of software development and IT operations, cloud-native technologies have opened the door to incredible opportunities while also presenting new challenges. These innovations bring unmatched agility, scalability, and efficiency but also introduce complexity, especially when managing microservices in hybrid cloud environments. Traditional monitoring, even when rebranded as observability engineering, often falls short due to outdated design philosophy and use case. This is where cloud-native observability platforms step in as game changers, bringing order to the chaos and ensuring your systems not only operate efficiently but truly thrive.

Observability Engineering with Cilium is not another technical manual or a coding book. It's a comprehensive guide designed to bridge the gap between theory and practice, helping you navigate the intricate landscape of cloud-native environments with confidence. Whether you're a seasoned engineer or a decision maker exploring the next leap in cloud-native observability, this book offers actionable insights and real-world strategies by critically understanding and applying Cilium and eBPF resource.

Cilium, powered by eBPF (extended Berkeley Packet Filter), is at the forefront of this transformation. Originally designed to address the networking and policy challenges in Kubernetes environments, Cilium has evolved into a versatile stack that brings unprecedented visibility and control over distributed systems. This book dives deep into how you can leverage Cilium and its ecosystem (including Hubble, Tetragon, plus other tools like Grafana Beyla) to create an observability platform that is not just robust but revolutionary.

Unlike other resources, this book doesn't teach you *where and how* to install tools; it empowers you to understand *what and why* they matter in the larger context of cloud-native evolution. You'll explore

- The philosophical and historical context of cloud-native computing and observability
- A road map for transitioning from basic monitoring to a cloud-native observability engineer, mastering the art of uncovering hidden system behaviors
- Strategic insights into aligning observability efforts with business outcomes, tackling socioeconomic and sociotechnical shifts head-on

This book is not a vendor-sponsored marketing piece. It is rooted in my personal experiences, insights, and independent research within the domains of cloud-native transformation and observability engineering. While I delve into tools like Cilium, Grafana, and others, my evaluations and recommendations are grounded in firsthand use cases, unbiased guidance, and professional expertise, not driven by affiliations or sponsorships. Additionally, I have drawn upon a wide array of resources, papers, and research to further inform my analysis and provide a comprehensive, validated, and well-rounded perspective.

I'm eager to learn from your journey in cloud-native transformation, your challenges, successes, and lessons learned. Your observability engineering stories, challenges with hybrid cloud platforms, and feedback are not only valuable but also help foster a deeper understanding of this evolving field. Feel free to connect with me and share your thoughts at `https://www.linkedin.com/in/mehdighane`.

CHAPTER 1

The Groundwork

A well-defined scope and a structured path turn dreams into achievable milestones.

In this chapter, we will delve into the blueprint, structure, essence, and roots that make Cilium and cloud-native observability approach a perfect match. We explore the strategic distinctions between the contents of Cilium configuration repositories, blogs, technical manuals, and documentations in relation to the primary objectives of this book. Additionally, we discuss the factors influencing the decision to adopt Cilium into your platform, covering both technical and nontechnical requirements outlined. Finally, we review the structured learning path designed to enhance your understanding and implementation of Cilium and how to efficiently utilize other available online resources and books. A guideline on how this book's content will tactically support your journey with Cilium, eBPF, and cloud-native observability will be provided.

This chapter will cover the following topics:

- Adopting Cilium is a strategy-dependent decision
- Decision matrix and logical dependencies and risks
- The knowledge tree of cloud-native observability engineering

Dr. M. Ghane, *Observability Engineering with Cilium*,
https://doi.org/10.1007/979-8-8688-1258-3_1

Hello Cilium World!

Technology-related content often starts with easy-to-follow technical tasks that yield fast visible results. These initial steps are usually followed by printed code lines, and if we're lucky, those codes are mapped to a dedicated GitHub repository. However, I've encountered many books where, after a few basic code snippets, the next offered code no longer works, the books' referenced repository is not maintained and is outdated, and there are missing dependencies or poorly scripted codes, requiring hours of troubleshooting. This frustration has led me to skip chapters or even abandon entire books.

Nowadays, we have tools like ChatGPT and Copilot to write and debug code and YAML files and answer precise questions. Most open source tools also have chatbots to assist with troubleshooting. This raises the question: *Do we really need a book to learn how to use a tool?* The calm answer might be: not essentially, especially for well-documented tool stacks like Cilium, Grafana, Kubernetes, or Linux. The wiser answer, however, is more nuanced: when you have all key technical and nontechnical requirements identified, prepared, evaluated, and your success metrics well-established, you can likely find all the technical know-how you need from freely available resources, including community and vendor-based technical manuals and AI assistants.

These resources are typically tested across numerous scenarios and platforms, maintained, and updated by large teams of community and paid experts. Contrasting many books or YouTube channels with dedicated GitHub repositories, freely accessible vendor-backed sites offer up-to-date and reliable information. Replication of these code bases and contents into a book format is unnecessary. In my opinion, if you cannot find an answer related to working with their tools in these resources and AI assistants, it is unlikely you will find it in a book.

On the other hand, it's rare to find a comprehensive, **human-centric**, solution-agnostic list of technical and nontechnical requirements, deployment maturity metrics, growth plans, risk registers, and master and action plans in any of these vendor-backed sites. For example, Grafana's website focuses on its stack products, manuals, learning content, use cases, and free and commercial services. The same goes for Cilium, AWS, Azure, GCP, and others, where the primary focus is on increasing the user base and resolving onboarding issues. However, none of these resources extend support for the pivotal first steps, such as understanding your company culture and acknowledging nontechnical requirements and risks. Their business models revolve around enticing you to adopt their services, not inspecting your existing organizational structure nor highlighting the risks of failure, product debt, organizational debt, technical debt, or maybe technical bankruptcy.

This information gap is precisely what *Observability Engineering with Cilium* aims to address. The goal is to move beyond replicating the tools manual and delve into the under-addressed aspects of observability engineering for cloud-native deployments. Firstly, it aims to provide a clear understanding of what can be tagged as cloud-native environments. What is the relation of cloud-native with microservice and cloud service providers with DataCenters? Throughout, we demystify key definitions and paradigms and shed light on the socioeconomic and sociotechnical change, Conway's law, maturity models, and the less-discussed aspects to guide you in designing, building, and operating the comprehensive observability platform, leveraging technologies like Kubernetes, service mesh, and eBPF and tools like Cisco Cilium, Hubble, Tetragon, Prometheus, OpenTelemetry, Cribl, Splunk, Pixie, Falco, Grafana Beyla, and Alloy.

KEY NOTE

While this book contains only a few lines of code, YAML, or commands, readers are strongly encouraged to refer to freely available official web sources for technical content, which are continuously updated. The main focus is to deliver strategic and engineering knowledge that helps to plan, design, build, and operate the cloud-native observability platform with eBPF-based auto-instrumentation approaches using Cilium stack.

So far, I have used many buzzwords without even defining them! It's ok; I will describe them in detail in the next few chapters.

Are You Ready to Jump In?

I promise to introduce Cilium and eBPF background from scratch later in this book. But for now, let's take a quick glance at them. Cilium is nothing but a perfect complement product to most of cloud-native architectures. It's the most powerful use case of eBPF and honestly the most successful use case of eBPF so far. Let's see what eBPF is and why it is adopted massively in recent years!

You know, technologies are often invented when there is a big problem or a chain of problems somewhere. In this case, the chain of big five problems started in Linux kernel release and lifecycle, which is too slow; production-grade Kubernetes networking, which is a nightmare; reliable tracing distributed traffics, which are resource consuming; and lack of a single source of truth for policy-making and visibility. eBPF was invented to help those issues generally, later a group of eBPF creators built Cilium on top of eBPF for the cloud-native market to relieve these pains in production grade. In 2024, Cisco acquired Isovalent, the creator of Cilium which was founded by the team of talented engineers and business professionals.

In next few chapters, you will gain insights to design, build, and operate cloud-native observability platform, incorporating elegant technologies, tools, and concepts like event-driven microservice, art of silent alerting, Conway's law, dynamic distributed tracing, Cilium mesh, unified policies as code, and service flow visualization. Don't worry, we will talk about these problems in this book and you will see how Cilium stack helps.

In the dynamic realm of software deployment, the rise of cloud-native technologies has transformed technological and cultural standards. This shift, while bringing innovation and agility, also introduces paradigms and complexities with the interplay of microservices in on-premises, multi-, and hybrid cloud. The Cilium stack is a versatile toolbox applicable to various use cases. Our focus is on exploring how to overcome observability engineering challenges in production, extending even beyond Kubernetes. To address these challenges, observability engineering (often referred to as O11y, similar to K8s for Kubernetes; it's O and 11 other letters ending with Y and pronounced like Ollie) is now a necessity crucial for survival in the competitive world of Industry 4.0, AI enabled, cloud-native and very soon AI Native. In the end, you'll transition from a conventional application monitoring specialist to a sophisticated cloud-native observability engineer.

Where Is My Holistic Mindset?

Observability is a key concept in modern software systems, borrowed from other engineering disciplines. Cloud-native is another crucial type of software and service architecture which has roots in cloud and DataCenter disciplines. Imagine cloud-native environment as a football game in a stadium, with many players, spectators, and cameras. Observability acts as the referee team, ensuring the game is played fairly and transparently. Cilium, in this analogy, is the VAR (Video Assistant Referee). If not used correctly, it can complicate things. However, when employed by a skilled referee at the right moment, it provides decisive and clear insights.

Cilium is not a golden hammer, but it's important to understand that adopting Cilium in production does not automatically ensure that your software or service is observable. Similarly, deploying a fully microservice-based application in a well-managed cloud does not necessarily qualify as a true Cloud-Native 1.0 environment (details on this will be provided later, I promise!). However, in an original Cloud-Native 1.0 environment, services are inherently observable, and Cilium can be a critical tool for achieving this.

Socioeconomic Change and Cilium

The era of cheap money for startups ended with the COVID blackout. These days, entrepreneurs cannot easily find investors who bear with them for years waiting for a light! MVP and first paid clients for months. They want things agile; fail fast is acceptable. Entrepreneurs have a unique skill of adaptation. They understand the importance of testing business ideas in a real scenario, observing the risk, scale, and do them all as fast as possible. All seconds and euros count. Cloud-native application architecture is created to answer this need. Almost all enterprises constantly strive to find the **equilibrium of speed and risk**. Cilium is one of the sociotechnical triggers that influence cloud-native business risk mitigation and stabilize this new business model and lifestyle.

Sociotechnical Changes and Cilium

I will later explain how cloud service providers have disrupted traditional DataCenter and how cloud-native solutions have transformed the landscape dominated by hyperscalers. This shift has addressed challenges with hybrid clouds and, in some cases, has even encouraged **service repatriation**. Cloud-native architectures have also significantly impacted developers' workflows. The interconnection between human life and technology has created a ripple effect, leading to profound changes in the software landscape. Cilium is one of the sociotechnical sparks that facilitate the human supervision and policy-making roles in a chaotic distributed service traffic.

Mapping Out the Itinerary

In Chapter 2, "Cloud-Native Phenomena," and Chapter 3, "Cloud-Native Maturity Models," I will describe the historical developments that have led us to the ***cloud-native*** era. This information and critical perspective can help strategic decision-makers gain a better understanding of trends and deeper insights into current hypes. In Chapter 4, "Observability Engineering Fundamentals," and Chapter 5, "Instrumentation Engineering Fundamentals," I will outline the landscape of ***observability*** and its older sister, ***instrumentation***. These essentials help technical leaders, CIOs, and CTOs devise effective growth plans and invest resources wisely.

If you are not currently in a strategic position or do not anticipate being in one soon, but are interested in learning about Cilium functionalities, you can skip directly to Chapter 6, "Demystifying Cilium's Spellbinding Nature," and continue to Chapter 9, "Observing the Unseen with Cilium and Grafana," where I explain how the Cilium stack and other key toolsets can empower a production-grade observability platform.

But the story doesn't end there. Cilium is not the only player on this stage. If you understand the context of Chapters 1 through 5 but cannot use Cilium community edition nor enterprise edition for any reason, there are other tools to consider. Chapter 10, "Cilium Outstanding, Yet Not Alone," discusses these alternatives. Let's dive in!

Summary

The chapter begins by establishing why Cilium is ideally suited for cloud-native observability. I discuss the strategic rationale for adopting Cilium and emphasize aligning it with observability objectives in cloud-native environments. Factors influencing the decision to implement Cilium, both technical and nontechnical, are explored.

The primary goal of the book is to fill gaps left by existing resources, offering insights into strategic and engineering aspects of observability. This includes understanding cloud-native environments, microservices relationships, and the socioeconomic and sociotechnical changes influencing technology adoption. This work target is to offer a comprehensive guide for designing and operating an observability platform using Cilium and related tools, with a strategic focus on assessing risks, benefits, and costs.

Cilium is introduced as a powerful application of eBPF, addressing major challenges in Kubernetes networking, which we will talk about later, and observability. It outlines the issues eBPF and Cilium tackle, such as slow Linux kernel updates and the complexities of distributed traffic tracing. Cilium's main value proposition lies in providing deep, cost-effective, and reliable 360-degree service visibility at the kernel level and serving as a single source of truth for action and traffic policy-making. These two values strengths captured the interest of Cisco leadership.

Cloud-native technologies are transforming software deployment standards, bringing new complexities, particularly in hybrid and multi-cloud environments. These changes affect business risk mitigation and developer workflows, highlighting the need for adaptable cloud-native architectures. Cilium is portrayed as a catalyst in these transformations, supporting effective policy-making and supervision in complex environments. Effective observability engineering becomes crucial for managing these complexities, with Cilium playing a vital role. In the next chapters, I will guide you from basic monitoring to advanced cloud-native observability.

CHAPTER 2

Cloud-Native Phenomena

Defining the goal is half the battle; unveiling the required change completes it.

In this chapter, we will learn about the impact of cloud-native and microservice architecture on the IT industry, as well as its implications for other businesses and people's lives, which is remarkable. We will conduct a thorough review and analysis of this trend from a philosophical perspective.

This chapter will cover the following topics:

- Role of DataCenter business in Industry 4.0
- The emergence of cloud computing industry
- Introducing Cloud-Native 1.0
- Cloud transformation with 10 R's framework
- Secrets of a 12-factor container

Dr. M. Ghane, *Observability Engineering with Cilium*,
https://doi.org/10.1007/979-8-8688-1258-3_2

The Industrial Revolution Timeline

Before delving into the concept of "cloud-native ontology," let's briefly touch on the history of computing technology from the Industrial Revolution timeline to the current state of Industry 4.0. However, I understand that not everyone may find the exploration of engineering philosophy and history appealing these days. So let's keep it concise. First, let us understand what the Industrial Revolution is all about.

The **industrial revolutions** were periods of significant *socioeconomic* and *sociotechnical* change characterized by the emergence of new manufacturing processes, increased mechanization, the transformation of economies, and dataism. There were four main industrial revolutions:

- **First Industrial Revolution (Late 18th to Early 19th Century):** Marked by the transition from agrarian economies to industrialized ones, powered by the mechanization of textile production and the use of *steam power*. In this era, mechanized agrarian practices revolutionized human societies, triggering profound lifestyle transformations. The advent of mechanization ushered in an array of new employment opportunities and business avenues, catalyzing unprecedented economic growth. Concurrently, industries with limited adaptability found themselves migrating toward obsolescence, gradually retreating into the annals of history.
- **Second Industrial Revolution (Mid-19th to Early 20th Century):** Notable for the expansion of industries like steel, railroads, and electricity. It saw the development of mass production, the telegraph, and the beginning of the *assembly line*. The conventional understanding of work and productivity has undergone

a significant upgrade. The antiquated mindset of "*what worked before will work tomorrow*" has been cast aside by forward-thinking businessmen.

- **Third Industrial Revolution (Late 20th Century):** Characterized by the rise of electronics, computers, robotics, and automation. In this new era, a flag of innovation flies high, symbolizing the dawn of a groundbreaking business model: the *DataCenter*. Hidden within its walls lies the clandestine chamber of innovation, where the secrets of thriving enterprises are safeguarded. As time unfurls, telecommunications service providers ascend to dominance, shaping and nurturing this burgeoning market by erecting numerous multitenant DataCenters, each a bastion of network, processing, and data storage advancement. The use of information technology and the development of the Internet played a significant role. The advent of ***computerization*** has permeated both business operations and daily human life. Once more, technology has supplanted traditional labor roles, reshaping the workforce landscape.
- **Fourth Industrial Revolution (Ongoing, Starting in the Late 20th Century):** Involves the integration of cloud services, digital technologies, artificial intelligence, and the Internet of Things (IoT) into various aspects of industry and society, leading to increased connectivity, availability, and automation. In this round, the focus transcends mere computerization; it delves into the profound impact of ***digitalization*** with agile delivery by *cloud* service providers. Embracing advancements such as LLM models,

Tabular AI, image processing, and the expansive domain of big data, we step into the era of dataism – a realm defined by transformative data and related sociotechnical prowess. Here's where we stand now. Let's delve further into the key components of our contemporary epoch.

Key Components of Industry 4.0

Industry 4.0 encompasses several key components and aspects that drive its transformational impact on manufacturing, human lifestyle, and other industries.

Some of the key components include

- **Big Data, Machine Learning, Artificial Intelligence (AI), and Deep Analytics:** The vast amount of data generated by social media, DLT platforms, Digital Twin, connected devices and machines, and Web 2.0 and Web 3.0 traffics is analyzed using sophisticated algorithms to learn, adapt, and perform tasks without explicit rigid programming. Utilizing data analysis enables lightning-fast, data-driven decision-making, streamlining processes, enhancing overall efficiency, and, of course, exponentially accelerating the growth rate of DataCenters.
- **Cyber-Physical Systems (CPS):** This involves the integration of physical systems with digital technologies, mainly cloud-based services. Machines and devices are connected via the IoT (Internet of Things) devices and sensors embedded within machines and products collect data, allowing for monitoring, analysis, and remote control. This interconnected network enables

data-driven decision-making, enabling communication and data exchange, often in real time, and boosts the DataCenter's growth rate again.

- **Augmented Reality (AR), Virtual Reality (VR), Additive Manufacturing, and 3D Printing:** These technologies are used for training, simulation, and maintenance, providing immersive experiences that enhance productivity and reduce errors and rapid prototyping and production of complex components, leading to more flexible and customized manufacturing. Organically increased the demands for more DataCenters.
- **Cloud Computing:** The quiddity and utility of DataCenter, which originated during the Industry 3.0 era and experienced exponential growth during the Industry 4.0 revolution, have profoundly impacted human societies, business paradigms, geopolitical landscapes, and strategic development plans. Pioneer DataCenter service providers offered computing, storage, and networking facilities "as a service" on demand. This business model was later named *cloud services*. Originally, the term "*cloud*" stemmed from conventional Internet access diagrams, where a symbolic cloud was drawn at the center of diagrams to represent the Internet, with other sites connected to it. While this depiction was quite literal, today, "***cloud***" has evolved into a distinct and well-defined concept with various interpretations and variations. There are six major architectures of cloud platforms currently: *public, multi-cloud, community cloud, edge distributed cloud, private,* and *hybrid*. We will describe them later in detail.

To envision Industry 4.0 from a strategic perspective, one could assert that any society incapable of effectively managing and harnessing its data and information systems stands at a distinct disadvantage when it comes to competing with others in the contemporary global landscape. The availability of high-quality data-driven services has become as crucial as classic roles of oil on the international energy and politics stage. Data and information systems are intricately woven into the fabric of economies and society structures, and political dynamics. The pervasive religion of the world today is ***dataism***. So where are the temples of dataism? The answer is **DataCenters**.

DATACENTER

Not every location with a bunch of servers in rows of racks can be considered a DataCenter. Imagine a well-balanced supersystem of ***operational technology (OT)*** and ***information and communications technology (ICT)*** resources fortified by fit-for-purpose physical structures, utilities, facilities, energy transmission and storage, heat management (cooling), data networks, security, and safety systems, all equipped with control and observability capabilities. When this supersystem and its collective framework designed to deliver information services to authorized users while meeting the specified Service-Level Agreements (SLAs), named DataCenter. Various terms such as 'Data Center', 'Data Centre', 'Datacentre', 'Server Room', 'Computing Centre', 'Data Hotel', 'Data Hub' and even 'Data Hall' are often used interchangeably, although they may differ slightly in scope or regional usage. I would like to adhere to the ***DataCenter*** format and writing style throughout this book.

DataCenters: The Unsung Hero of Industry 4.0

DataCenter, often regarded as the sanctum of the Information Era, came into existence during the late 20th century to mainly host mainframes. During that time, DataCenters were meticulously designed, constructed, and operated by vendor-accredited engineers, primarily located in headquarters. This model proved to be perfect for mainframe manufacturers like IBM, allowing them to offer long-term vendor lock-in services and revenue streams, especially when the second active site, standby sites, disaster recovery sites, and cold backup sites were mission critical and crucial.

Two decades later, the next generation of computing processes became ubiquitous worldwide, and mainframe-based applications gradually evolved into x86-based applications. along with many newly designed software. However, this transformation was not without challenges. At least two major obstacles impeded its progress. The first was a widespread misunderstanding of the complex relationship between infrastructure redundancy and service reliability. The second was the dominance of monopolistic hardware vendors who resisted open transformation. The first one was marked as a favorable period for DataCenter infrastructure industry (electrical, mechanical, and OT equipment manufacturing), mainly with Uptime Institute Tier I to IV classification system and EIA/TIA 942 rated 1 to 4 concepts of redundancy and later ANSI/BICSI 002 Facility class F0 to F4 superficial analysis. Let me call it a *historical entertaining mathematical misunderstanding in reliability engineering*: An excessive focus on OT and infrastructure redundancies occurs alongside insufficient attention to modern ICT, software, and virtualization technologies capabilities. For over three decades, this persistent misconception has served as the benchmark for market leaders in DataCenter construction, bringing significant profits to infrastructure vendors including power distribution system, genset, batteries and UPS, chiller and cooling systems, racks, cabling, and other vendors. That, later significantly challenged by BICSI 002:2019, EN 50600, and ISO/IEC 22237, underwent substantial evolution. The second major obstacle to DataCenter transformation lies in the entrenched control of legacy hardware empires. These companies tend to release new products only after their current flagship offerings have reached peak sales and when there is strong, often carefully engineered, demand for higher-performance solutions. In many cases, performance ceilings are intentionally built into products through hardware or software restrictions, as part of a licensing strategy that locks advanced capabilities behind future version of products. This deliberate throttling creates artificial bottlenecks, ensuring a predictable upgrade cycle and sustained stable revenue streams. Although this model has long been tolerated in traditional enterprise IT environments, it was significantly disrupted by the Open Compute Project (OCP). OCP sparked a fundamental shift in DataCenter design by promoting open standards, greater hardware efficiency, and a transparent, collaborative development model, directly challenging the closed, vendor-controlled ecosystems that had previously dominated the industry. However, during that time, mainframes held certain unfair advantages, such as central management, native virtualization, and process segregation, which slowed down the adoption of x86 platforms in some of iconic DataCenters. Later, when virtualization hypervisors, clustering, **HPC,** and **SDN** (**Software-Defined Networking**) technology providers like VMware and OpenStack matured that the era of mainframes began to fade, making way for the rise of cloud providers like Amazon AWS and Microsoft Azure and Google GCP. My earlier phrasing was, "*cloud transformation*" along with *dataism,* is a key mainstream force in the Fourth Industrial Revolution, marking a major sociotechnical and socioeconomic milestone. I have frequently referenced the term "*dataism*" throughout this chapter. Now, it's imperative to delve deeper into its origins and trajectory to gain a fuller understanding of its significance.

DATAISM

Dataism is a concept that emphasizes the increasing importance of data in contemporary society, suggesting that data is becoming the fundamental substrate of the world. Coined by the philosopher and historian Yuval Noah Harari in *Homo Deus: A Brief History of Tomorrow*, dataism proposes that the value and significance of entities, including individuals and organizations, are increasingly determined by their ability to generate and manipulate data. In the era of dataism, the immense volume of data generated by various digital interactions, sensors, and devices is seen as the key driver of insights, decision-making, and progress.

The key value propositions of dataism lie in its potential to harness and analyze vast amounts of data to derive meaningful patterns, correlations, and insights. This approach enables more informed decision-making, personalized user experiences, and advancements in fields such as artificial intelligence and machine learning or lets name it as AI-Native model. Dataism emphasizes the efficiency and effectiveness of data-driven processes, fostering innovation and optimization across diverse sectors. However, it also raises important considerations related to privacy, security, and ethical use of data, as the reliance on data in decision-making becomes more pervasive. As organizations increasingly embrace dataism, balancing the benefits with responsible and ethical data practices becomes crucial to harnessing its full potential.

Unveiling the Public Cloud Ontology: It's simply someone else's DataCenter!

From a technological standpoint, a typical cloud service provider can be seen as a multi-location facility class 1 or 2 DataCenter service provider, incorporating virtualized computing services and augmenting its offerings with outsourced provisioning and reliability wherever feasible.

Cloud computing transcends mere technological progress; it embodies a transformative business paradigm that adopts innovation, scalability, and agility. While this represents a significant operational shift, the fundamental technological landscape remains largely unchanged!

Given that cloud provision is essentially a business model facilitating the dissemination of distributed DataCenter services more efficiently and swiftly through public networks, *why does it warrant recognition as a disruptive force in computing history?* To excel in industrial revolutions and commercial competitions, enterprises constantly strive to find the equilibrium of *speed* and *risk*.

What does a CEO desire? Most likely, it's the ability to implement requested changes rapidly, reduce costs, pivot swiftly, respond to market demands promptly, expedite market entry, and minimize risk management, cost structure transparency, and outsourcing non-core functions heavy lifting, all while aiming for a quick exit when time comes. Public cloud providers offer a more favorable speed and risk equilibrium compared to traditional DataCenter service providers in the market with metered pricing, so you pay only for the resources you consume. Naturally, cloud service providers win. That's a **Darwinism game rule**.

So far, it may seem that I am attempting to undermine the perceived magic of cloud providers and critiquing the Tier classification DataCenter contraction business concepts. However, as an experienced DataCenter technology architect who has constructed numerous DataCenters globally for large enterprises, public sector, and hyperscale cloud providers, I possess a deep understanding of this ecosystem. Considering the focus of this chapter, it's important to note numerous remarkable iconic innovations and value propositions within the DataCenter construction industry and the realm of hyperscale cloud providers that have not been addressed here. You might find further insights in my other works, such as *DataCenter Project and Agile Delivery Management Handbook, AI Native DataCenter Base of Design*, and *MLOps Computing*, or through attending my lectures and seminars.

We've journeyed through the timeline of the Industrial Revolution, delving into the transformative era of Industry 4.0. Along the way, we've explored the foundations of traditional DataCenter and the towering advancements of cloud computing. Our next destination? *Cloud migration* – a realm closely intertwined with its predecessors but charting a distinctive path forward.

Cloud Migration Strategy Playbook

In the traditional realm, harking back to the mainframe era, applications adhered to a monolithic structure. They were constructed on a singular code base and implemented within a three-tier architecture involving the user interface (today called *Web* or *App UI*), application logic (*app codes*), and database (*storage*). Should alterations be necessary – a new feature introduction, bug fixing, or amending an existing feature – the entire code base would require redeployment into the production environment. Even if the change was confined to a small segment of the code, the entire application had to undergo redeployment. Consequently, this process often led to planned downtime for code updates and, at times, unanticipated system interruptions if issues arose post-deployment.

Rectifying these disruptions demanded extensive collaboration between development, QA, and operations teams, resulting in substantial efforts to rectify and resume operations. The resulting inefficiencies consistently led to delays, directly impacting on the business's revenue, much to the frustration of CEOs. Traditional mainframe DataCenters were originally designed to accommodate monolithic applications. Despite hardware architecture transitions to x86 and other distributed processing units, the fundamental architecture of applications has largely retained its old-school monolithic structure.

Two decades ago, a release cycle of over six months was the norm, posing significant obstacles to agile operations and innovation. With the advent of digital transformation, present-day CEOs seek a faster release cycle, aiming to introduce new features and secure market share ahead of competitors. Accelerating the release cycle necessitated a fundamental shift – breaking down the monolithic application code into smaller, more manageable code chunks. The "*divide and conquer technique*" stands as a remarkably successful aspect of software engineering. The substantial action of segmentation facilitated a more agile development process compared to managing the entire code base. This approach not only achieved an equilibrium point that resonates with the CEOs' vision of balancing speed and risk but also enhanced operational efficiency and excellence.

Picture your CEO's smiling face, gleaming with a shrewd and friendly gaze, whispering softly to the winds: "*the speed and safety at scale and in harmony!*"

The seismic shift in approach became apparent during the evolution from a traditional model. The simple migration of a monolithic application from virtualized on-premises DataCenter servers (sometimes called *cloud ready*) or a hyperscale cloud provider (called *cloud migrated*) to a microservice architecture (sometimes called *cloud enabled*) marked a significant start.

However, the real transformation emerged with the segregating the control and worker planes and embracement majority of cloud-native principals (called *cloud scaled*). Several major service providers, such as Microsoft with her CAF framework, Azure Migrate, and AWS Migration Hub and Refactor Spaces, tout their ability to streamline this transformation process while minimizing risks. However, despite these claims, the reality remains that significant effort is required to undertake such endeavors.

Presently, cloud-born companies operate by required automated release cycles that can occur as frequently as multiple times a day, a paradigm that enables businesses to swiftly introduce enhanced functionalities to their audience. This agility translates to increased revenue generation and the ability to promptly address customer concerns, thereby ensuring the retention of their existing customer base. Harnessing "*speed and safety at scale and in harmony!*" is undoubtedly a top priority for many in this realm. However, before delving into the nitty-gritty, it's crucial to identify the optimal strategy for your cloud migration journey. I highly recommend perusing the 10+1 R's menu and selecting based on your unique preferences and the realities of your situation.

Decoding Cloud Migration Strategies: Unveiling the 10+1 R's Rationalization Framework

The **10+1 R's framework** in cloud migration rationalization refers to a set of strategies for transitioning applications and workloads from on-premises environments to the cloud. Each "*R*" represents a different strategy, helping organizations determine the most suitable approach for their specific needs and requirements. The 11 R's playbook provides a structured approach for organizations to make decisions about their existing applications. These strategies are explained below:

- **Retire:** Retiring involves decommissioning or discontinuing applications that no longer serve a purpose or are deemed obsolete. For example, when a high risk of technical bankruptcy is observed (described later in this chapter), you should assess the impact of retiring an application on users and data, ensuring a seamless transition to alternative solutions.
- **Retain:** Retaining tactic signifies keeping existing applications without any significant changes. This approach is suitable for applications that meet current requirements and don't require immediate updates. For example, you may choose to retain applications

temporarily or as part of a long-term strategy if it's planned to decommission soon or needs no load scaling or cost improvement.

- **Rehost:** Rehosting, often referred to as *"lift and shift,"* involves migrating applications to the cloud without making substantial modifications. While it offers a quick transition, you should evaluate whether this approach maximizes the benefits of cloud services and adjust configurations and FinOps accordingly.
- **Relocate:** Relocating entails moving applications to different cloud environments or regions to optimize performance, compliance, or cost. You must assess the specific needs of their applications and select the appropriate cloud location to meet those requirements.
- **Repurchase:** Repurchasing, often referred to as *"drop and shop,"* involves replacing existing software or technology with commercial off-the-shelf SaaS, API, or service mesh solutions or switching to a different service model. You should evaluate the cost, functionality, and compatibility of available alternatives before making repurchasing decisions.
- **Replatform:** Replatforming, also known as *"lift, tinker, and shift,"* involves making minor adjustments to applications to optimize them for the cloud environment. This approach aims to enhance performance and take advantage of specific cloud services without a complete overhaul, for example, leveraging cloud storage, SSO service providers, secret management, or load-balancing services.

- **Refactor:** Refactoring or *rearchitecting* involves modifying the application's code or architecture to make it cloud-native. This approach often includes breaking down monolithic applications into microservices while leveraging well-architected cloud delivery service offerings. You need to carefully plan and execute the refactoring process to ensure improved efficiency and scalability.
- **Rebuild:** Rebuilding requires rewriting the application from scratch, often using different programming languages, core technologies, or frameworks. This approach is chosen when existing applications are outdated and technically bankrupt or when you seek to fully leverage cloud-native capabilities for innovation and scalability.
- **Replace:** Replacing involves substituting an existing application with a new one, often chosen from a different vendor or developed in-house with some adjustments for compatibility or optimization, but without completely changing the underlying technology stack. Repurchasing and Replacing are complementary strategies, both aimed at enhancing a service component while preserving its core values. The key distinction lies in whether you choose to embrace entirely new cloud-native solutions (Repurchasing) or integrate cloud-offered components into existing systems (Replacing). When implementing this approach, it is crucial to conduct a comprehensive evaluation of the functionality, integration potential, and sustainability of replacement options. This exercise ensures a seamless transition and long term.

- **Reimagine:** Reimagining goes beyond traditional approaches and involves completely rethinking business processes, workflows, and applications to leverage cutting-edge technologies and cloud-native paradigms. This approach aims to drive innovation and transform the organization's digital landscape fundamentally. It requires a visionary strategy and a commitment to embracing emerging technologies. Reimagining and Rearchitecting stand as sibling strategies, each with the shared goal of birthing a novel product. The key divergence lies in their approach: Rearchitecting preserves the intrinsic values of the existing service, leveraging cloud-native technologies, while Reimagining ventures into uncharted territory, crafting a fresh product adorned with innovative business models and user stories.

In addition, it's crucial to incorporate step 11: **Revisit** (Revert). Periodically reassessing cloud migration decisions is essential for organizations. They may find it necessary to revert to a previous state, engage in *cloud repatriation*, or even reconsider their entire migration strategy book. This ongoing review ensures adaptability and alignment with evolving business needs. After selecting the optimal set of strategies for migrating your application to the cloud, it's time to embark on the journey toward cloud-native excellence. This is where we encounter the fundamental principles of microservices and embrace the pillars of cloud-native architecture.

The Paradigm Shift: Cloud-Native Dynamics

Cloud-native architecture orchestrates a collection of cloud-based components and old-school methods tailored for optimal performance within the cloud environment. It's more than just cloud-hosted servers; it revolves around services. Embracing cloud-native isn't solely a technical shift – it's an organizational journey to the next FMO. It encapsulates the current aspiration for enterprises aiming to revolutionize their infrastructure, processes, and cultural foundations. This endeavor involves a scrupulous selection of computer science and cloud technologies tailored to meet their distinct requirements.

However, while this represents the current pinnacle, it's imperative to acknowledge the dynamic nature of the tech landscape. One of the primary merits of Cloud-Native Application CNA 1.0 is the substitutability which mitigates vendor lock-in and legacy system change concerns in the future. This is achieved through its commitment to continuous improvement capacities facilitated by change compatibility and the utilization of loosely coupled microservices and service mesh architectures. In the foreseeable future, Cloud-Native Application 'CNA 2.0' may give way to a novel paradigm, reshaping our approach to tasks once again.

CMO, TMO, and FMO

The **Current Mode of Operation** (**CMO**) refers to the existing state or processes within an organization. It encapsulates the present methods, workflows, and operational practices. Understanding the CMO is essential for change managers as it provides a baseline for identifying areas that need improvement or modification.

On the other hand, the **Future Mode of Operation** (**FMO**) represents the envisioned state or desired future state after the implementation of proposed changes. It outlines the anticipated improvements, efficiencies, and outcomes that the organization aims to achieve through the change initiative.

Transitioning between CMO and FMO involves the **Transition Mode of Operation** (**TMO**), which refers to the period during which the organization is in flux, adapting from the current state to the future state. This transitional phase involves managing potential disruptions, training employees on new processes, and ensuring a smooth shift from the old to the new.

Let's delve into the precise definition of CNA 1.0 to deepen our understanding. In the following section, we'll explore how this definition can provide clarity and insight into the concept. Please note that in this book, CNA refers to cloud-native architecture generally and CNA 1.0 refers to this definition.

Demystifying CNA 1.0: Understanding Its Core Attributes

In the tech landscape, buzzwords like "*cloud-native*" are often defined through various industry references. Notably, authoritative bodies such as CNCF, NIST, and Gartner provide differing yet influential perspectives on its definition. Here are the definitions of cloud-native from each of these authoritative bodies:

- **Cloud-Native Computing Foundation (CNCF):** *"An approach to building and running applications that exploits the advantages of the cloud computing delivery model"*
- **National Institute of Standards and Technology (NIST):** *"A software development approach that focuses on building applications that are scalable, reliable, and resilient, and that can be easily deployed and managed scalable applications in modern dynamic environments, such as public, private, and hybrid clouds"*

- **Gartner:** *"A software delivery approach that emphasizes the use of containers, microservices, declarative APIs, DevOps practices, and resilience to build and run applications that are cloud optimized"*

Cloud-Native Application CNA 1.0 represents a group of software architectural patterns where applications are developed, operated, and maintained as *event-driven microservices* within the *well-architected cloud delivery framework.*

In accordance with the definition of CNA 1.0, the emphasis lies in harmonizing the event-driven approach with a well-architected cloud delivery framework. In the subsequent paragraphs, we delve into both aspects in detail, supported by illustrative examples. Throughout this book, it's important to clarify that when we refer to CNA, we're specifically addressing cloud-native architecture. When we mention CNA 1.0, we are specifically referring to the Cloud-Native Application definition outlined within this section.

What Exactly Defines Event-Driven Microservices Systems?

The CNA 1.0 definition relies explicitly on the concepts of event-driven microservices and well-architected cloud delivery framework. Assuming we share a common understanding of microservice concepts, as a software design approach organizing applications into small, independently deployable services, each dedicated to a specific business capability, these services communicate through well-defined APIs over a mesh network. The microservices architecture promotes autonomy, allowing for individual development, deployment, and scaling. Its resilience ensures that the failure of one service does not impact the entire application, enhancing fault isolation. The scalability feature allows services to scale independently, optimizing resource utilization, and the acceptance of diverse technologies enables the use of the most suitable tools for specific tasks.

On the other hand, **event-driven architecture (EDA)** is a design pattern where events, representing occurrences or state changes significant to a system's functioning, drive the operation and interaction between components asynchronously. The six key elements include the following:

- **Event Producers:** Spanning from applications and services to external systems. Events, encapsulating actions or state changes like user interactions, sensor data, or system notifications, are their brainchild.
- **Event Channels or Brokers:** Acting as intermediaries, event channels facilitate seamless communication between producers and consumers. Employing message brokers such as Apache Kafka, RabbitMQ, or cloud-based services like Amazon SNS or Azure Event Grid, they ensure efficient event flow.
- **Event Consumers:** These vital components or services react promptly to incoming events. By subscribing to specific event types, consumers tailor their actions to event triggers, spanning from simple handlers to intricate workflows or microservices.
- **Event Processors:** Tasked with processing and responding to events, event processors come in various forms, including event-driven microservices, serverless functions, or traditional applications adapted for asynchronous event handling.
- **Event Stores:** Designed for optimal event storage and retrieval, event stores serve as databases or data storage systems. They offer persistence for events, enabling functionalities like replayability, auditing, and comprehensive event analysis.

- **Event Schema and Metadata:** Events are accompanied by metadata and adhere to predefined schemas delineating their structure and content. This adherence ensures interoperability and consistency among event producers and consumers, facilitating seamless integration.

Microservices, typically characterized by their synchronous nature, pose a challenge when aiming for asynchronous and nonblocking functionality. Addressing this challenge requires an intersection between **microservices architecture (MSA)** and **event-driven architecture (EDA)**. This intersection manifests as a proliferation of event-driven microservices - sometimes referred to as loosely coupled - essential for the realization of real-world, real-time, and resilient applications.

In contrast to **synchronous microservices**, which engage in direct interaction, **asynchronous microservices** necessitate an intermediary for indirect communication. The asynchronous microservices facilitate the implementation of a *"fire and forget"* pattern, enhancing flexibility and responsiveness. The seamless integration of MSA and EDA styles harmoniously provides both synchronous and asynchronous communication capabilities, contributing to the versatility and effectiveness of modern distributed systems.

Event-driven microservices architecture integrates microservices principles with event-driven communication patterns. It leverages the publish-subscribe model, allowing microservices to publish events to a central bus and others to subscribe to events of interest. Event sourcing ensures events become the source of truth, and asynchronous communication between microservices enhances decoupling and scalability. The architecture provides flexibility by supporting the addition or modification of microservices without disrupting the entire system. Additionally, scalability is achieved as components can scale independently based on the volume of events.

Embracing **event-driven architecture (EDA)** fosters loose coupling between components, leveraging events as the primary mode of integration. This paradigm shift from traditional request-response models results in architectures characterized by enhanced flexibility, scalability, and resilience.

What Exactly Defines a Well-Architected Cloud Delivery Framework?

All hyperscalers as well as most other cloud service providers offer *a set of best practices* that can help you design, build, and run secure, reliable, efficient, and cost-effective cloud applications. An updated well-architected framework is based on the following seven pillars:

1. **Operational Excellence:** This pillar focuses on the ability to run and manage systems effectively and efficiently. It includes best practices such as automation, monitoring, and incident response.

2. **Security:** This pillar focuses on protecting data, systems, and applications from unauthorized access, use, disclosure, disruption, modification, or destruction. It includes best practices such as identity and access management (IAM), data encryption, and network security.

3. **Reliability:** This pillar focuses on ensuring that systems are available and perform as expected. It includes best practices such as redundancy, load balancing, and disaster recovery.

4. **Performance Efficiency:** This pillar focuses on optimizing systems to deliver the desired performance at the lowest cost. It includes best practices such as choosing the right instance types, caching, and **content delivery networks (CDNs)**.

5. **Observability:** All systems have some level of mandatory monitoring, visibility, and accounting capabilities. Along with alerting, reporting, and notification features, we can have a great high fidelity.

HIGH-FIDELITY VISIBILITY (HFV)

High-fidelity visibility in observability systems is a linchpin for maintaining the health, reliability, and efficiency of modern distributed systems. It represents the precision, granularity, and completeness of the data collected and analyzed within the observability framework. To attain this, observability systems employ a combination of advanced instrumentation and monitoring techniques, which are covered in Chapter 5, "Instrumentation Engineering Fundamentals." These instrumentation points provide a detailed view of the system's internal states, allowing for precise identification of bottlenecks, errors, and performance anomalies.

Furthermore, the concept of high-fidelity visibility extends to the correlation and contextualization of observability data. Advanced observability systems employ sophisticated algorithms to correlate telemetry signals across diverse components of a distributed system. This correlation enables engineers and operators to trace the flow of transactions, identify the root causes of issues, and comprehend the intricate relationships between different system elements. Contextualization involves associating observability data with relevant contextual information such as user transactions, deployment changes, or infrastructure events, which are covered in Chapter 4, "Observability Engineering Fundamentals." By combining these elements, high-fidelity visibility allows for a holistic understanding of system behavior, facilitating proactive issue resolution, optimizing performance, and ensuring a seamless user experience in complex and dynamic computing environments.

6. **Cost Optimization:** This pillar focuses on optimizing costs to avoid unnecessary spending. It includes best practices such as rightsizing resources, using reserved instances, and spot instances.

7. **Sustainability:** This pillar focuses on reducing the environmental impact of cloud computing. It includes best practices such as choosing energy-efficient resources, recycling unused resources, and using renewable energy.

Each pillar is comprised of a series of design principles, which serve as the foundational guidelines for the design and construction of an application. These design principles are further reinforced by a compilation of best practices, offering detailed recommendations for the implementation of these principles. Additionally, they provide insights into patterns, cloud tools, and technologies that facilitate the application of these principles in practice.

In addition to best practices, the well-architected framework offers another invaluable resource known as **lens**. Each lens zeroes in on a specific aspect, where it provides distinct perspectives or dimensions through which to evaluate cloud architectures. Lenses are essentially sets of tailored tools, services, and assets that enable users to pinpoint potential risks and opportunities within their architectures and ensure alignment with the well-architected framework's seven pillars: operational excellence, security, reliability, performance efficiency, observability, cost optimization, and sustainability.

There are currently seven lenses available for the AWS Well-Architected Framework. They are as follows:

- **Serverless Lens:** This lens helps you assess and improve the architecture of serverless applications.
- **SaaS Lens:** This lens helps you assess and improve the architecture of software as a service (SaaS) application.

- **Container Lens:** This lens helps you assess and improve the architecture of containerized applications.
- **Data Analytics Lens:** This lens helps you assess and improve the architecture of data analytics workloads.
- **Machine Learning Lens:** This lens helps you assess and improve the architecture of machine learning workloads.
- **Networking Lens:** This lens helps you assess and improve the architecture of networking components and solutions.
- **Storage Lens:** This lens helps you assess and improve the architecture of storage components and solutions.

Lenses can be used at any stage of the development lifecycle, from design and planning to deployment and operations. They can also be used to assess existing workloads, as well as new workloads that are under development. To use a lens, you first need to define the workload that you want to assess. Once you have defined the workload, you can answer the questions in the lens. The lens will then provide you with a summary of your results, as well as recommendations for improvement. Lenses can be used individually or in combination. For example, you might use the Serverless Lens and the Data Analytics Lens to assess the architecture of a serverless data analytics workload. By using lenses, you can ensure that your workloads are well-architected and aligned with the well-architected framework's pillars.

Most hyperscale cloud service providers recommend using microservices, containers, serverless computing, monitoring, and observability services, but it's not limited or mandated by these services.

We will discover more about them later, but here are some examples of how the components of a well-architected framework can be used together:

- **Design Principle:** Decouple the different parts of an application.
- **Best Practice:** Use microservices.
- **Pattern:** Use a service mesh to coordinate communication between microservices.

Any service delivery platform that adheres to the well-architected framework patterns and operates seamlessly within a diverse range of cloud infrastructures, including public, private, hybrid, community, federated, and multi-cloud environments, can be classified as a well-architected cloud delivery framework.

In truth, neither microservices nor CNA 1.0 mandates that containerization is an absolute necessity to be a part of the ecosystem. Instead, these approaches offer a plethora of design patterns, tools, and technologies suitable for crafting a well-architected cloud delivery framework and constructing an event-driven microservices deployment. Is it achievable even only with virtual machines and serverless functions or WebAssembly? The answer is: technically, *yes*. But such an approach would likely receive a significantly lower rating in the metrics of a well-architected cloud delivery framework if not designed, deployed, and maintained carefully. Hence, it's not commonly recommended in most established patterns.

To summarize our discussion thus far, the evolving global computing market consistently seeks heightened reliability, flexibility, and agile transformations expedited in Industry 4.0 revolution, while simultaneously aiming to reduce costs and risks (speed and risk equilibrium points in Game Theory). In response to this surging demand, cloud providers have emerged to meet these evolving desires. In the era of Industry 4.0

revolution and dataism, we framed the integration of cloud services as an evolutionary shift, akin to a Darwinian progression from traditional DataCenter services.

However, cloud-native architectures have transcended their origins in ***DataCenter*** engineering, pivoting primarily toward a focus on software engineering. Concurrently, each industrial revolution introduces a suite of buzzwords, which we have collectively delineated, including concepts like microservices, event-driven architecture, well-architected cloud delivery frameworks, ***FinOps***, and various stages of cloud integration such as being cloud ready, cloud enabled, and achieving CNA 1.0 status. Nevertheless, this represents just the initial phase of this transformative journey.

Simply labeling a cloud-deployable application as ***"cloud-native"*** based on the baseline CNA 1.0 definition is insufficient. To comprehensively assess its alignment with cloud-native value propositions, it's imperative to establish a maturity model. This model allows for dynamic evaluation, enabling a precise determination of whether an application meets the benchmarks for cloud-native maturity. Moreover, it facilitates the creation of a tailored road map for each application, charting a clear path toward achieving optimal cloud-native norms. This pivotal shift will be comprehensively explored in the next chapter. Before delving into that, we will first examine established maturity models for cloud-native products.

Until now, our perspective on CNAs has largely focused on CloudOps and SRE/DevOps considerations. Now, let's delve into what architects and developers specifically need to understand. One of the best ways is 12-factor methodology.

What Is the 12-Factor Container?

When engaging with developers and application architects in the cloud-native passage, it's imperative to articulate both the guiding principles and the pitfalls. This conversation should not solely revolve around ambitious end goals and groundbreaking aspirations but also encompass the practical road map from our current state to the realization of a CNA 1.0. This comprehensive approach is what we refer to as the cloud-native journey.

Fortunately, your team isn't the first to embark on this wondrous journey. Many travellers have ventured on this path before, and pioneering individuals have created maps and detailed accounts of their travels. In 2012, Adam Wiggins, the CTO of *Heroku*, along with others, introduced the "12 Factor App" methodology. This concept provides a road map and a foundational set of principles that developers and software architects should adhere to when steering toward a microservice application architecture.

This innovative idea was warmly welcomed by the industry. Over time, it evolved from "*12 Factor App*" to "*15 Factor App*" to encompass a broader domain and later re-converged back to the "*12 Factor App 2.0*," paying homage to the fortuitous number 12 and the efforts of the Heroku teams maybe. The 12 Factor App 2.0 is inherently programming language and cloud platform independent, focusing on its agnosticism. However, it explicitly emphasizes the utilization of containerization and container orchestration system principles. Hereafter, we will refer to it as "*Twelve Factor Container*."

Adhering to these 12 factors within an application ensures its readiness for enterprise-grade production continuous integration (CI) setup and primes it for a seamless continuous deployment (CD) in a microservice environment.

The 12-factor container encompasses five key objectives that render it highly suitable for deployment and operation on CNA 1.0 platforms:

- Utilization of GitOps, declarative formats, API, and automation.
- Establishing a clean contract, event-driven approach with the underlying infrastructure and backing services.
- Alignment between development and production environments and separate configuration, credentials, and code.
- Observability in-depth involves the comprehensive collection of distributed application metrics, tracing data, logs within the deployment context, and health checks.
- Dynamically scalable and concurrent without significant change in tooling, architecture, or development practices.

I aim to present the revised concept of the 12 Factor App 2.0 as Twelve Factor Container within the context of Kubernetes architecture.

1. One code base, One application; maintain one Git repo per application, and use segregated environment-base deployment configuration and parameters. When you can express applications and infrastructure as code and configurations that are being version controlled by Git, you can apply techniques such as GitOps and continuous integration/continuous deployment (CI/CD) with greater ease. Making Git the single source of truth helps prevent promoting unexpected changes, makes your application state reproducible, and provides accountability for changes introduced in your environments and roll-forward compatible deployment and release engineering.

GITOPS

GitOps represents a framework of methodologies and principles that harnesses version control systems, notably Git, for the streamlined management and automation of infrastructure and application deployment. The nomenclature "GitOps" stems from the amalgamation of "Git," a widely embraced distributed version control system, and "Ops," denoting operations.

Key tenets and fundamental concepts integral to GitOps encompass the utilization of version control systems (VCS) as a source of truth coupled with declarative configuration, alongside the seamless integration of continuous integration and continuous deployment (CI/CD). By employing GitOps, organizations establish the version control repository as the authoritative source of truth, ensuring that the declared state, codified as infrastructure and application configurations, serves as the baseline for operational changes.

One of the hallmark features of GitOps is its emphasis on observability and monitoring. Through the incorporation of monitoring tools, GitOps provides valuable insights into the well-being and performance of both applications and infrastructure. Leveraging these insights, automated responses can be triggered based on monitoring metrics, facilitating real-time adjustments to maintain the desired operational state. In essence, GitOps not only enhances collaboration between development and operations but also fosters a continuous and auditable evolution of the entire system, making it particularly well-suited for dynamic and containerized environments.

2. **SDLC Parity:** Design, Build, Release, and Run phases, strictly separation between each by CI/CD toolchains.

3. **Environment Parity:** Striving to maintain as much uniformity as possible across the Development (Dev), User Acceptance Testing (UAT), and Production environments, maybe with namespaces.

4. **API First:** Define service contract, developing APIs as a first-class artifact that is consistent and reusable, giving the ability to work against public contracts without interfering with the internal development processes.

5. One stateless functional process, one SBOM, per container. Containers, by nature, are ephemeral, meaning the data stored inside a container dies when the container goes away. Leveraging containers makes application developers think of better ways to store state in their application, whether they're storing data in a database or maintaining the state within an external cache. Minimizing state in containerized workloads helps ensure that applications can scale up and down easily without affecting the user's experience.

SOFTWARE BILL OF MATERIALS (SBOM)

A **Software Bill of Materials** is a detailed inventory or listing of all software components, their versions, and dependencies contained within a specific containerized application. It serves as a comprehensive record of all the software elements used to build the container image. The goal of an SBOM in containers is to enhance transparency, security, and traceability in the software supply chain. Having an updated SBOM is a crucial part of software components versions and dependencies, structure and format (where standards like CycloneDX or SPDX help), security and compliance, supply chain transparency, and lifecycle management.

6. Administrative processes, by K8s native functionalities and resources. Implement Helper Container, CronJob, and Jobs.

7. Configuration, Credentials, and Code files segregation by K8s functionalities and resources to distinctly isolate them; enforce ConfigMaps, environment variables, and secrets resources.

8. **Backing Services:** By K8s functionalities and resources, treat backing service as an attached resource by services and API. Whenever possible, communicate interactions with external services using APIs with consistent contracts.

9. Policy in-depth, by K8s functionalities and resources, such as port binding, service exposure, routing, and traffic flow control via service mesh.

10. Security in-depth, by securing Code, Container, Cluster, and Cloud configuration and data across all hardware, network, platform, runtime, and software layers.

11. Observability in-depth, by design telemetry, means gathering performance and functionality metrics from inside the app. Logs are a stream of events; make sure your containerized workloads are dumping their logs to STDOUT/STERR.

12. Disposability and concurrency, by K8s functionalities and resources, such as ReplicationControllers, Horizontal Pod Autoscaling, package manager, liveliness, and readiness probes.

Use a circuit breaker, retry transient failures, degrade gracefully, throttle high-volume users, and apply compensating transactions and testing for resiliency.

The adoption of the 12-factor methodology in the last ten years marked a pioneering approach to microservice software development. This methodology revolutionized the foundational principles for building and deploying microservice applications. With the subsequent evolution to Twelve Factor Container, a comprehensive guide was established to introduce new developers to the fundamental concepts of the Cloud-Native 1.0 ecosystem.

With this, we have come to the end of the chapter.

Summary

As rock star cloud-native observability engineers, it's imperative that we possess a comprehensive understanding of key domain concepts. This entails not only grasping these concepts but also illustrating their interrelations and backgrounds with precision and clarity. The chapter commenced with a well-known timeline of the industrial revolutions, shedding light on the pivotal role of DataCenter and subsequent cloud service providers in the Industry 4.0 era and the emerging dataism doctrine. We delved deeper into essential terminologies such as cloud service providers' business model, cloud-native 1.0, event-driven microservices, well-architected framework, 12-factor containers, and cloud migration strategy playbook employing the 10+1 R's framework. The chapter's focal points encompass understanding these key terms and elucidating their relevance in both the present and future realms of technology, business, and societal landscapes. In the forthcoming chapter, we delve deeper into the cloud maturity model and the core principles of transformation planning. Moreover, we've underscored the significance of observability at each juncture thus far. As we weave these threads together in Chapter 3, "Cloud-Native Maturity Models," a comprehensive picture emerges. Please bear with me as we embark on the journey to our next destination. Get ready to immerse yourself in the adventure and embrace the experiences that lie ahead.

CHAPTER 3

Cloud-Native Maturity Models

> *Only the most culturally mature organizations assess their technology maturity level frequently, taking deliberate steps toward enhancement.*

In this chapter, we will explore the diverse landscape of Cloud-Native Maturity Models, examining paradigms and the inherent trade-offs associated with them. The discussion will extend beyond the technological aspects, addressing the sociotechnical dimension by exploring the architecture of people and organizations.

The entanglement between culture and technology stands as one of the most complex factors determining the success or failure of digital transformation projects. By gaining insight into potential pitfalls and exploring pathways for improvement, we can heighten awareness and tailor our journey to navigate challenges with greater resilience and preparedness.

The key topics covered in this chapter include

- The **Cloud-Native Maturity Model (CNMM)** paradigm
- Cloud Maturity Models per CNCF and OACA
- The Kanban Maturity Model and documentation model

Dr. M. Ghane, *Observability Engineering with Cilium*,
https://doi.org/10.1007/979-8-8688-1258-3_3

- The influence of Conway's law and Reverse Conway Manoeuvre on SaaS businesses
- Offering the cloud-native maturity matrix and measurement methods

The CNMM Paradigm

CNMM stands for **Cloud-Native Maturity Model**. It is a software development approach that combines cloud services, microservice principles, and mesh networking to build scalable, reliable, and resilient applications. The CNMM paradigm is a set of principles and best practices for building and running applications in the cloud era. These principles include containerization, microservices, mesh networking, declarative APIs, DevOps methods, and observability features. The CNMM paradigm is designed to help organizations build CNAs that are scalable, reliable, and efficient. In Chapter 2, "Cloud-Native Phenomena," we explored the definitions of microservices and Cloud-Native Application CNA 1.0, as well as the principles outlined in the 12-factor container methodology.

Now, let's delve into the concept of mesh networking to gain a clearer understanding. Mesh networking is a type of networking that provides a layer of abstraction between the services and the underlying infrastructure. This allows services to be easily deployed and managed, regardless of the specific infrastructure that they are running on. Microservice applications use a variety of networking technologies to communicate with each other and with the outside world. The service mesh would provide features such as load balancing, service discovery, and fault tolerance. We will delve into the extraordinary capabilities of Cilium within the realm of mesh networking in greater detail in Chapter 6, "Demystifying Cilium's Spellbinding Nature" and later chapters. In the next chapter, we will recreate the observability definition for CNA 1.0 products. Before exploring these technical intricacies, let's revisit the cultural domains integral to the sociotechnical transformation toward cloud-native paradigms and examine the corresponding maturity models.

CNCF Approach to Cloud-Native Maturity Model

The **Cloud-Native Maturity Model (CNMM)** is a framework developed by **the Cloud-Native Computing Foundation(CNCF)** to help organizations assess and improve their cloud-native maturity. The CNMM is a five-level model that covers the following areas:

- **Business Outcomes:** Focuses on how well the organization's cloud-native practices are aligned with its overall business goals
- **People:** Emphasizes on the skills, knowledge, and culture of the organization's workforce
- **Policy:** Concentrates on the organization's policies and procedures related to cloud-native development and operations
- **Processes:** Focuses on the organization's development and operations processes for microservices
- **Technology:** Emphasizes on the organization's use of cloud-native technologies and tools

The CNCF version of CNMM was originally published in 2021 and has been updated twice since then, most recently in Autumn 2023. The latest version of the CNMM places *Business Outcomes* at the top of the model, recognizing that cloud-native transformation should be driven by business goals. The original four sections become the pillars upon which Business Outcomes are designed, developed, and delivered.

Definition of the five levels of cloud-native maturity according to CNMM GitHub:

- **Level 1: Build**

  Organizations at Level 1 are just beginning to explore cloud technologies and practices. They may have some microservices in production, but these applications are typically managed in silos or pre-production stages and are not fully integrated with the organization's overall IT infrastructure.

- **Level 2: Operate**

  Organizations at Level 2 are actively developing and deploying microservice applications in production stage. They have established some cloud-native best practices, but they are still working to mature their processes and tools.

- **Level 3: Scale**

  Organizations at Level 3 have established repeatable processes for developing and deploying applications. They have also implemented several cloud-native best practices, such as SRE, Disciplined Agile Delivery (DAD), continuous integration and continuous delivery (CI/CD), and observability in-depth.

- **Level 4: Improve**

  Organizations at Level 4 have fully automated their application development and operations processes. Security, manageability, and observability are not treated as additional properties; they are key elements integral to all components. They have also implemented several advanced CNA 1.0 practices, such as service meshes and chaos engineering.

- **Level 5: Adapt**

  Organizations at Level 5 have mastered cloud-native development and operations. They can rapidly deliver new features and innovations in CNA 1.0 products to their customers while maintaining a high level of reliability and security.

Harmonizing CNMM and CNCF Landscape

There is a correlation between an organization's maturity level and the recommended maturity levels of CNCF products. Each level represents a progression in cloud-native maturity, with organizations moving from initial exploration to full optimization of cloud-native practices and technologies. When exploring the CNCF products landscape, please note that sandbox projects are not recommended for low maturity organizations (i.e., organizations that have not achieved Level 4 or 5 yet). It is my general decision-making advice to improve users' experience with well-established tools (CNCF graduated tools) while also encouraging exploration and potential contribution to emerging CNCF projects when capacity and interest allow.

The CNMM includes references only to CNCF graduated or incubating projects and will not include any references to commercial products.

CNMM AND 12-FACTOR CONTAINER

The CNMM model by CNCF may evoke memories of the 12-factor container concept introduced in Chapter 2, "Cloud-Native Phenomena." If this rings a bell, you're right on track.

Cloud Maturity Model of Open Alliance for Cloud Adoption (OACA)

The **Cloud Maturity Model (CMM)** is a structured and comprehensive framework. According to the latest version of the **Open Alliance for Cloud Adoption's (OACA)** Cloud Maturity Model guidelines, companies can use CMM to assess their cloud maturity and develop a road map for improvement. The CMM is based on industry best practices and is aligned with the **Cloud Adoption Framework (CAF)** v2.0. The model assesses a company's maturity across 12 domains with 12 key strategic questions:

1. **Strategy:** How the organization defines and prioritizes its cloud adoption strategy
2. **Governance:** How the organization establishes policies, procedures, and roles to manage cloud adoption
3. **People:** How the organization develops the skills and knowledge of its workforce for cloud adoption
4. **Processes:** How the organization streamlines its processes for cloud adoption
5. **Technology:** How the organization evaluates, selects, and deploys cloud technologies
6. **Infrastructure:** How the organization designs, builds, and manages its cloud infrastructure
7. **Operations:** How the organization operates and maintains its cloud infrastructure and applications
8. **Security:** How the organization protects its cloud environment from security threats

9. **Data:** How the organization manages its data in the cloud
10. **Compliance:** How the organization ensures compliance with regulatory requirements
11. **Measurability:** How the organization measures and tracks the success of its cloud adoption
12. **Continuous Improvement:** How the organization continuously improves its cloud adoption process

The CMM supports each domain across five maturity levels:

- **Ad Hoc:** The organization has no formal processes or governance for cloud adoption.
- **Initial:** The organization has some basic processes and governance for cloud adoption, but there is no alignment with business goals.
- **Managed:** The organization has mature processes and governance for cloud adoption, but there is still room for improvement.
- **Optimized:** The organization has optimized its processes and governance for cloud adoption, and it is able to achieve its business goals.
- **Continuously Optimizing:** The organization is constantly improving its processes and governance for cloud adoption, and it is always looking for new ways to enhance its cloud capabilities.

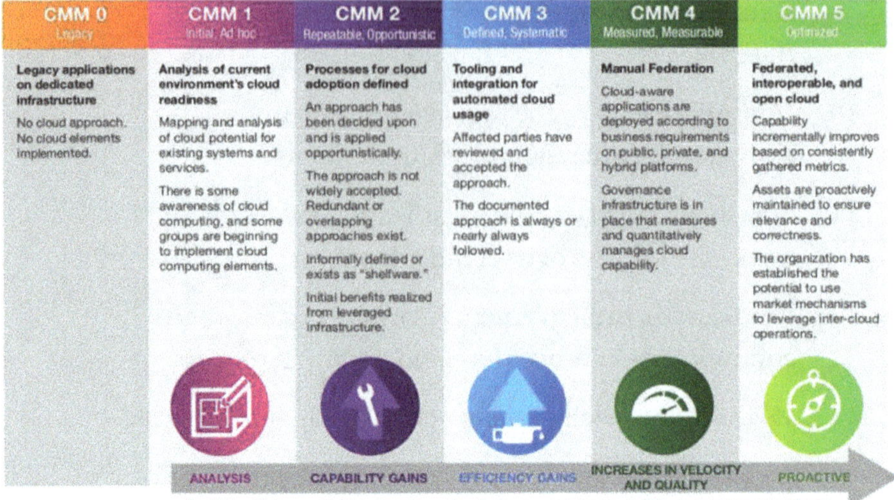

Figure 3-1. *CMM Maturity Levels*

The **Open Alliance for Cloud Adoption (OACA)** has released version 4.8.2 of the **Cloud Maturity Model (CMM)** which now includes an enhanced analysis and assessment questionnaire available as a free Excel spreadsheet. This update introduces several key improvements, with a particular emphasis on hybrid cloud adoption, offering a more detailed exploration of its complexities. Additionally, the new version provides a more nuanced assessment of security aspects and features a comprehensive evaluation framework for DevSecOps practices. These advancements underscore OACA's commitment to providing a comprehensive and up-to-date model that aligns with the evolving landscape of cloud technologies, offering organizations a nuanced and effective tool for evaluating their cloud maturity.

CMM AND WELL-ARCHITECTED CLOUD DELIVERY FRAMEWORK

The CMM model by the OACA might trigger your memory of the meticulously well-architected cloud delivery framework discussed in Chapter 2, "Cloud-Native Phenomena." If it does, you're right on track.

In pursuit of the objectives outlined in this chapter, our aim is to delve into the intricacies of designing a road map for the development and operation of a CNA 1.0 provider organization. Here, we'll explore how the CNCF's **Cloud-Native Maturity Model (CNMM)** serves as a guiding framework, along with the **Organizational Adoption and Change Acceleration (OACA)** approach, to facilitate the seamless integration of cloud services. The CMM offers invaluable insights for organizations seeking to enhance their cloud adoption journey. By leveraging this model, entities can pinpoint areas ripe for improvement, craft a strategic road map for transformation, and gauge their advancement over time. Harnessing the power of the CNMM and CMM ensures that organizations maximize the returns on their cloud investments.

Microsoft Cloud Adoption Framework (CAF)

Microsoft has introduced the **Cloud Adoption Framework (CAF)**, an essential tool for navigating the complexities of cloud adoption. At its core, the CAF serves as a guiding framework for the entire lifecycle of cloud adoption, ensuring alignment between business objectives and cloud adoption efforts to facilitate successful outcomes.

The CAF encompasses best practices, documentation, and tools designed to support organizations throughout their cloud adoption journey. While it consists of several distinct phases, there is no definitive endpoint, as cloud adoption is an ongoing process characterized by continuous improvement and evolution.

In the initial phase of the CAF lifecycle, known as the *Strategy* phase, organizations collaborate with business leaders to understand their motivations for cloud adoption. Objectives and key results are identified and documented, laying the groundwork for the adoption journey. Financial and technical considerations are explored and documented to create a robust business case, with an emphasis on cloud-agnostic strategies that transcend specific technologies.

The subsequent phase, *Assess*, involves evaluating the organization's existing digital estate to develop an actionable plan aligned with the established business objectives. This phase sets the stage for informed decision-making regarding the adoption process.

The often-overlooked *Ready* phase focuses on preparing the organization for cloud adoption. This includes defining the operating model, identifying necessary roles and responsibilities, and implementing training programs. Additionally, the target environment is prepared through the deployment of Landing Zones, which serve as the foundation for successful Azure deployments.

The *Adopt* phase entails the implementation of necessary changes, whether through migrating existing workloads or developing new ones to meet business requirements. This phase represents a pivotal step in the adoption journey, where strategies are put into action to drive tangible outcomes.

In the Adopt phase, you'll find yourself navigating through one of two loops, each catering to distinct objectives.

Firstly, there's the migration loop, meticulously designed for the seamless transition of existing workloads to the cloud. This loop begins with an earnest assessment of the current workload, followed by the deployment of resources tailored to facilitate its migration based on the assessment's findings. Subsequently, rigorous testing ensues before the workload is released into its new cloud environment. This iterative process unfolds repeatedly, possibly in batches, until the entirety of your migration endeavor is successfully concluded.

Alternatively, there's the innovation loop, a realm dedicated to fostering rapid evolution and responsiveness to customer demands. Should the decision not to migrate existing workloads be the route taken in the Plan phase, the innovation loop beckons. The cloud serves as an ideal playground for agile experimentation and innovation. Here, you'll embark on a journey of continuous iteration, starting with the construction of new features, perhaps even mere minimally viable products. These features are meticulously measured using diverse metrics, such as uptake, and insights gleaned from the data inform subsequent iterations. This cycle perpetuates indefinitely, ensuring either the solution's eventual feature completeness or the continuous refinement and enhancement of the solution based on ongoing learning and improvement efforts by your teams.

Running parallel to these four main phases are three additional phases that persist throughout the entire lifecycle. The *Govern* phase focuses on ensuring compliance with corporate policies, establishing guardrails, and implementing cost management controls. The *Manage* phase involves defining business requirements, establishing management baselines, and developing specialized operations for critical workloads. Finally, the *Secure* phase aims to continuously improve workload security, ultimately striving to implement a zero-trust architecture.

Together, these phases and components of the Cloud Adoption Framework provide organizations with a structured approach to cloud adoption, empowering them to achieve their business objectives efficiently and effectively in the ever-evolving landscape of cloud computing.

Figure 3-2. *Cloud Adoption Framework*

In addition to cloud-centric maturity models, we'll also shed light on the **Kanban Maturity Model (KMM)**, a cornerstone framework renowned for its efficacy in driving continuous improvement across software development and service operations within contemporary enterprises.

The Methodological Approach to Service Maturity

In the ever-evolving landscape of agile methodologies, service management and documentation emerge as formidable challenges in CNA teams. Among the myriad of established solutions and methodologies, three stand out: **Kanban Maturity Model (KMM)** by David J. Anderson, founder of Kanban University; **C4** by Simon Brown; and **ARC42** by Dr. Gernot Starke and Dr. Peter Hruschka, which will facilitate technical and strategical readiness.

Kanban University Methodology

The **Kanban Maturity Model (KMM)** serves as a comprehensive framework designed to evaluate and enhance the efficiency of Kanban and Lean methodologies within an organizational context. Comprising seven distinct maturity levels, each delineated by its unique characteristics and corresponding Kanban practices, KMM provides valuable insights into the evolution of agile practices. While KMM doesn't explicitly focus on cloud-native application delivery, it serves as a versatile tool for comprehending the organization operational landscape. Particularly relevant for companies embracing service-based deliveries, KMM facilitates the development of organizational and cultural road maps. The model is structured around five pivotal dimensions, enabling a holistic assessment and strategic improvement across various facets of the organizational workflow (in the team and intra-team) by five strategic inquiries.

1. **Visibility:** Does the organization have good visibility into its work and its workflow?

2. **Flow:** Does the organization have a smooth and efficient flow of work?

3. **Feedback:** Does the organization (intra-team and inter-team) have a good system for collecting and responding to feedback?

4. **Agility:** Is the organization able to quickly adapt to change?

5. **Continuous Improvement:** Is the organization constantly looking for ways to improve its practices?

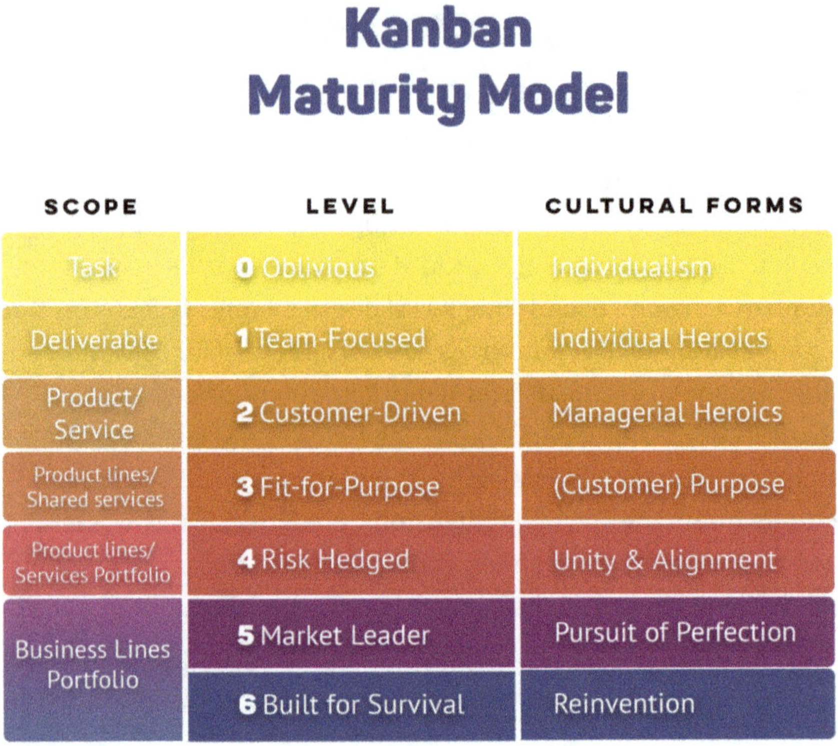

Kanban Maturity Model

SCOPE	LEVEL	CULTURAL FORMS
Task	0 Oblivious	Individualism
Deliverable	1 Team-Focused	Individual Heroics
Product/ Service	2 Customer-Driven	Managerial Heroics
Product lines/ Shared services	3 Fit-for-Purpose	(Customer) Purpose
Product lines/ Services Portfolio	4 Risk Hedged	Unity & Alignment
Business Lines Portfolio	5 Market Leader	Pursuit of Perfection
	6 Built for Survival	Reinvention

***Figure 3-3.** Kanban Maturity Model*

The Kanban Methodology Maturity Model defines seven levels of maturity:

Level 0: Oblivious

At the Oblivious level, work is managed in an ad hoc manner without formal processes. Individual contributors focus on their own tasks, often lacking collaboration or awareness of workflow and system constraints. This stage is characterized by a strong sense of individualism, with little to no coordination among team members. For example, in a small startup, individual developers might work on tasks independently without a structured workflow, leading to inefficiencies and a lack of team collaboration.

Level 1: Team-Focused

The Team-Focused level marks the beginning of collective task management. Teams start to visualize work and manage it together, relying on individual efforts and heroics to achieve goals. Basic understanding of workflow emerges, though coordination remains limited. This stage often depends on individuals going above and beyond to ensure success. In a growing tech company, teams might begin using basic Kanban boards to visualize work. While team members collaborate more, they still heavily rely on individual efforts to meet deadlines, with some members taking on more work to ensure success.

Level 2: Customer-Driven

In the Customer-Driven level, the focus shifts to understanding and delivering customer needs. Managers play a crucial role in driving process improvements, and customer-focused practices and feedback loops begin to develop. This stage aligns services and products with customer expectations, emphasizing the importance of meeting their needs. For example, a mid-sized software company might prioritize customer feedback and adjust products accordingly. Managers drive initiatives to align projects with customer needs, fostering a culture where customer satisfaction is a key focus.

Level 3: Fit-for-Purpose

The Fit-for-Purpose level is characterized by aligning services and products with customer purpose and value. Processes are tailored to meet specific customer expectations, fostering collaboration across teams to enhance service delivery. The organization focuses on delivering consistent value, closely aligning with customer goals. A service provider, for instance, might align its offerings with customer goals, customizing processes to enhance value delivery. Cross-functional teams collaborate closely to ensure products and services meet specific customer purposes, improving overall satisfaction.

Level 4: Risk Hedged

At the Risk Hedged level, organizations engage in proactive risk management and resource optimization. There is a unified approach aligning teams with organizational objectives, leading to improved coordination and communication across departments. This stage is marked by strategic alignment and a strong emphasis on managing uncertainties. A financial institution, for example, might implement proactive risk management strategies to ensure resources are optimized and aligned with business goals. Teams work in harmony, with clear communication across departments to mitigate risks and capitalize on opportunities.

Level 5: Market Leader

The Market Leader level is where organizations set industry standards and lead in innovation. Continuous improvement and refinement of processes are central, with high agility and responsiveness to market changes. This stage represents an organization that is not only efficient but also adaptive, consistently pursuing excellence and perfection. An innovative tech company, for instance, might set industry standards through continuous improvement and agility, leading the market with cutting-edge solutions and adapting quickly to changes to maintain their leadership position.

Level 6: Built for Survival

Built for Survival is the pinnacle of maturity, focusing on sustainable practices and long-term resilience. Organizations at this level have the ability to reinvent and adapt in the face of challenges, supported by a culture that encourages continuous evolution and change. This stage ensures that the organization is robust and capable of thriving in dynamic environments. For example, a multinational corporation might focus on sustainable practices to ensure long-term resilience. They continuously reinvent themselves, adapting to market disruptions and maintaining a robust culture that supports ongoing evolution and change.

I've utilized the Kanban Maturity Model extensively throughout my career. It's user-friendly and delivers impressive results for service-oriented organizations. I highly recommend it for transitioning from traditional software production to a cloud-native approach.

The C4 Documentation Model

The **C4 model** stands out as a widely embraced framework for crafting software architecture documentation, offering a lucid and succinct visual representation of intricate system structures. Particularly advantageous for microservices, characterized by their distributed nature and reliance on diverse cloud services, the C4 model excels in elucidating the intricacies of these complex systems. The "C4" stands for Context, Containers, Components, and Code.

- **Context:** This represents the highest level of abstraction and provides an overview of the system and its surrounding environment. It includes things like system boundaries, external dependencies, users, and key interactions.
- **Containers:** Containers are the next level of detail down from Context. They represent the runtime elements of the system, such as web servers, application servers, databases, etc. Containers encapsulate and host Components.
- **Components:** Components are the building blocks of the system and represent the major functional units or modules. They typically consist of sets of related code and data structures that perform specific tasks within the system.

- **Code:** This is the lowest level of detail in the C4 model and represents the actual implementation details of the system. It includes the source code, database schemas, configuration files, etc.

The C4 model comprises four distinct levels of diagrams:

- **Level 1: Context Diagram**

  The context diagram offers a holistic perspective of the system within its broader context, depicting both the external actors interacting with the system and the external systems with which it interfaces. This diagram serves as a valuable tool for gaining a high-level overview of the system and comprehending the interrelationships among its constituent parts.

- **Level 2: Containers Diagram**

  Focusing on deployable units, the containers diagram delineates the system's containers, with each container encapsulated within a box. The arrows interconnecting these boxes signify the dependencies between containers, facilitating a nuanced understanding of deployment strategies and scalability considerations. It's important to clarify that while the C4 model's concept of containers shares similarities with the Docker container concept, they are not identical. The C4 model's container concept serves as an abstraction for deployable units within a software system, encompassing a broader scope beyond the specific characteristics and functionalities associated with Docker images. Nevertheless, there exists a mapping between the two, allowing users to draw parallels and establish connections between the C4 model's containers and microservice containers for enhanced understanding.

- **Level 3: Components Diagram**

  Zooming further into the software architecture, the components diagram delineates the system's individual components – distinct software units deployed within containers. Each component is visually represented by a box, and the arrows connecting them convey dependencies, providing insight into the implementation details of the system.

- **Level 4: Code Diagram**

  The code diagram delves into the granular details of the system's code base, showcasing classes, functions, and other code elements. This diagram proves instrumental in comprehending the system's implementation at a fine-grained level, aiding developers in detailed analysis and troubleshooting.

  The C4 model exhibits flexibility and scalability, making it applicable to systems of varying sizes. Its adaptability is particularly advantageous in the documentation of microservices, effectively capturing the intricate nature of these systems while maintaining a clear and concise representation of their architectures.

The C4 model offers several benefits for microservice architectures. First, it enhances communication and collaboration among developers, architects, and stakeholders. The visual nature of C4 diagrams promotes a shared understanding of the system's architecture, making it easier for all parties to communicate effectively and work together.

Second, the C4 model aids in the early identification and resolution of architectural issues. By providing a clear, structured view of the system, it allows teams to spot potential problems early in the development lifecycle. This proactive approach helps in addressing technical debt and other challenges before they become significant obstacles.

Third, C4 diagrams serve as effective documentation tools. They provide a comprehensive reference that stakeholders can use throughout the system's lifecycle to understand its architecture. This ongoing reference ensures that everyone remains aligned and informed about the system's structure and design.

Fourth, the C4 model enhances code maintainability and comprehension. By offering a structured representation of the system, it helps developers navigate the architecture more easily. This clarity facilitates efficient code analysis and modifications, leading to better overall maintainability.

The other interesting software documentation method that I can recommend to you is ARC42. ARC42 is a widely used framework for documenting software architecture, emphasizing pragmatism, clarity, and utility. It consists of a set of templates and guidelines for documenting software architecture in a way that is comprehensible to both technical and nontechnical stakeholders. This makes ARC42 an excellent complement to the C4 model in different phases of CNA production for comprehensive and effective documentation.

The ARC42 Documentation Model

The objective of **ARC42 documentation** is to provide a complete overview of the software system, explaining its purpose, business context, and the problem domain it addresses. This documentation identifies stakeholders (end users, administrators, developers, and managers) and explains their roles, responsibilities, and concerns. ARC42 recommends a core template format that can be used for all CNA products.

The ARC42 template provides a structured approach to documenting software architectures. Its core structure typically includes the following sections:

- **Introduction:** Provides an overview of the document, its purpose, and its intended audience. It may also include a brief introduction to the system being documented.
- **Goals and Constraints:** Outlines the objectives and constraints that shape the architecture. This section clarifies what the system aims to achieve and any limitations or requirements it must adhere to.
- **Context and Scope:** Describes the business context in which the system operates, including the problem domain it addresses and the stakeholders involved. It defines the scope of the system, its boundaries, and its interfaces with external systems.
- **Solution Strategy:** Discusses the high-level strategy or approach used to address the system's requirements and constraints. This may include architectural styles, patterns, or frameworks chosen for the solution.

- **Building Blocks:** Provides detailed descriptions of the major components or building blocks of the system. It includes information about their responsibilities, interfaces, dependencies, and interactions.
- **Runtime View:** Describes the dynamic behavior of the system, including its runtime structure and how components interact during execution. This may include sequence diagrams or other visualizations.
- **Deployment View:** Explains how the system is deployed and configured in different environments. It may cover deployment topologies, infrastructure requirements, and deployment processes.
- **Crosscutting Concepts:** Addresses crosscutting concerns such as logging, security, performance, and scalability. It explains how these concerns are addressed and integrated into the architecture.
- **Quality Attributes:** Discusses the quality attributes of the system, such as performance, reliability, maintainability, and scalability. It describes strategies and mechanisms used to achieve and measure these attributes.
- **Risks and Technical Debt:** Identifies potential risks, vulnerabilities, and areas of technical debt within the architecture. It discusses mitigation strategies and plans for addressing these issues.
- **Glossary:** Provides definitions for key terms and acronyms used throughout the documentation to ensure a common understanding among stakeholders.

Here's an example of how this structure might be applied to document a CNA product. The introduction outlines the document and the CNA it describes, highlighting its innovative architecture designed for scalability and resilience in cloud environments. The goals and constraints section specifies the application's objectives, such as achieving high availability, scalability, and rapid deployment, while also addressing constraints like compliance requirements or resource limitations.

The context and scope section delves into the business context, describing the application as a platform for e-commerce services. It defines the scope of the application, including its interfaces with external payment gateways and inventory systems. The solution strategy section discusses the chosen microservices architecture, which leverages containerization and orchestration technologies like Kubernetes for scalability and resilience.

The building blocks section describes the major components of the application, such as microservices for catalogue management, user authentication, and order processing, detailing their responsibilities and interactions via RESTful APIs. The runtime view provides sequence diagrams that illustrate typical user interactions with the application, showing how requests are routed between microservices and data stores.

The deployment view explains how the application is deployed across multiple cloud regions for redundancy, with automated deployment pipelines using tools like Argo CD and Ansible. Crosscutting concepts address concerns such as centralized logging with Splunk, security using OAuth2 for authentication, mesh networking with Cilium mesh, and scalability through horizontal scaling of microservices.

The quality attributes section discusses strategies for monitoring performance with Cilium Hubble, Tetragon, and Grafana, ensuring reliability with circuit breakers and retries, and maintaining scalability through autoscaling. The risks and technical debt section identifies potential risks like vendor lock-in with cloud providers and technical debt from rapid feature development, outlining plans to address these risks through periodic architecture reviews and refactoring. Finally, the glossary provides definitions for terms like "containerization," "observability," and "event-driven microservices" to ensure clarity for all stakeholders involved in the development and operation of the application.

By including these additional technical details, the ARC42 documentation becomes more comprehensive and informative, providing valuable insights into the architecture and design of the software system.

With a solid understanding of modern maturity models and documentation methods, we are equipped with both theoretical and practical industrial knowledge, allowing us to effectively plan for the transformation to cloud-native platforms. This perspective emphasizes the significance and challenges of modern observability theory. In the final section of this chapter, we will explore this topic further through the cloud-native maturity matrix. However, before proceeding, I would like to examine the sociotechnical aspects of cloud-native transformation, specifically focusing on the Reverse Conway Manoeuvre and the effects of Conway's law in the next section.

From Mainframes to Mindfulness

Over half a century ago, Dr. Melvin Conway, a computer scientist with education in physics and mathematics, conducted pivotal observations. His keen insight led to the formulation of *Conway's law*, which underscores the critical importance of harmonizing organizational structure with system design to optimize outcomes in software development and other realms of system design.

Delving into more advanced perspectives, the proposition is that an organization's structure and communication dynamics inevitably manifest in the architecture of the systems they conceive. Consequently, if an organization's communication is fragmented or inefficient, it is highly probable that the systems they develop will exhibit analogous traits. In essence, Conway's law illuminates the intricate interplay between organizational dynamics and system architecture, underscoring the need for cohesive alignment to foster success in complex design processes. Later an organizational behavior researcher, Daniel Coyle, the author of Talent Code (*The Talent Code: Greatness Isn't Born. It's Grown*) and Culture Code (*The Culture Code: The Secrets of Highly Successful Groups*) books, provides insights into how successful groups create a positive and high-performing culture by focusing on interpersonal dynamics, communication, and a shared sense of purpose. He said: "*Culture is not something you are—it's something you do.*" In a business context, the "*do*" of your culture encompasses key practices that collectively shape and define how your business and people operate.

The success of a cloud-native journey hinges on meticulous planning, precise execution, and a transformative cultural shift, as eloquently elucidated in the invaluable insights provided by Reznik, Dobson, and Gienow in *Cloud-Native Transformation: Practical Patterns for Innovation.* In this comprehensive exploration, the authors articulate a set of patterns designed to enhance scalability, bolster resilience, and significantly increase the likelihood of organizational success.

Succeeding as a cloud-native entity necessitates a fundamental transformation from traditional hierarchical processes or even relatively modern agile practices to a decentralized organizational structure. Conway's law succinctly asserts that the architecture of a system will inevitably mirror the structure of the organization that houses it. In the realm of cloud-native architecture, the mandate for distributed systems is non-negotiable; it's not a choice but a requirement dictated by the very nature of cloud-native systems.

Embarking on the cloud-native journey entails embracing a profound shift toward human-centric organizational charts and processes. This transition involves moving away from rigidly defined KPIs to a more nuanced understanding of target ranges, striking a sandbox between overserving and underserving in a healthily dynamic manner. Bid farewell to micromanagement in all its forms; this paradigm shift is a game changer and a formidable challenge for most tech enterprises. Another illustration of this concept can be found in the **Reverse Conway Manoeuvre**. This phenomenon suggests that when an organization's structure and departments are loosely coupled, it may have a stronger tendency to produce microservices that are also loosely coupled!

WARNING

Software rot, also known as **software entropy**, refers to the gradual decline in software quality over time or its diminishing responsiveness, ultimately resulting in the emergence of faults within the software. Cloud service providers offer little assistance in this critical area. Whether it's Amazon Web Services, Google Cloud Services, Azure, or others, their primary focus is on anticipating and resolving onboarding issues. However, none of them extends support for the pivotal first step: understanding your company culture and acknowledging Conway's law. Their business models revolve around enticing you to adopt and utilize their systems, not scrutinizing your existing organizational structure, nor highlighting more risk of failure or product debt, organizational debt, technical debt, or even technical bankruptcy.

Technical debt is the accumulation of shortcuts and workarounds made during software development to meet deadlines or release features quickly. These shortcuts may involve using outdated technologies, writing inefficient code, or failing to thoroughly test and document the software. While these decisions may seem beneficial in the short term, they can have long-term consequences for the software's maintainability, performance, and overall reliability. Technical debt can manifest in various ways, including code complexity, unstructured code, and inflexible architecture. Rigid or outdated system architecture can limit the ability to adapt to changing business requirements or incorporate new technologies, hindering the software's long-term viability. As you recall from the microservice documentation section using the *ARC42* core template, there was a dedicated chapter for documenting and monitoring technical debt throughout the software lifecycle.

If debts manifest at the product level, they are termed **product debt**, while process or structural issues in team operational quality or communication are referred to as *organizational debt.* In general, having a certain level of debt is not inherently negative. It can be considered a normal aspect of system development. However, the risk arises when these debts are either overlooked, underestimated, or surpass the tolerable levels set for them, leading to hard charge-off or bankruptcy. Vigilance in recognizing and managing these debts is paramount to mitigate potential risks and maintain a healthy system development environment.

One of the advantages of CNA 1.0 products that leverage loosely coupled or event-driven microservices is the minimization of change risk and legacy component lock-in. This means that when there's a need to replace any component of CNA 1.0 products due to technology depreciation or **CVEs (Common Vulnerabilities and Exposures)**, it's much easier compared to monolithic applications burdened with legacy component architectural debt.

Technical bankruptcy is the extreme state of technical debt where the accrued costs of maintaining and fixing the software become overwhelming, significantly impacting the organization's ability to deliver value or stay competitive. At this point, the software has become an anchor, weighing down the organization's agility and innovation.

The symptoms of forthcoming technical bankruptcy include

- **Constant Firefighting:** Most development efforts are focused on resolving urgent issues and preventing system failures, leaving little time for innovation or strategic initiatives.

- **High Maintenance Costs:** The overhead of maintaining the convoluted and buggy software becomes a significant financial burden, diverting resources away from other business priorities.
- **Inability to Adapt to Change:** The organization is trapped in a reactive mode, unable to respond to evolving business needs or leverage new technologies due to the limitations of the legacy system.

In summary, navigating the cloud-native path demands not only technological adaptation but a holistic transformation of organizational culture and structures. It's a challenging journey that requires a keen understanding of your unique business environment, distinct culture, and the intrinsic relationship between organizational structure and system architecture.

Now that we've established a thorough understanding of Cloud-Native Maturity Models, service management, and documentation methods, which have proven invaluable, it's time to venture into the lesser-explored aspects of CNAs. Let's navigate through the realm of trade-offs and alternatives.

Balancing Act: The Trade-offs

In the 1950s, Genrikh Altshuller and his colleagues introduced the groundbreaking TRIZ method, along with the inventive principles and patterns of evolution. Through extensive analysis of innovation paradigms and registered patents, they developed schemas for problem-solving and innovation thinking. TRIZ posits that there are fewer than 40 generic engineering problems and a handful of recurring inventive standards that can systematically address most new engineering challenges. The methodology emphasizes the importance of clearly defining the problem and identifying its key challenges. By breaking down the problem into smaller, generic components and mapping them onto the generic problems and TRIZ matrix, practitioners can then strive to achieve an Ideality state using well-introduced TRIZ inventive standards. TRIZ methods have seen widespread adoption across various industries, including prominent companies like Toyota, Samsung, Siemens, and Boeing. While TRIZ's origins lie in physics and manufacturing problems, its principles can be adapted for use in the software realm as well. This book does not delve deeply into TRIZ; readers interested in further exploration can refer to my other papers on *TRIZ and the CNA 1.0 Innovative Enterprise Architect Handbook.*

One of the fundamental principles of TRIZ is the recognition that "innovation arises from contradictions." When two or more values are in conflict - such as security vs. accessibility or production speed vs. quality risk - a contradiction exists. By focusing on finding a balance within the constraints of existing solutions, we design with trade-offs. However, true innovation occurs when we transcend these limitations and develop solutions that elevate the current balance points, thus innovating in the face of contradictions.

CNA products and operations offer a multitude of undeniable advantages. However, alongside these benefits come certain trade-offs that cannot be overlooked. The pivotal question isn't whether cloud-native approaches are favorable or not. Instead, the focus should be on the essential preparations required during the transition from existing applications to a genuinely CNA 1.0 environment. A deep understanding of these trade-offs is essential when considering the adoption of a cloud-native transformation strategy. I will lead you through this complex landscape, detailing the essentials needed for each stage of the journey and during travel.

- **Complexity:** The nature of cloud-native architectures and event-driven microservices is inherently complex, a complexity that can be further compounded by the requirements for multi- or hybrid cloud deployment, increased components, and intricate service dependencies. In addressing these challenges, I present Kubernetes and service mesh (Cilium mesh) as key solutions within this complex landscape.

Observability Tool Fragmentation presents a significant challenge within Kubernetes and CNA observability. I aim to tackle the pervasive issue of "*tool sprawl*," where each tool employed may contribute to the creation of data silos and UI silos. These silos necessitate complex interpretation, terminology and reference point mapping, and manual data translation across platforms, resulting in bottlenecks and other impediments to seamless integration and best practices in platform engineering.

The uncontrolled proliferation of tools brings about increased complexity, operational costs, expenses for enterprise support, and the burden of managing multiple licenses or subscriptions. Moreover, it consumes valuable time communicating with various vendors, hindering scalability and standardization and resulting in potential security risks and integration challenges. To tackle these issues head-on, organizations should prioritize the consolidation and standardization of their toolsets to cultivate a more secure, cost-effective, and efficient containerized application ecosystem.

- **Ensuring Security:** With an expanding array of tools and technologies, maintaining consistent security policies becomes increasingly challenging, potentially exposing vulnerabilities and risks.

- **Enhancing Efficiency:** Uncontrolled tool growth can lead to heightened operational costs and complexities, adversely affecting the efficiency of containerized applications.
- **Managing Complexity:** Tool sprawl introduces layers of complexity, making it daunting for IT teams to navigate and comprehend the overall system architecture.
- **Lowering Operational Costs:** An abundance of tools and technologies may result in elevated infrastructure, maintenance, and support expenses.
- **Mitigating Potential Security Risks:** Inconsistent security measures across disparate tools can heighten exposure to threats and vulnerabilities.
- **Facilitating Scalability:** As the tool landscape expands, organizations may encounter difficulties in scaling their containerized applications to meet evolving business needs.
- **Promoting Standardization:** Tool proliferation often leads to a lack of standardization across teams, fostering inefficiencies and potential misconfigurations.
- **Simplifying Tracking and Monitoring:** Managing numerous tools can complicate the monitoring and tracking of various aspects of the Kubernetes environment, diminishing visibility and control.
- **Addressing Integration Challenges:** Integrating multiple tools and technologies can be intricate and time-consuming, potentially causing delays and reducing overall effectiveness.

CILIUM IS NOT ONLY A CNI

In Chapter 2 till 10 of this book, we will delve deeper into how Cilium can effectively address tool sprawl within a Kubernetes environment by offering a comprehensive and unified solution for networking, security, and observability. By harnessing Cilium's capabilities, organizations can reduce dependency on multiple tools, streamline operations, and bolster efficiency in their Kubernetes deployments. Furthermore, Cilium offers compelling replacements for various existing tools, such as

Replacing Calico for Advanced Networking: Cilium provides high-performance and scalable networking capabilities, eliminating the need for additional networking plug-ins or overlays, thereby simplifying the networking stack.

Replacing Istio or Linkerd for Observability: Cilium offers multi-tenant connectivity data and metrics, providing real-time and historical insights without impacting applications, deployments, or clusters.

Replacing Istio or Linkerd Transparent Encryption: Cilium leverages eBPF to offer transparent, efficient, and secure encryption for containerized applications without sacrificing performance, making it an ideal solution for modern cloud-native environments.

Replacing Sysdig/Falco for Runtime Security: Cilium's capabilities enable rapid threat identification and response, offering complete visibility into network and runtime environments for informed decision-making and threat investigations.

From a **business perspective**, reducing tool sprawl yields significant benefits by streamlining operations, reducing costs, and enhancing efficiency. Through tool consolidation and standardization, organizations can achieve better resource management, simplified workflows, and increased standardization across teams, leading to reduced operational expenses, improved security, and faster decision-making. Ultimately, this enhances an organization's agility and competitiveness in the market.

- **Operational Overhead:** Managing a CNA 1.0 environment necessitates proficiency across diverse tools, platforms, and technologies. This often translates to heightened operational demands, encompassing monitoring, tracing, debugging, infrastructure maintenance, and managing performance issues. I propose leveraging cloud-native friendly observability (Cilium Hubble), CI/CD, and IaC as pivotal solutions to address these challenges.
- **Cost Management:** Although cloud-native architectures offer long-term cost-effectiveness through scalability, the initial expenses can be higher. Implementing FinOps best practices becomes crucial, particularly in scenarios where proper resource optimization or management is lacking. This process is critical for effective cost control and management.
- **Security Concerns:** The escalating complexity of cloud-native architectures brings about a corresponding rise in security vulnerabilities. It is imperative to employ robust security measures to effectively mitigate these risks. In this context, I propose

the utilization of sophisticated security protocols such as advanced network policy (with Cilium) and runtime security (Tetragon) to address and counteract potential threats.

Addressing trade-offs and challenges such as vendor lock-in necessitates a strategic approach that minimizes reliance on proprietary technologies. Embracing CNCF products like Cilium and leveraging open source technologies such as eBPF, widely adopted by various supply chain vendors and enterprises, indicates a proactive stance toward reducing future risks associated with exit plans and vendor lock-in. As my mentor wisely conveyed, when a solution fails to meet your expectations, adjustment might be necessary, either within the solution itself or within your expectations! Notably, while hybrid cloud deployment stands out as a cost-efficient and compliance-friendly option, its feasibility should be a **non-functional requirement (NFR)** integrated into the comprehensive supply chain review checklist.

Fear not, for as the saying goes, with every technological challenge comes at least one solution capable of either resolving or mitigating it. In the following chapters, we will delve into each of these solutions, emphasizing cutting-edge instrumentation technology and well-established observability methods. So, please, stay with me on this journey. It's crucial to remain vigilant about the limited flexibility and portability between diverse cloud platforms and toolsets. Opting for established, well-documented, and mature production-grade tools with the latest stable versions over low community-supported products or over-reliance on emerging technologies is fundamental. This approach ensures a more predictable landscape but demands careful consideration, potentially leading to a steep learning curve for development and SRE teams.

The Future Is Now

Platform and infrastructural transformation, alongside SDLC modifications, necessitate careful consideration of trade-offs and cultural shifts. Before venturing further into this transformative journey, it's essential to scrutinize the implications. Are you confident in pursuing a more extensive transformation, and what benefits await you on this path? Have you explored the option of maintaining the current mode of operation for a few more years? It's plausible that many of our competitors may not be as daring as us to embark on such a journey. Is this assertion accurate? Delving into these questions will guide us in making informed decisions about the direction of our cultural-technological evolution.

When confronted with a state of uncertainty, the inclination to perceive it as excessively risky and consider postponing decisions or actions is a common response. The impulse to transfer the risk to another party or delay actions under the guise of a "wait-and-see" approach often surfaces. However, is this a feasible option, and is it truly in your best interest?

Ultimately, the decision lies squarely in your hands. In the dynamic landscape of businesses, survival hinges on adaptability to the constant flux of change. As aptly articulated by David Anderson in the book *Kanban Maturity Model*, embracing evolutionary changes emerges as a prudent approach, particularly when navigating the interconnected realms of people, technology, and processes within a shared framework.

In essence, the safest path forward involves recognizing the inevitability of change and strategically evolving alongside it. This approach not only fosters resilience but positions individuals and businesses to thrive in an environment characterized by perpetual improvement journey and transformation.

> *Change is inevitable. Growth is optional.*
>
> –John C. Maxwell

It is strongly advised to invigorate and align your organizational change readiness, adapting to a lifestyle of continuous change. Prioritize the design of processes that seamlessly interconnect your goals, cultures, and technologies. Only after establishing a robust foundation should you consider the integration of new toolsets, ensuring they harmonize effectively within your dynamic framework.

There are many types of company culture in software-based businesses, but let's browse four types: *waterfall* (heavy planning upfront), *agile* (plan, act, and correct frequently), *semi-agile* (Scrumfall), and *cloud-native* (built microservices to optimum advantage of functioning in cloud technologies and services according to the CNA 1.0 definition). In a rapid cadence of deployment AI enabled world, software developers are no longer coders; they understand observability, networking, security, SDLC, and they are FinOps-aware well-architected cloud microservices design managers. Today, problem-solving; it's not just about finding the "*right*" solution or tools; it's equally crucial to foster the "*right*" culture. Our daily interactions within an organization are profoundly influenced by its collective culture. When the "*right*" solution and tool, or perhaps a blend of various toolsets, is implemented within the "*wrong*" culture, conflict ensues, stifling progress and leading to gridlock. It's imperative to recognize that what may be advantageous or expected in one context can prove detrimental in another.

Amidst the advent of Industry 4.0, work paradigms, regulations, and lifestyles undergo significant transformations. Enter the **Culture Clash Conundrum:** the convergence of waterfall and agile methodologies. While the involvement of product managers (owners) remains pivotal in both approaches, the fundamental issue persists - teams lack true autonomy over their projects. Agile teams may boast the capacity to handle greater complexity compared to their waterfall counterparts, yet they too often find themselves constructing monolithic structures with superficial agility. Consequently, central planning prevails, necessitating extensive coordination and joint delivery efforts spanning multiple sprints. Conway's law rings true here: any shortcomings in a software product can often be traced back to deficiencies in organizational communication and structural integrity within the responsible company. One notable method to visualize your cloud-native maturity matrix is to illustrate the CMO line in this chart. The red line is the CNA 1.0 FMO expectations, the blue line is your current state of CMO, and the colored area is what you need for evolutionary change.

Style \ Culture	Random	Waterfall	Agile	Cloud native 1.0	Cloud native 2.0 (perhaps)
Company	Individualistic	Predictive	Iterative	Collaborative	Generative
Leadership	Heroic	Shared Purpose	Unity	Alignment	Holacracy
Team	Single Contributor	Hierarchy	Cross-Functional Lean/Kanban Teams	DAD base SRE	Internal Supply Chains
Architectural	Trial and error	Tightly coupled monolith	loosely coupled monolith	Event base microservice on well-architected cloud framework	Distributed Serverless / FaaS and WebAssembly
Product	Arbitrary	Vision Driven	Feature Driven	Event Driven	AI Driven
DataCenter and availability zone	Single DC and AZ	data syncs (Active Standby)	service async (Active Standby backup)	platform syncs (Hybrid Cloud)	Cloud provider Agnostic and Distributed Edge
Provisioning	manual	scripted	Config management	Orchestration	IaC & PaC
Delivery	Irregular releases	Periodic release	Continuous integration	GitOps and Continuous Delivery	NoOps and Continuous Deployment
Operation	Responsive to user's complaints	Ad-hoc monitoring	alerting	Observability & self-healing	Preventive AI
Exemplar company status:			Current Status	Gap	Strategic Plan

Figure 3-4. *Cloud-Native Maturity Matrix*

The focal point of this chapter was to explore the intricate dynamics of the contemporary computing industry, investigating the foundations of DataCenter, the rise of cloud service providers, and the perpetual human pursuit of heightened speed and diminished risk. We navigated through the inherent trade-offs in this landscape, placing a spotlight on the cloud-native paradigm – a sophisticated technological concept with profound cultural implications. To thrive in this environment, it is highly recommended to conduct a thorough assessment of your organization's cloud-native readiness and maturity. This involves elucidating your product visions, refining your road map, and strategically enhancing your approach iteratively to align with the evolving needs of your organization. Fear not, a deeper understanding of how modern observability engineering can propel you to success in the cloud-native arena, coupled with the spirit offered by strong Cilium Swarming, will empower you in this dynamic landscape. (For a more comprehensive insight into the Holacracy, please refer to my other papers or books.)

Cloud-native computing satisfies crucial properties, encompassing essential attributes like extensibility, interoperability, portability, simplicity, malleability, and composability. It also embraces cloud federation and reliability, addressing the imperative requirements of modern distributed systems. This is just the beginning of the journey. As you delve into the upcoming chapters, your experience with cloud-native observability engineering using Cilium will not only deepen but also instill a heightened sense of confidence. Get ready to explore and enhance your understanding further for an enriched and rewarding journey ahead.

Summary

Modern cloud-native observability extends beyond the realm of software engineering; it necessitates a deep understanding of management principles, strategic foresight, and a keen awareness of evolving trends. By delving into maturity models and team orchestration methods, principal observability engineers are equipped to guide their teams and organizations along a path aligned with overarching company objectives. This chapter provided a practical approach for delineating, assessing, and enhancing our cloud-native maturity level through the integration of both social and technical catalysts for evolutionary smart changes. The exploration involved gaining insights into Holacracy, Disciplined Agile

Delivery capabilities, the pivotal roles of enterprise architecture, the impact of Conway's law, and the influence of organizational culture on product development. This comprehensive understanding enables the establishment of robust product **Key Performance Indicators (KPIs)** and team **Objectives and Key Results (OKRs)** for sustained continuous improvement.

In the next chapter, we will apply the same methods to delve into the realm of observability engineering.

CHAPTER 4

Observability Engineering Fundamentals

Any app lacking purpose-driven observability is just Code.

The product labeling with technical buzzwords like event-driven microservice architecture, immutable containerization infrastructure, orchestration platforms with declarative APIs, segregated control and data planes, multi-cloud mesh networking, self-healing, and resiliency platforms may be beneficial in marketing theory and SEO. Similarly tagging the organization with cultural buzzwords such as decentralized management, distributed authority, Holacracy, Disciplined Agile Delivery method, DevSecOps, and SRE contributes to this effect. Not good enough? Name enablers like progressive release delivery, declarative automation, GitOps, CI/CD, FinOps, graceful degradation of service capability, and integrated configuration management, minimizing operational toil and moving toward NoOps, in documents and talks. These are undoubtedly valuable concepts, but only if they "operationally exist" and "create values."

Dr. M. Ghane, *Observability Engineering with Cilium*,
https://doi.org/10.1007/979-8-8688-1258-3_4

Dear readers, achieving such a paradigm shift isn't feasible without a well-architected observability deployment facilitated by skilled cloud-native observability engineers. In this and the next chapter, we'll delve into the principles, disciplines, and methods of observability engineering and its transformative impact on cloud-native application delivery.

This chapter covers the following topics:

- Roots and background of observability engineering
- Conventional observability systems and cloud-native
- Observability system's components and objectives

Observability Engineering Philosophy

The success of a truly streamlined and efficient cloud-native ecosystem relies heavily on the meticulous implementation and maintenance of observability engineering practices. We will discuss the engineering foundation of cloud-native observability in this chapter. To establish a robust foundation, begin by adopting the ontology lens to delve into the roots and fundamentals of observability.

Observability Engineering in the Control Fields

Historically, the term "*observability engineering*" originated in the realms of control systems and algebra, later making its way into the domain of software business with certain foundational modifications. Consequently, many software engineering textbooks still lack a precise and nuanced definition of observability. The transference of this concept from its original context has led to an imprecise understanding within the software engineering community, highlighting the need for a more accurate and updated characterization in contemporary literature. When thinking about observability in the control theory context, it is a feature of an **H-system** - which is a mathematical way of describing a system that can switch between different modes, has both continuous and discrete states, and is affected by various inputs and outputs. This kind of system modelling is often used in control engineering to analyze and design systems that exhibit both continuous and discrete behaviors where we are looking for "*state space*" and "*observability matrix*." This refers to the set of all possible states that the system can occupy. To address the Zachman enterprise architectural questions of observability (why) in the hybrid state space, each state is a combination of a discrete state (what) and a continuous state (when).

Observability in classic control theory refers to the ability to determine the internal state of a system based on its outputs (measurements). In the context of state-space representation, observability is closely related to whether the entire state of the system can be reconstructed accurately from the available outputs.

The observability of a system is analyzed using the observability matrix, which is derived from the system's state-space representation. This matrix helps determine if the internal states of the system can be uniquely determined or observed based on the available outputs by observing its external outputs over time. Observability is crucial for designing effective control strategies and it is a desirable property of the system. If a system is not observable, it means certain internal states cannot be accurately determined from the outputs, making it challenging to design controllers that ensure the desired system behavior. While this definition remains valid for many systems in control theory, adjustments are necessary for software systems, as they may not conform to the mathematical H-system model.

Observability Engineering in the Software Fields

Recall the **software development lifecycle (SDLC)** parity and environment parity concepts introduced in Chapter 2, "Cloud-Native Phenomena," within the 12-factor container 1.0 definition. In each phase of the SDLC and for every container in each environment associated with a specific code base, distinct states of functionality can be recognized and documented in an explorable, high cardinality time series datasets. Continuous development of "observability matrix" enables the accurate description of all software services and dependencies, forming the basis for an observable application.

As per the classic characterization, observability is the harmonious integration of a suite of well-architected monitoring technologies, tooling, policies, IT Service Management (ITSM), and visibility, where it serves to bring the internal states of a system into the human realm, addressing the fundamental questions of "what," "when," and "why," enabling a comprehensive understanding of behavioral patterns and the ability to anticipate potential issues.

Observability, abbreviated as **O11y** (similar to Kubernetes, or K8s, with the O, 11 characters, and Y, pronounced as "Ollie"), is more than just an architectural topic; it's a cultural-technical concept, akin to the ethos of cloud-native development. Organizational culture, a collection of behaviors that are rewarded, tolerated, or sanctioned, is deeply intertwined with O11y. It goes beyond mere tooling; it's a mindset.

O11y isn't simply about real user monitoring (RUM) coupled with backend monitoring, sometimes dubbed application performance monitoring (APM). It encompasses synthetic monitoring as well. Rather than being merely a service, it's a capability, a feature that demands proactive development and maintenance across all stages of the software development lifecycle (SDLC) and parity in environments.

In their illuminating book on observability engineering, Majors et al. passionately argue against reducing observability to just another term for telemetry, indistinguishable from monitoring. They contend that this reduction oversimplifies the concept, failing to capture its true essence and breadth. This critique exposes a marketing ploy that seeks to integrate new buzzwords into outdated toolsets, underscoring the necessity for a more nuanced understanding and application of observability in modern software development.

Observability Is Not Monitoring!

Majors aptly points out the limitations of metrics-based monitoring systems, drawing a clear line between monitoring and observability. Monitoring tackles the known unknowns, whereas observability has capability for unveiling the unknown unknowns. Monitoring focuses on predefined signals, thresholds, and alerts. It is about keeping track of the system's health and performance based on those signals and rules. Observability goes beyond monitoring by enabling a deeper understanding of system behavior, even when the specific questions or issues are not predefined. It's about having the capabilities and data necessary to recognize and potentially resolve problems or patterns you didn't anticipate. Traditional monitoring tools often falter here, as they're confined to a narrow scope of metric interpretation. This deficiency presents a significant hurdle in maintaining and debugging microservice applications amid the complexities of distributed computing platforms, especially when dealing with high dimensionality and cardinality datasets.

While cardinality pertains to the uniqueness of values within datasets, dimensionality focuses on the number of keys present in that dataset. High cardinality information consistently proves most valuable for pinpointing data during debugging or gaining insights into system behavior. In a microservice observable systems, telemetry data manifests as a structured event with arbitrarily extensive dimensions. The greater the dimensionality of your dataset, the higher the likelihood of uncovering hidden or elusive patterns in application behavior, troubleshooting, and debugging.

In these systems, where potential failure permutations are virtually boundless, limiting telemetry data to only a few basic dimensions proves inadequate. Generally speaking, an effective practice is to exclude attributes with high cardinality from metrics and instead utilize them within spans or logs. This is because spans and logs typically don't encounter issues with cardinality explosions. Moreover, having more structured metadata regarding the significance of each metric signal is highly advantageous. Rest assured, all of these terms will be thoroughly explained in this chapter.

The broader the event, the more expansive the context captured at the time of occurrence, facilitating a profound and hypothesis-driven debugging process. This depth is often beyond the reach of conventional, metric-based, and time series database-oriented monitoring tools that typically excel in handling low cardinality dimensions at a smaller scale. In the time of monolithic applications, where issues commonly stem from component failures, reactive monitoring, which depends on individual debuggers' skills and institutional knowledge for troubleshooting and built around the concept of alerts and outages, emerged as the predominant operational method for decades. For simplicity's sake, we can say that microservices are made up of resources and transactions (address of known unknown). However, in the dynamic landscape of microservices and cloud-native applications, challenges primarily revolve around user behavior and intricate code, deployment, configuration, bugs, and interrelations (address of unknown unknown). As a result, there is a growing need for observability solutions that can adapt to the nuanced complexities introduced by this shift in architecture.

The Shifting Terrain of Cloud-Native Era

In the realm of cloud-native systems, the prevalence of unpredictable and unconventional failure modes far outweighs those that are somewhat foreseeable. These unforeseeable failures occur frequently enough to be a common occurrence, yet their patterns are so infrequent that most SRE and developer teams struggle to establish relevant dashboards for explorability. Such dashboards are essential for providing engineering teams with a clear view of the system's state and a critical responsibility in ensuring continuous uptime, reliability, and satisfactory performance of production applications. Emphasizing the human factors essential for cultivating observability practices, now it's time to walk through key areas of these engineering processes.

Imagine you are operating a mission-critical application like a core banking platform or the online payment system of an international retail bank or maybe the trading engine of a stock exchange company, or even a large scale e-commerce platform in a cloud-native world. There are some peak hours and there are some quiet times in the year. To manage computing resources efficiently, you probably use many techniques including autoscaling to keep the working instances right-sized according to real temporal loads. It means you allowed frequently destroying and initiating telemetry data sources with different IP addresses and locations, which is a noise for reactive monitoring. On the other hand, the combination of overlay and underlay network in SDN, K8s service mesh, or multi-cloud environments - which is another noise when troubleshooting based on conventional monitoring tools - with the distributed network nature of microservices creates more volatility and low visibility. Creating policies, routing, and security roles base on IP or MAC addresses which is very usual in almost all current systems, are not that reliable in microservice systems for telemetry where other methods like ID base networking to overcome these noises. It's a game changer.

Rosemary Wangan, in her book on *Infrastructure as Code, Patterns and Practices,* defines IaC as the cornerstone of modern DevOps/SRE methodologies, emphasizing its role in automating infrastructure changes. IaC, she explains, embodies the principles of scalability, resiliency, and security by codifying infrastructure setups. A notable facet she explores is event-driven IaC, where a modular infrastructure configuration responds dynamically to specific events.

On the other hand, GitOps emerges as a pivotal solution within this paradigm, offering automated responses to configuration drifts. Its core features include version control, continuous deployment, declarative configuration, and drift detection. Through GitOps and modern IaC, any configuration changes are managed via a declarative definition, ensuring version control and seamless deployment to production environments.

The book also delves into the practice of rolling forward DevSecOps configuration changes, which allows for the efficient resolution of issues by reverting changes and leveraging immutability. Additionally, GitOps's role in troubleshooting is discussed, highlighting common challenges such as configuration drift, unexpected dependencies, and environment discrepancies. At the zenith of automated event-driven Infrastructure as Code (IaC) and GitOps, with a keen focus on security awareness, lies the domain of observability.

Simply put, no robust CNA security, GitOps, or IaC strategy can exist without meticulous attention to observability configurations. Every alteration in infrastructure or application settings must seamlessly trigger corresponding changes in observability configurations, all managed meticulously through the GitOps methodology.

Enterprise Architecture and Cloud-Native

Drawing upon the discussions in Chapter 2, "Cloud-Native Phenomena," regarding Conway's law, it becomes evident that the journey toward cloud-native transformation requires a sociotechnical architectural approach and recall the mission of your enterprise architecture team. The central mission of a contemporary enterprise architecture (EA) team within an organization is to strategically align business and technology facets, ensuring a seamless integration where the IT infrastructure and systems robustly support overarching business goals.

The principal objectives of an EA encompass business, culture, and IT integration, along with strategic alignment, maintenance of a technology road map for optimized operations and cost efficiency, innovation enablement, agility, adaptability, change management, and standardization for consistency. Functioning as a crucial liaison between business and IT, the team offers a comprehensive perspective that empowers decision-makers to make well-informed choices aligned with the strategic vision of the organization. Remarkably, this team's mission shares several parallels with the well-architected delivery frameworks in the cloud, as discussed in Chapter 2, "Cloud-Native Phenomena," and aligns closely with the definition of Cloud-Native 1.0, doesn't it?

It's important to highlight that roles and teams designated as "enterprise architect" typically hold a consultative level of authority within organizations. To foster alignment among teams, business objectives, and architectural plans, it is imperative to have architects who exude charisma and embed a coaching-style leadership approach. These architect roles should be complemented by seasoned domain veterans and flexible realistic individuals with a keen understanding of emerging technology trends, ensuring a forward-looking perspective.

This combination of leadership qualities and expertise plays a pivotal role in orchestrating synergy across diverse facets of evolutionary transformation success. This architecture necessitates the harmonious evolution of technical, business, and social aspects within the management, production, and operation realms to align people, processes, and technologies with new standards. One critical facet of this transformation is observability, a factor contributing significantly to the enhancement of team characteristics and capabilities. Many enterprise architecture frameworks advocate for a clear delineation between governance processes and management processes, with observability serving as a unifying framework overarching both domains.

Allow me the privilege of presenting to you a marvelous book summary, *The Conference of the Birds*, a poetic masterpiece crafted by Attar of Nishapur, a Persian mystic and poet from the 12th century, which stands as an allegorical exploration of the spiritual and social path within the enlightenment teachings of the Sufi tradition. The narrative intricately weaves around a flock of 30 high-inertia birds led by the wise Hoopoe bird, embarking on a profound quest to find their legendary hero, Simurgh. Each bird symbolizes distinct human personalities, representing the rich and diverse nature of human existence.

Renowned for its philosophical depth, spiritual insights, and timeless allegorical storytelling, *The Conference of the Birds* emerges as an original and impactful guide for enterprise architecture. In this metaphorical landscape, the Hoopoe bird, serving as a charismatic coach, transformation architect, and pathfinder, assumes a role devoid of formal authority. Instead, the unpretentious Hoopoe intimately communicates with each bird, understanding their unique needs and challenges. It conducts blameless counselling sessions, crafts, and maintains a development road map toward the elusive hero.

The term "Simurgh" in Persian linguistics is imbued with the essence of biluminosity - a poetic concept of light radiating from two sources - representing simultaneous illumination from two perspective. It conveys *30 birds*, embodying the collective power of each of the organizational stakeholders, and at same time it symbolizes a parallel with the mythical Phoenix, a legendary bird known for its cyclical regeneration and rebirth, encapsulating the timeless essence explored in this story.

Through human-centric leadership, the Hoopoe transforms a community of proud, envious, slothful, gluttonous, and timid members into a healthy, arrogant, and semi-autonomous organization walking on the path of excellence. As the birds progress on their shared quest, facing trials that rigorously test their commitment and faith, the Hoopoe's art of leadership and architectural prowess become evident.

At the end of the book, the birds may not encounter any transcendental Simurgh, but through self-awareness, they discover themselves on the rail of continuous improvement. This destination, pursued by the Hoopoe, mirrors the journey of many enterprise architects striving for organizational excellence. I have long regarded this literary work as a key reference in enterprise architecture and coaching courses, finding enduring relevance in its profound lessons on leadership, transformation management, and the intricate tapestry of human nature.

In today's software operation world, the SRE team shifts its focus from mere component alerts to addressing user pain points. This shift involves examining structured events, which encompass meticulously formatted log data for machine parsability as well as adopting distributed tracing methodologies to comprehend system interdependencies. But before going deep on tracing and talking about what exactly tracing, telemetry, and instrumentation entail, let's look on observability concepts and testing method.

Observability-Driven Testing

Consider the concept of observability-driven testing as an alternative approach to traditional unit and integration testing. While the latter aims to validate application responses to predefined inputs, observability-based testing leverages traces and metrics to achieve similar outcomes.

In observability-driven testing, tests serve as a means to compare system behavior against a known, desirable state. Employing distributed tracing, you trace your services and capture traces reflecting predefined states, such as a typical customer order in an e-commerce platform. These traces are stored for future use. Periodically, perhaps after a deployment or as part of a canary release process, you re-run these tests with identical states and compare the new traces against the saved ones.

This methodology can be adapted and expanded in various ways. For instance, you may record specific metric measurements or define acceptable value ranges, comparing them at strategic points in the application or service lifecycle. These measurements can then serve as inputs to a continuous delivery tool, enabling the establishment of quality gates for canary releases. This ensures that new code does not degrade performance or introduce issues before reaching all users.

To enhance observability-driven testing approach further, consider integrating distributed tracing and profiling functionalities into your continuous integration and delivery pipeline. This enables the profiling of deployments and builds, providing deeper insights into system behavior and performance.

In the upcoming section, prepare yourself for a masterclass in observability terminology, methods, and concepts. If you encounter a new term that hasn't been explained yet, don't fret. Simply continue reading, and within a few paragraphs, it will be thoroughly elucidated. Alternatively, feel free to consult ChatGPT or her alternatives for immediate clarification.

Software Observability 101

When delving into conventional observability literature or attending most of marketing-focused seminars and conferences, one often encounters a familiar scene – a classic Greek pediment supported by a few columns or as they love to name, *pillars*. However, a swift exploration of these materials reveals their historical marketing significance to many in the business realm. It is advised to approach them with caution, refraining from unwarranted touch or criticism, as such actions may prompt a defensive reaction by mainstream observability vendors.

When talking about the conventional component of observability platforms, monitoring is one of the key objects from both the tooling perspective and the philosophical view. We can list three categories of monitoring systems, two styles of endpoint data gathering deployment architectures, and five types of monitoring services.

Primary Observability Pyramid

The **observability triangular pyramid** offers a structured framework for organizing and comprehending observability data within intricate systems. It consists of three layers, each serving a specific function within the observability framework.

- **Base Layer:** Positioned at the foundation of the observability pyramid, this layer encompasses fundamental data collection and monitoring mechanisms. It involves gathering raw telemetry signals from various components and subsystems within the system being observed. These signals encompass metrics, traces, logs (structured or semi-structured events), and other pertinent data points, ensuring accurate monitoring of the system's basic operational aspects.
- **Analysis Layer:** Situated above the base layer, the analysis layer focuses on examining and interpreting the collected observability data to detect and diagnose issues or irregularities within the system. This involves correlating data from different sources to uncover the root causes of problems or performance degradation. Through techniques like log analysis and correlation, distributed tracing patterns, and anomaly detection, teams can pinpoint areas needing attention and take corrective measures effectively.

- **Anticipation Layer:** Positioned at the top of the observability pyramid, the anticipation layer endeavors to predict potential issues or trends before they escalate into critical problems. This involves utilizing advanced analytics, machine learning algorithms, and predictive modelling techniques to forecast future system behavior based on historical data and present trends. By pre-emptively identifying patterns indicative of impending issues or performance bottlenecks, organizations can proactively implement preventive measures and optimize system resilience and efficiency.

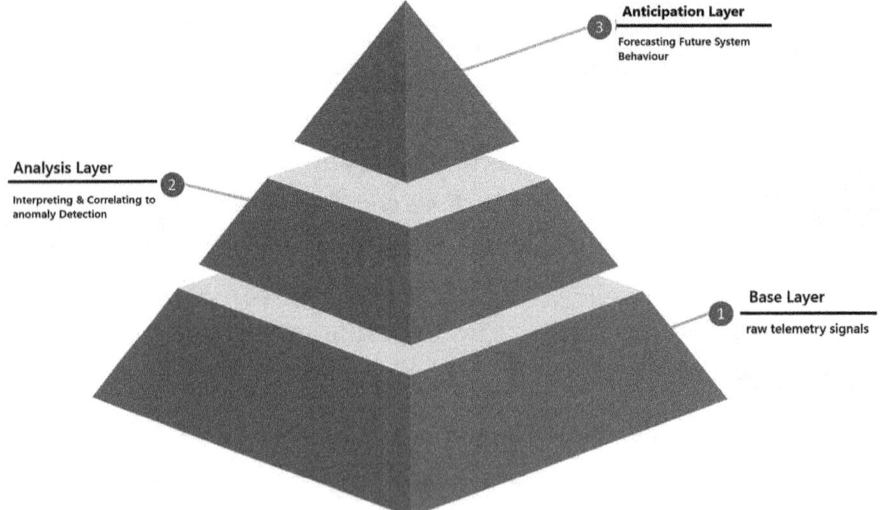

Figure 4-1. *Observability Pyramid*

The observability pyramid provides a structured guide for navigating observability data complexities, assisting teams in efficiently monitoring, diagnosing, and predicting their systems' behavior to ensure reliability, performance, and operational excellence.

Two Endpoint Data Gathering Deployment Architectures

Endpoint monitoring, also known as target system or instrumented asset monitoring, can be implemented using two primary architectures: **agent-based** and **agentless**. While agentless monitoring might suggest that monitoring tools can magically extract telemetry data from thin air, it actually employs generic protocols like SSH, SNMP, HTTP, or gRPC to gather information. The crucial aspect of agentless monitoring is ensuring that target systems provide access via the appropriate protocol versions and service APIs.

Agent-based monitoring, on the other hand, gains greater control over instrumented endpoints by installing lightweight agents on each endpoint. Agents such as Prometheus node exporter, Metricbeat, Telegraf, Grafana Beyla, and OpenTelemetry Collector act as intermediaries between the monitoring services or observability middleware and the endpoints, enabling data collection and command injection. Agent-based monitoring offers enhanced capabilities but also incurs additional costs associated with licensing, resource allocation, and maintaining the monitoring platform. This line-item cost contributes to the broader cost category commonly referred to as the "**observability tax**," a topic we will delve into in more detail later.

We have the flexibility to establish telemetry data collection through agent-based and agentless methods, utilizing either push-based or pull-based approaches. In **push-based** collection, data continuously emit metrics, logs, and traces to observability backend via HTTP post APIs to servers. This proactive approach normally used with agent-based or simple scripts and cronjobs. Conversely, **pull-based** systems rely on observability backends initiating requests to retrieve telemetry data from target hosts as needed. While pull-based systems offer more control over data retrieval frequency, volume, and leveraging vault secret management systems, they may introduce latency and resource overhead due to periodic polling.

Additionally, push-based systems are well-suited for handling high-frequency data streams and provide a more scalable solution for large-scale and cloud-native environments. In contrast, pull-based systems offer greater flexibility in managing backends and data integrity and can be more efficient in resource-constrained environments.

Three Monitoring Systems Catalogs

To unravel the intricacies of monitoring tools and system classes within the service domain, we typically classify them into three distinct categories: *ITIM*, *RUM*, and *BAM*. These catalogs serve as invaluable frameworks for comprehending the diverse facets of 360-degree monitoring and optimizing performance across various IT environments.

IT infrastructure monitoring (ITIM) serves as a continuous evaluation of the availability, performance, and resource utilization of IT infrastructure elements and services. Availability transcends mere uptime, encompassing a system's capacity to function within predetermined performance parameters known as SLOs (service-level objectives) in the realm of Site Reliability Engineering (SRE). Conversely, a system that is up but operates below SLOs is deemed unavailable due to performance degradation or sluggishness. API monitoring, a subcategory of ITIM, plays a pivotal role in ensuring that APIs deliver uptime, consistent performance, and data accuracy.

View SRE as a distinct deployment of the DevOps philosophy; however, it transcends being just another implementation of DevOps. The fundamental distinction lies in the distribution of continuous integration (CI) tasks: while pure DevOps typically shifts these tasks to the operations (Ops) team, SRE predominantly shifts them leftward, empowering Development (Dev) teams.

Real user monitoring (RUM) furnishes a comprehensive understanding of application performance from the user's standpoint. Synthetic user monitoring employs bot technology or other user-mimicking techniques to simulate real-time interactions with the application or web service, enabling the detection of user-impacting issues. Real user monitoring (RUM), also known as digital experience monitoring (DEM), tracks user interactions within the application and through the user interface (UI), providing a granular grasp of the actual user experience.

You may have heard about application performance monitoring (APM) as application functionality and heartbeat reader by capturing the entire interaction flow. According to Gartner in their Magic Quadrant for Application Performance Monitoring and Observability research, they defined APM as "software that enables the observation and analysis of application health, performance, and user experience. The targeted user roles are IT operations, site reliability engineers, cloud and platform ops, application developers, and product owners. These solutions may be offered for self-hosted deployments, or vendor-managed, hosted environments; via software as a service (SaaS)." I'm not particularly fond of categorizing a collection of tools and services under a buzzword like APM. While it may serve well in terms of upselling and marketing, it doesn't necessarily hold substantial meaning for most O11y enthusiasts. In this book, I'll refrain from utilizing APM to tackle any aspect of observability.

Business activity monitoring (BAM) is tasked with assessing business Key Performance Indicators (KPIs) and typically builds upon the insights gleaned from ITIM and user monitoring. FinOps monitoring (focusing on cost drivers, which are the factors or activities that affect your total cloud computing cost), as a BAM subcomponent, focuses on evaluating the financial performance of IT infrastructure and applications, primarily in cost center or usage-based pricing model environments. To effectively gauge business activity, it is crucial to map key business metrics to underlying services, assets, processes, costs, and mathematical formulas. This empowers organizations to track critical indicators such as average revenue per user (ARPU), average cost per user (ACPU), total addressable market (TAM) percentage, user churn rate, net promoter score (NPS), power usage effectiveness (PUE) per application, carbon offset per application, average cost of acquisition (ACoA) per user, and average user lifetime value (AULV). Relying on these metrics requires a robust, data-driven observability framework that is intelligently designed and implemented to meet the demands of modern applications and services.

Four Levels of Cloud-Native Observability

Understanding cloud-native observability intricacies across different levels is paramount for effective system management and optimization. At the foundational level of CloudOps, observability revolves around monitoring and analyzing the performance, health, and utilization of cloud infrastructure resources. Known as BaseOps in some circles, this level ensures visibility into the underlying infrastructure components such as virtual machines, containers, networks, and storage systems, facilitating proactive issue identification and troubleshooting. When having DCIM features, it can also be recognized as DataCenter level observability. Moving up to DevSecOps, observability extends to software and deployment, focusing on monitoring the behavior and security posture of applications, components, and APIs. Here, the goal is to detect and respond to security threats, vulnerabilities, and compliance issues in real time, ensuring continuous security monitoring throughout the software development lifecycle. Next, DataOps brings observability to data quality, emphasizing practices such as data profiling, standardization, and monitoring to optimize data workflows and processes. By leveraging metadata and data quality principles, observability engineers can refine their DataOps strategies, unlocking greater value from their information resources. Lastly, ServiceOps, where integration of user expectation according to SLM and deliverables is observed.

CloudOps: This level focuses on observability at the infrastructure system and component level. It involves monitoring and analyzing the performance, cost, health, and utilization of cloud infrastructure resources such as virtual machines, containers, networks, and storage systems. CloudOps observability - sometimes called BaseOps - ensures visibility into the underlying infrastructure to identify and troubleshoot issues effectively.

DevSecOps: At this level, observability extends to software and components. Observability within DevSecOps involves monitoring the behavior and security posture of applications, deployments, and APIs. It aims to detect and respond to security threats, vulnerabilities, and compliance issues in real time, ensuring continuous security monitoring throughout the software development lifecycle CI/CD as well as quality and availability performance indicators and SLOs. All this must be achieved without losing the traditional monitoring aspects of the observability platform, ensuring linked outputs to effectively manage application deployments in case of failures in nodes or application components.

DataOps: This level emphasizes observability in the context of data quality. As often stated, "*Platform Operations are a software engineering issue, while observability is a data engineering concern.*" Among the 11 domains outlined in the DAMA wheel for data management and governance, two are particularly relevant to observability engineering: *data quality principles* and *metadata management.*

Conventionally, DataOps entails a spectrum of practices including data profiling, standardization, geocoding, monitoring data quality, and establishing time frames. As a senior observability engineer, you likely possess a solid understanding of each of these practices.

Metadata assists as the concept of "*data about data,*" enhancing, contextualizing, correlating, and reducing the burden of nonvaluable loads and contents. Broadly categorized into three types, descriptive metadata includes elements such as geocoding and time frame, while structural metadata encompasses details like events and JSON format machine logs and administrative metadata and pertains to crucial information such as logins and access permissions.

By recognizing and harnessing the diverse facets of data quality principles and metadata, observability engineers can optimize their DataOps strategies and unlock greater value from their information resources.

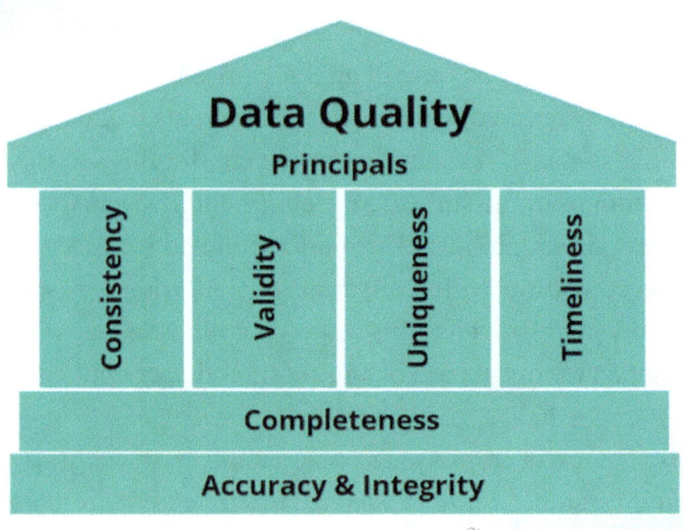

Figure 4-2. *Data Quality*

DataOps emphasizes the automation, collaboration, and optimization of data workflows and processes. Observability in DataOps involves monitoring and analyzing data pipelines, datasets, and data processing operations to ensure data quality, consistency, and reliability. It enables organizations to identify data anomalies, errors, and inconsistencies promptly, facilitating data-driven decision-making and ensuring the integrity of data-driven applications and analytics.

ServiceOps: This comprehensive level focuses on business-driven metrics observability. Generally, The director's dashboards fed by ServiceOps signals related to achieved SLAs, error budget, uptime, future risks, and more, which we will discuss in the next chapters.

Five Types of Monitoring Services

There are five basic types of monitoring services crucial for maintaining system health and performance within established service-level objectives (SLOs) while minimizing operational toil and fatigue. First, visualization services serve as the primary interface for observability, providing intuitive dashboards and graphs to empower Site Reliability Engineers (SREs) in identifying patterns and anomalies. Analytical services work behind the scenes to analyze telemetry data using machine learning models and artificial intelligence (AI) to detect anomalies and provide insights. Data management services organize, store, and aggregate telemetry data, crucial for analyzing system insights. Profiling services delve into application execution to pinpoint performance bottlenecks, while Incident Response Management (IRM) ensures prompt response to operational and security incidents, maintaining service quality and upholding SLOs. Together, these monitoring services form the backbone of observability, extending beyond component monitoring to encompass service SLOs and status, ensuring robust system performance and reliability.

Visualization Services: The Eye-Catching Face of Observability

Visualization services are the primary interface for observability, providing dashboards, graphs, and gauges with built-in statistical models to present and compare system status in a human-centric manner. These tools empower SREs to identify patterns and anomalies with intuitive UX and ergonomic design, enabling them to maintain system health and performance within established service-level objectives (SLOs) ideally with minimized toil, fatigue, and frustration.

Analytical Services: Unravelling Insights from Data

Behind the scenes, analytical services work tirelessly to analyze telemetry data, combining it with other sources and employing machine learning models to detect anomalies and their root causes in real time. They may even leverage artificial intelligence (AI) to uncover patterns, provide guidelines, and predict potential issues.

Data Management Services: The Silent Guardian of System Insights

Cloud infrastructure, services, and applications generate a wealth of metrics and unstructured and structured events throughout their lifecycle. Despite concerns about where to store telemetry data, They contain crucial information about performance status, state changes, user interactions, resource usage, billing, and security events. Data management services organize, store, ingest, and aggregate them, enabling analysis of combined traces.

While log structure conventions exist, such as timestamps, log levels, and JSON formatting, message formats and contextual information may be delivered unstructured. It's essential to ensure logging services are capable of reliable search functionality for high cardinality and dimensionality events. Data correlation, rotation, retention, and security considerations are also paramount during service selection.

Tracing and distributed tracing functionalities, often integrated within logging services, provide a holistic view of system behavior by capturing and analyzing dependencies of applications and resources. This capability is crucial for identifying performance bottlenecks and resolving complex issues.

Profiling Services: The Unsung Hero of Observability

Profiling services delve into the execution of applications to gain insights into their behavior, pinpoint performance bottlenecks, analyze resource utilization, and identify optimization opportunities. Typically, when integrated with load testing; profiling involves capturing detailed code execution information, including performance telemetry data at the function and method levels.

Load testing and profilers empower developers and operators to understand where the most resource-intensive sections of code reside, enabling optimizations to enhance performance and identify potential issues. This profiling data can be seamlessly integrated into observability platforms for a comprehensive understanding of application performance.

Incident Response Management (IRM): Promptly Responding to Outages

Incident Response Management (IRM) serves as the backbone of monitoring, encompassing an ITSM systematic process for identifying, responding to, and resolving operational and security incidents that impact the normal operation of applications and platforms. This includes monitoring various types of incidents and the health status of components, evaluating service performance and costs, and filtering out any incidents that impact service-level indicators (SLIs) or risk breaching service-level objectives (SLOs). To promptly detect any SLO breaches, dedicated channels per service or product management team are necessary, although not all incidents warrant alerting.

All high-severity alerts are considered in Incident Response Management (IRM) and trigger the escalation rules. Alerting primarily emphasizes user impact, while incidents are concerned with maintaining service quality. O11y extends beyond component monitoring, encompassing service SLOs and status, rather than just status and alerting.

Alerts, triggered by IRM services, serve as notifications to inform on-call operators of abnormal or undesirable system states. By facilitating swift responses to incidents, alerts help teams maintain system health and performance. Later in this chapter we will talk about more human-centric approaches in IRM as art of silent alerting.

The debate over which monitoring suite is best is often contentious. As observability engineers and SREs, we recognize that there is no one-size-fits-all approach. A structured decision-making process is essential to determine the appropriate monitoring types and categories, considering the specific needs and complexities of the system.

Classic Golden Signals

With a foundational grasp of monitoring taxonomy, we can now explore the renowned golden signals, which stand as a cornerstone in the history of observability. These signals offer a unified framework for measuring and analyzing endpoints, providing insights into core system health and characteristics, fostering continuous improvement and resilience.

Coined by Google's Site Reliability Engineering (SRE) team, the term "golden signals" underscores the exceptional importance of four key metrics: Latency, Errors, Traffic, and Saturation (LETS). These metrics are deemed crucial for monitoring any user-facing system or subsystem, with their acronym facilitating easy memorization and consistent reference.

Latency: Latency refers to the time a system takes to respond to a user request. For instance, the time it takes for an online banking portal to appear after a button click. Latency is critical for user-facing systems, and any degradation directly impacts user experience. Distinguishing latency for successful and unsuccessful responses is essential.

Errors: Focus lies on the ratio of error (HTTP 50x codes) to successful (HTTP 20x) responses rather than the absolute number of errors. This metric, known as the error rate signal, presents the percentage of successful responses relative to total requests. Customizable conditions can define when a response is considered a failure.

Traffic: Interpretation depends on the system or subsystem being monitored. For web-based interfaces, the number of HTTP requests per second is an example. It directly correlates with the system's workload and activities within a given time frame.

Saturation: This metric quantifies the current load on a system. It's based on understanding the system's breakeven point concerning available IT resources. In CPU-constrained systems, exceeding 100% CPU utilization leads to service degradation. In modern applications with autoscaling, network bandwidth may be the limiting factor.

Beyond the Classic Golden Signals

Venturing beyond the foundational golden signals framework, we encounter *STELA*, *USE*, and *RED* methodologies. STELA expands the original signals by integrating availability, streamlining resource allocation. USE employs checklists for assessing system performance, ideal for IT resource monitoring. RED tailors metrics for each microservice, focusing on rate, errors, and duration.

STELA (Saturation, Traffic, Error rate, Latency, and Availability)

Expanding the original golden signals by incorporating availability. Assessing availability first determines whether measuring other golden signals is relevant, saving valuable resources.

USE (Utilization, Saturation, and Errors)

Developed by Brendan Gregg, the USE method utilizes checklists to evaluate system performance, especially for monitoring IT resources like compute nodes.

RED (Rate, Errors, and Duration)

Created by Tom Wilkie, RED defines three metrics for each microservice: request rate, request errors, and request duration.

While these methods don't directly derive from the golden signals, they provide complementary perspectives. SREs rely on LETS, STELA, RED, and USE to understand system behavior through data and guide the placement of monitoring metrics. Regrettably, these approaches pose challenges when applied to streaming APIs. With the rise in popularity of streaming Remote Procedure Calls (RPC), such as gRPC, there arises a need for innovative methodologies and tools tailored specifically for monitoring these systems.

Four Pillars of Classic Monitoring: LDTM

Monitoring system components generate various data types collectively known as *LDTM*: Logs, Dumps, Traces, and Metrics. (Mnemonic says: **L**ooks **D**azzling **T**o **M**e!) These serve as the architectural pillars supporting the observability pediment. While the term "pillar" is not commonly employed by principal observability engineers to denote primary signal data types or telemetry, it has a rich history of extensive usage in the field.

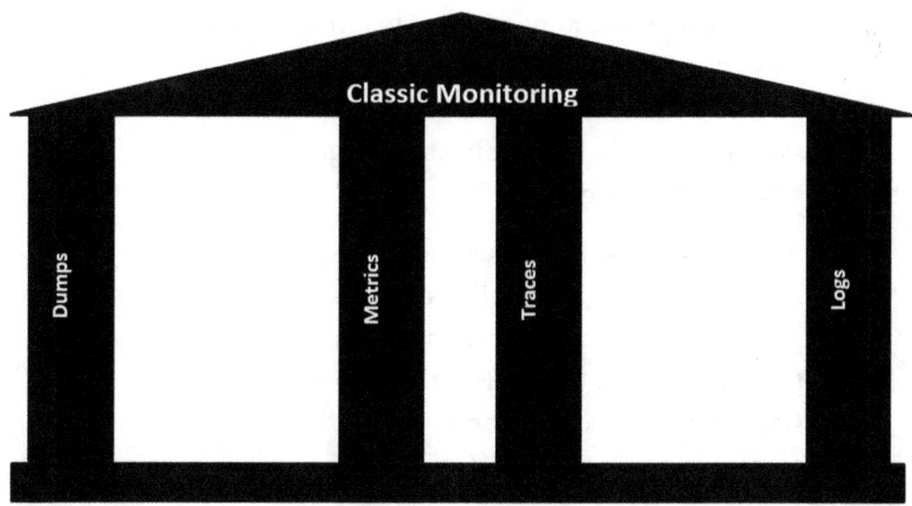

Figure 4-3. *Classic Monitoring*

Logs

Textual records containing detailed information about events, transactions, or activities within a system. Timestamped entries with context-specific details. These entries can be classified into various categories, including

> **Application Logs:** Generated when an event occurs within an application, aiding developers in comprehending and assessing application behavior during development and post-release phases
>
> **Security Logs:** Created in response to security-related events, encompassing failed log-in attempts, password changes, authentication failures, resource access, and administrative alterations, with customizable configurations by system administrators

System Logs: Documenting events within the operating system, covering kernel-level messages, boot sequences, authentication processes, and system activities, facilitating fault diagnosis and status monitoring

Audit Logs: Also known as audit trails, maintaining records of events and modifications, capturing the performer, nature, and system response of activities, typically tailored by administrators to meet organizational requirements

Infrastructure Logs: Integral to infrastructure management, overseeing physical and logical components impacting an organization's IT infrastructure, sourced from on-premises or cloud environments via APIs, Syslog, or host-based agents

Logs serve various purposes, including metric derivation, security audits, and debugging, offering insights into application and system events for comprehensive understanding and potential reproduction of specific scenarios.

Despite the unstructured nature of log data, attempts to impose schemas have been made over the past three decades to facilitate information extraction. These efforts involve parsing, segmenting, and analyzing log text, with potential conversion into metrics or traces for enhanced observability and analysis.

Log levels enable the classification of log statements based on their significance, ranging from ERROR for failure notifications to DEBUG for detailed troubleshooting information, aiding in hypothesis-driven debugging, root-cause analysis, core analysis loop, and troubleshooting efforts.

In the past, we tracked errors using log messages and focused on making them human readable. However, in cloud-native environments, error messages are now sent to STDERR in machine-readable formats like JSON.

To manage logs effectively, several forwarding methods are available, including direct streaming to a central location, routing through message queues for filtering or enrichment, or employing open source data collectors for centralized repository storage, complementing other observability signals for comprehensive system monitoring.

Security considerations are paramount in logging solutions, necessitating encryption of log data at rest and in transit, avoidance of storing personally identifiable information (PII), and ensuring critical data redundancy beyond logs' reliability limitations.

EVENTS

In certain older sources, events are regarded as one of the classic pillars, defined as distinct incidents or signals that capture specific occurrences or changes in a system. They denote moments such as system startups, user interactions, or error conditions as events. While logs usually consist of unstructured textual records documenting activities and offering a detailed historical account, events are structured data that pinpoint particular happenings, emphasizing real-time monitoring and analysis. As we progress through this book, we will adopt "logs" as the overarching term for both unstructured and structured textual records.

Dumps

In the realm of software development, core dump files serve as vital tools for diagnosing program issues, particularly when a process crashes unexpectedly. Traditionally, when a crash occurs, the operating system captures a snapshot of the process's memory, guided by certain configurations like file location, naming conventions, or file size. However, in cloud-native environments, the aggregation of core dump files across a large cluster can pose challenges, potentially leading to storage bottlenecks or network congestion, depending on the architecture of the storage attached to cluster nodes. For instance, applications with high processing demands may generate core dump files of considerable size, often reaching double-digit gigabytes.

In Linux-based systems, the handling of core dump files has evolved with the introduction of core dump handlers since kernel version 2.6 and beyond. This approach differs from the conventional method by shifting the responsibility of file collection from the operating system to designated core dump handler applications. In Debian-based distributions, this process can be facilitated through systemd or abort, while RedHat-based distributions utilize the ABRT framework. Despite these advancements, the cloud-native community still grapples with efficient core dump collection. A request for comments (RFC) issued approximately seven years ago (referenced here: `https://lore.kernel.org/patchwork/patch/643798/`) underscored the need for namespaced core_pattern support within the Linux kernel community, advocating for a departure from the current global system setting approach.

Traces

Software traces work by a sequences of timestamped events tracing the path of a request through various components in a distributed system. It includes information about the duration and interactions of the request. Distributed tracing is a valuable technique for gaining insight into the intricacies of distributed transactions. It enables the understanding of how requests initiated by end users propagate through various microservices and data stores, influencing system behavior along the way.

One of the key advantages of distributed tracing is its versatility. It can be applied across different programming languages, runtimes, and deployment environments, making it compatible with a wide range of applications and services. Moreover, distributed tracing enhances collaboration and coordination within teams while also streamlining the process of identifying and addressing performance issues within applications.

Traces are typically visualized as trees of "tracing data points" or spans, offering detailed insights into the path of a specific transaction instance within a program. These spans are rich in context, recording information about their parent spans and establishing causal relationships between various components of a distributed system, such as services and databases.

A crucial aspect of distributed tracing is context propagation, which ensures the persistence of relationships across different actors within the system. While various monitoring systems have historically employed proprietary methods for trace context propagation, there's now widespread agreement within the industry on the importance of standardization. The adoption of standards like the W3C Trace Context format by pioneering projects underscores the importance of standardized trace-context propagation for effective monitoring and analysis.

Metrics

Quantitative measurements capturing specific aspects of the system's performance over time called *Metrics*. Numeric values associated with dimensions like CPU utilization, memory usage, and error rates. Metrics, ideal for addressing known unknowns, prove efficient in terms of predictable processing costs across various operations such as retention, emission, transmission, and storage. Within the CNCF ecosystem, two prevalent metric data models, Prometheus and OpenTelemetry, manifest in three distinct forms:

> **Gauge:** Representing a single numerical value capable of fluctuating arbitrarily, gauges find application in measuring parameters like temperature or current memory usage, as well as "counts" subject to fluctuation, such as concurrent request numbers.

Counter: Serving as a cumulative metric, counters track a monotonically increasing value, reset only upon system restart. Examples include counts of requests served, tasks completed, or errors encountered.

Histogram: Having sampling observations, such as *request durations* or *response sizes*, when histograms categorize them into configurable or exponential buckets while providing a summation of all observed values are very helpful. They facilitate advanced analysis, enabling insights into distributed observations like percentiles and heatmaps.

Metrics primarily adhere to structured or semi-structured formats and are employed in two primary ways.

Metrics play a crucial role in visual dashboard overviews, enabling users to delve into data and triggering alerts or notifications for human or automated responses when systems surpass predefined thresholds or exhibit anomalous behavior.

Over time, metrics facilitate trend analysis and long-term planning, offering insights into incidents post-occurrence to rectify underlying issues and establish preventative measures against future recurrences.

While metrics may not always pinpoint the root cause of an issue, they furnish a high-level perspective and serve as a starting point for identifying underlying problems.

If you're wondering when to utilize tracing and questioning the relevance of logs, consider this: logs remain essential for extracting signals from applications that can't be traced directly. Additionally, they play a crucial role in correlating infrastructure resources, such as managed databases or load balancers, with application events. Moreover, logs are indispensable for comprehending the behavior of an application beyond mere user requests.

As the fundamental signal of observability, trace is a type of distributed logging statement that's designed to model transactions across distributed systems that offer several semantic benefits. Traces encode the specific relationships between services in a microservice and the parameters that pass between them. Each trace is a collection of related logs for a given transaction and comprises many spans, or individual units of work. Each span, in turn, contains a variety of fields.

As the cornerstone of observability, a trace represents a specialized form of distributed logging that meticulously captures transactional activities across microservices, yielding numerous semantic advantages. Each trace aggregates associated logs pertinent to a particular transaction, consisting of multiple spans, which are discrete units of work. Within each span, a diverse array of fields further enriches the contextual information.

Each type of data provides unique insights into the performance and behavior of the software system. The process of collecting this data involves sampling techniques tailored to each data type and its associated characteristics. Sampling refers to the process of collecting a subset of data points or observations from a larger population or dataset. In the context of software monitoring and observability, sampling involves periodically gathering specific data points or measurements at predetermined intervals. This enables the assessment of the state and behavior of the software over time without overwhelming the monitoring system with an excessive amount of data.

Resampling, on the other hand, involves the re-evaluation or recalibration of the sampling process. It may entail adjusting the sampling intervals, changing the data collection methodologies, or revising the subset of data points being collected. Resampling is often employed to enhance the accuracy and reliability of the collected data, especially in scenarios where the initial sampling approach may not adequately capture relevant information or trends.

Furthermore, the concept of resampling can be applied to optimize the data collection process. This may involve adjusting the sampling intervals for different data types, refining the selection criteria for specific observations, or modifying the data collection pipelines to accommodate changes in the software environment. By continuously refining the sampling approach through resampling, organizations can improve the accuracy and relevance of the collected data, thereby enhancing their ability to monitor and analyze the software system effectively.

Cardinality and Dimensionality of Metrics

In the realm of metrics, cardinality denotes the count of distinct metric series amassed within a specific time frame. Prometheus, for instance, boasts scalability into the realm of tens of millions of active series, offering a notable advantage in processing efficiency compared to the vast number of logs or trace events required to represent each memory allocation.

The scalability of any proficient metric storage backend or vendor invariably correlates with metric cardinality; in essence, the genuine expense escalates alongside cardinality. Given the typical metric interval fluctuates between one second and one minute, the volume of samples also serves as a measure of cardinality for a given duration. Consequently, it's not uncommon to encounter vendors or systems billing based on per-sample metrics. Moreover, many systems impose limitations on the permissible cardinality within a specified time frame.

Metric cardinality is often singled out as the Achilles' heel of metric data. However, such a perception can be misleading, as every facet of observability data bears its associated cost. The efficacy of metrics hinges on the stability of dimensions and their values over time.

Instances of high cardinality issues frequently arise when users attempt to stretch their economical and efficient metric storage and pipelines beyond their intended scope by incorporating observability data with non-metric attributes. If we find ourselves contending with highly distinct labels, resulting in short-lived metric series with minimal samples, it behoves us to contemplate emitting events such as logs, traces, or profiles rather than persisting with metric samples.

Let's shift from the superficial notion of three distinct pillars and embrace a semantic analogy: envision a cohesive intertwining of all telemetry data in a context. Within this unified structure, we uncover correlations by intertwining all telemetry signals seamlessly. The essence of observability lies not merely in the accumulation of telemetry signals but in achieving the optimal level of signal coherence. This is where observability truly adds value to business operations. As previously discussed, the synergy between cohesive telemetry signals and thorough analysis culminates in a contemporary observability framework.

Six Pillars of Cloud-Native Observability: M3PLT

In the cloud-native observability domain, telemetry data types or observability pillars expand to include **m**etrics, service dependencies **m**apping, consistent targets **m**etadata model, **p**rofiling, **l**ogs, and distributed **t**races (*M3PLT*). Please note that core dumps are not widely available in the CNA platforms yet.

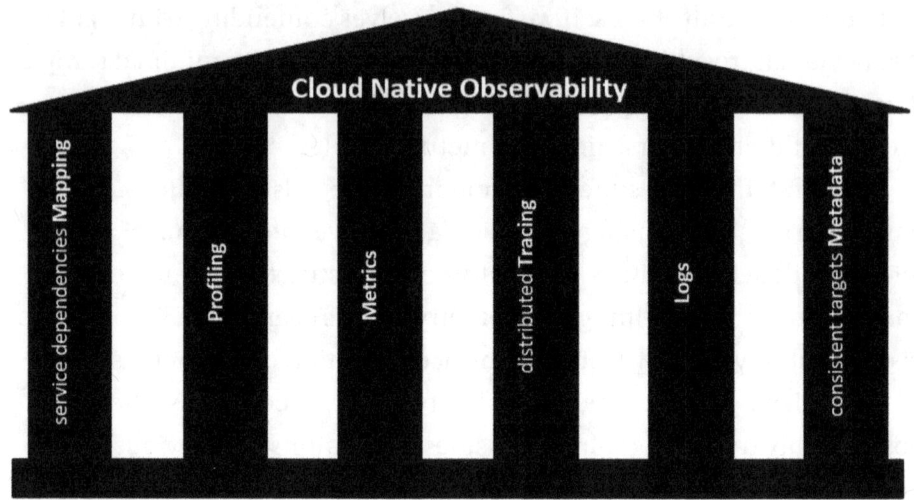

Figure 4-4. *Six Pillars of Cloud-Native Observability: M3PLT*

Metadata Model

A cohesive and easily referenced metadata model should be applied uniformly to all signals.

Ensuring uniform metadata is crucial for seamlessly transitioning between observability signals originating from the same source (e.g., a single application). This may involve utilizing pull-based frameworks such as Prometheus or the Prometheus receiver in OpenTelemetry (for metrics), as well as log tailing collectors like OpenTelemetry, Fluentd, or Fluent Bit. It's essential to guarantee that a consistent set of target labels or attributes, such as "cluster," "environment," "pod," and "container_name," are associated with your collector or agent. When working with push-based collections like OTLP (covering metrics, logs, and tracing), the instrumented application typically includes the necessary target information, ensuring continuity.

Consider establishing a standardized unique identifier such as Operation ID, Request ID, or Trace ID and connecting it seamlessly with both tracing and profiling, as well as logging systems. Investigate the potential of integrating your tracing and logging client instrumentation, enabling the tracing library to generate a Trace ID that signifies a distinct request journey across multiple microservices. Subsequently, this Trace ID can be attached to log entries when capturing events associated with the request.

Numerous domain-specific languages (DSL) cater to observability data systems, yet they lack consistency and interoperability. The OpenTelemetry (OTel) initiative emerges as a beacon, fostering interoperability across open source projects and vendors, ensuring compatibility from client interaction to data ingestion. Despite OTel's strides, there remains a need for standardization in data querying methods and the uniformity of schema and terminology. While metric databases like Prometheus, Thanos, and Cortex have reached maturity, the CNCF umbrella lacks logging, tracing, and profiling databases. Nevertheless, the observability landscape boasts a plethora of compelling solutions beyond the CNCF ecosystem, some offering more lenient licensing terms than others.

Service Dependencies Mapping

It involves visualizing the relationships and dependencies between different services or component interfaces in a system using UML or ARC42 tools. It provides a high-level overview of how services interact, aiding in understanding architecture, identifying critical paths, and visualizing the impact of changes. It is valuable for architecture planning, risk assessment, and system documentation. The process kicks off with the gathering of data pertaining to the various deployed services, encompassing details like their endpoints, communication protocols, and interconnections. Subsequently, this data undergoes thorough analysis to unveil the intricate relationships and dependencies among services. These relationships delineate which services lean on others for functionality or data exchange.

Armed with this insightful data, a visual representation is crafted, typically manifested as a dependency map or network diagram. This graphical depiction delineates the intricate web of requests and data transmissions among services, shedding light on dependencies, communication channels, and potential weak links.

Service dependencies mapping stands as a cornerstone in the realm of cloud-native application observability. It serves as a crucial tool for unravelling the architecture and dynamics of the system, aiding in the identification of performance bottlenecks, pinpointing root causes of issues, and optimizing resource allocation and communication pathways. This, in turn, leads to enhanced reliability and efficiency within the system.

Profiling

It involves analyzing the runtime behavior of an application to identify performance bottlenecks, resource usage, and areas for optimization. Profilers collect data on CPU usage; memory consumption, using Heap Profilers, Mutex profilers, IO profilers, and language-specific profilers; and execution times of functions or methods within the application. Traditionally, the concept of profiling faced hurdles in its application for real-time systems due to the significant overhead it incurred. However, with the rise in popularity of sampling profilers, particularly in CNA environments, the landscape is shifting. These profilers now impose only a minimal overhead, making real-time profiling a feasible option.

Integrating a temporal dimension into profiling data enhances the granularity and comprehension provided by static profiles. This augmentation enables individuals to scrutinize their data from both a detailed and an overarching perspective. In the realm of optimizing and debugging CNAs, grasping resources holistically is paramount for effective resource allocation.

Much like how tracing broadens the scope of understanding regarding latency issues within an application, profiling delves even deeper into the root causes behind these delays. Moreover, it sheds light on which segments of code are the most resource intensive, aiding in efficient resource management.

Profiling data generated by runtimes typically offers detailed statistics, including line-level information. Consequently, this data serves as a bridge from identifying the "what" to unravelling the "why" in terms of code behavior.

With normalized and consolidated M3PLT data, advanced data science techniques can be applied to unveil insights into a system based on discernible patterns in the dataset. Each signal has its purpose and best practices, and their misuse can lead to new problems when running software at scale, such as "alert fatigue" and "high cost."

Tracing, Telemetry, Instrumentation, and NoOps

At its core, a trace is a sequence of interconnected events. In an observable system, any collection of events can be seamlessly woven into traces.

To achieve effective tracing, three span identifiers and two chronological values of data are required for each tracing component:

1. **Trace ID:** This unique identifier, generated by the root span, serves as a mapping tool back to a specific request. It is propagated throughout each step taken to fulfill the request.

2. **Span ID:** For every individual span created, a unique identifier is essential. Spans encapsulate information captured during a unit of work in a single trace. The unique ID facilitates easy reference to each span as needed.

3. **Parent ID:** This field plays a crucial role in defining nesting relationships throughout the trace's lifecycle. Notably absent in the root span, the Parent ID signifies the initiation of the trace.

4. **Timestamp:** Each span must indicate the precise moment its work commenced, providing chronological context within the trace.

5. **Duration:** Record-keeping of the time taken to complete each span's work ensures a comprehensive understanding of the temporal aspects of the trace.

As the request exits your service, or returns an error, there are several bits of data about how the unit of work was performed: duration, response code, error messages, etc. It is common for events generated with mature instrumentation to contain even 300 dimensions per event.

Incorporating observability features into code to gather behavior and performance data relies on a key concept *called telemetry instrumentation*. This term, along with "instrumentation" and "signals," comes from instrumentation and control engineering, a field widely used in industries like power plants, oil refineries, and mega DataCenters.

In cloud-native environments, there are several ways to implement instrumentation:

Manual Hardcoding: Developers can write custom code during the development phase to collect metrics, data, and trace execution.

Using Annotations: Annotations in the source code can mark where instrumentation is needed, and tools or frameworks automatically insert the necessary code based on these annotations.

Pre-compilation Modifications: Instrumentation can be added before or during the compilation process using preprocessor directives or telemetry code generation tools.

Bytecode Instrumentation: During the build or compilation phase, tools can modify the program's bytecode to include telemetry objects, agents, or libraries.

Dynamic Instrumentation: More advanced methods use frameworks to inject code into running programs without requiring recompilation or redeployment.

Good news! Enhancing observability doesn't always mean extensive code changes. Modern tools make it easy to integrate telemetry instrumentation, whether in source code or bytecode, even before compilation. eBPF offers a highly efficient way to collect telemetry data from running applications with minimal resource use and no need for redeployment. With these tools, achieving better observability is simpler than ever. Rest assured, you have powerful solutions at your disposal! No worries! We've dedicated the next chapter to diving deeper into software instrumentation and exploring eBPF in greater detail.

Observability engineering methods and systems, through the lens of distributed tracing, empower developers, product managers, and SRE teams to navigate the complexities of a cloud-native transformation, debugging, and optimization with precision and clarity. View SRE as a distinct deployment of the DevOps philosophy; however, it surpasses being just another implementation of DevOps. The fundamental distinction lies in the distribution of continuous integration (CI) tasks: while pure DevOps typically shifts these tasks to the operations (Ops) team, SRE predominantly shifts them leftward, empowering Development (Dev) teams. Observability engineering skills are a must-have knowledge for both.

Mastering observability engineering skills is imperative knowledge for professionals in both DevOps and SRE realms, particularly in the contemporary landscape where IT-based businesses intersect with the revolutionary concepts of NoOps. NoOps, comprising five essential elements – *CNA 1.0, purpose-driven semantic observability, well-architected automated CI/CD, FinOps, and AIOps* – represents the quintessential recipe for streamlined operations in modern IT environments. At its core, NoOps is characterized by semantic event-driven automation of cloud-native operations, culminating in the automated management of posture. Looking ahead, CIOs will inevitably be confronted with inquiries such as, "What is the key value of observability without the integration of automation and AIOps?" Simply gaining visibility into context is not enough for future-proof businesses! These buzzwords have been elucidated in preceding chapters and will be further expounded upon in subsequent sections. However, let us delve deeper into the pivotal game changer, AIOps, and its profound impact on observability engineering.

AI, Machine Learning, and AIOps Work for Observability

Our cloud-native maturity road map epitomized through the evolution toward FinOps and NoOps methodologies, with AIOps emerging as their cornerstone. In this landscape, the essential essence of AIOps transcends mere functionality; it becomes the catalyst for transformative outcomes. At its core, AIOps promises fundamental deliverables: the eradication of noise and distractions, the seamless correlation of information spanning diverse data repositories, and the facilitation of frictionless collaboration across disparate teams. AI models have become a standard feature in most observability (O11y) suites, comprising specialized software constructed with artificial neural networks. These algorithms, when trained to recognize patterns, including anomalies, can predict failures before impacting the user by assessing the trending behavior. Efficient log management concepts like Ephemeral Log Storage and Diversity of Logs need AIOps too. Similar to other players, IBM Cloud Pak for Watson AIOps empowers organizations to achieve greater observability across their cloud-native applications and infrastructure, enabling them to proactively monitor, troubleshoot, and optimize their IT operations with confidence. Ninety-nine percent of O11y saved data is never queried (signal-to-noise problem data) where AIOps can help.

AIOps, utilizing M3PLT data for machine learning, involves training an AI model with a set of data (training data) to establish what is considered normal. The model then creates a hypothetical representation of the data to identify patterns. Subsequently, it is tested against real data to identify abnormal conditions.

Key AI-enabled features include

> **Events Correlation:** Duplicative events can be grouped using patterns and rules to decrease event noise. This includes scenarios where events are related to the same application transaction passing through multiple infrastructure elements and cloud providers.
>
> **Anomaly Detection (Predictability):** The AI model, after correlating M3PLT data, extracts pattern and identifies anomalies for further analysis, aiding in early intervention to mitigate root causes before incidents occur.
>
> **Topology Self-Discovery:** By adding metadata to M3PLT data, the system's topology can be ascertained, facilitating troubleshooting of problems affecting multiple subsystems.
>
> **Blast Radius:** With knowledge of the solution topology, the AI model determines which components are affected by an anomaly, assisting in isolating causes of service outages or slowdowns.

Monitoring effectiveness is gauged by how quickly anomalies are detected. Identifying potential issues before impacting system users reflects a robust monitoring system.

Modern monitoring systems work with structured, normalized monitoring data, with critical events triggering alerts. The principles for effective alerting and notification include

1. **User Perspective Notification Trigger Principle:** Alerts should be triggered only if end users experience symptoms of the event, directly affecting service performance.

2. **Predictability Condition:** For monitoring systems with predictability, trigger an alert if an event is predicted to lead to a system disruption or degradation shortly, even if there's no immediate impact on end users, based on the AI model's forecast.

These principles ensure that alerts and notifications are cost-effective and add value to end users, aligning with the user perspective and predicting potential disruptions.

Recently, generative AI has taken center stage as a hot topic. Organizations of all sizes are eagerly embracing the potential of ChatGPT or Copilot, anticipating how these technologies will revolutionize our daily lives and work routines. While I refrain from commenting on the accuracy of these predictions, it's evident that large language models like LLaMA and GPT offer significant value in simplifying human-computer interactions.

Upon detecting an anomaly, it becomes imperative to swiftly address and evaluate its origins. Typically, this involves a meticulous examination either manually or via automated methodologies. These methodologies sift through an array of data signals encompassing logs, metrics, and traces to pinpoint the primary culprit. Employing advanced strategies, such as event graph–based methodologies, enables the processing of data across multiple microservices. This results in expedited issue resolution within vastly distributed systems.

Despite the myriad legal, ethical, and moral debates surrounding AI, one thing is certain: for widespread adoption of these technologies, we require observability.

Observability in AI serves three primary purposes:

1. Understanding the intricacies of model training, including modifications or vectors, to effectively trace and monitor changes within the model itself
2. Analyzing the model's real-time functionality, utilizing traces to dissect input text tokenization and response selection processes
3. Evaluating user experiences with chat-like queries and assessing the model's responses

As conscientious technologists, it's imperative that we consider the economic and environmental ramifications of our software. Embracing Green Observability principles can significantly contribute to this endeavor. Current efforts in the financial operations (FinOps) sector are directed toward establishing standardized metadata concerning cloud expenditures, encompassing both on-demand pricing data and CO_2 emissions metrics. As this information becomes increasingly accessible in the coming years, it's essential to explore ways to leverage it not just for cost optimization but also for emission reduction. Anticipate that forthcoming regulations, particularly in the EU, may underscore the importance of this initiative even further.

AI-Native Observability

AI-Native Observability represents a fundamental shift in how modern DataCenters are monitored, optimized, and orchestrated. It introduces a new model that unifies infrastructure, hardware, software, models, and data into a single, intelligent service platform. Unlike general-purpose telemetry systems, AI-Native Observability is purpose-built for DataCenters with artificial intelligence-dominated workloads. It integrates deeply with large language models (LLMs) and deep learning frameworks to provide unprecedented visibility into model internals, including layer-level introspection, distributed tensor tracking, attention head profiling, and dynamic memory visualization. This new category of observability extends across heterogeneous compute environments - GPUs, CPUs, TPUs, FPGAs, and custom AI accelerators - and critically ties into infrastructure-level telemetry. This ensures a seamless alignment between application, hardware, and infrastructure layers. What truly differentiates AI-Native Observability is its model- and pipeline-specific telemetry. Semantic traces allow for precise mapping of data flow, model checkpoints, and resource contention across distributed clusters, making telemetry both workload-aware and context-rich. Integration with orchestration platforms such as Kubernetes, Ray, and Mosaic AI enables real-time insights into auto-scaling behavior, spot instance volatility, and inter-node communication, essential for optimizing large-scale machine learning workloads. Beyond infrastructure monitoring, AI-Native Observability is directly connected to key performance indicators such as model convergence, energy efficiency (measured as throughput per watt), and production latency. This transforms infrastructure dynamics from a cost center into a strategic advantage. During the training phase, observability has evolved to monitor data and model quality by detecting embedding and concept drift, validating real-time feature integrity, and surfacing anomalies using self-supervised learning. In the inference phase, AI models contribute to *operational intelligence* by generating natural language summaries of incidents, forecasting cascading failures, and recommending proactive actions to mitigate them. This event- and intent-driven model of observability links low-level telemetry to high-level KPIs such as experiment reproducibility, model fairness, FinOps optimization, and inference explainability. It is designed not only for scalable compute but also for intelligent, adaptive infrastructure that meets the dynamic demands of modern AI workloads. The convergence of observability, explainability, and automation enables cloud and AI infrastructure architects to run AI platforms that are not only resilient and high-performing but also transparent, efficient, and aligned with broader business goals. We define this emerging capability as *AI-Native Observability*, a potential successor to Cloud-Native 1.0 and a defining element of the next generation of observability for intelligent systems.

Quantum and Information Theory Effects

Observability is a cornerstone of data engineering, encapsulating the processes of quantification, measurement, and information manipulation. However, this concept didn't originate solely within the software domain. Its roots stretch across disciplines such as control theory, reliability engineering, mathematics, and even theoretical and experimental physics, as exemplified by Yang-Mills theory in quantum field theory. While the significance of observability in any of these disciplines is directly align with software practices, they share numerous similarities and foundational paradigms. In this section, I delve into three renowned dilemmas within this realm. These facts and quandaries invite discussions that can occur in brown-bag meetings with peers or prompt philosophical reflections on our daily interactions and expectations with observability systems, dashboards, and analyses.

Observer Paradox

The Observer Paradox encapsulates the dilemma inherent in monitoring a system without inadvertently influencing its behavior. This paradox stems from the unavoidable interaction between the act of observation and the system itself, potentially leading to alterations that can affect its performance or behavior.

The process of gathering data on a system's behavior inherently perturbs that behavior. This perturbation complicates the task of accurately capturing the system's true, unperturbed behavior. Leveraging instrumentation can introduce slight performance overhead and potentially security breach. Deployment of network probes may impact the flow of network traffic. Monitoring CPU usage can itself marginally increase CPU consumption.

Here are a few notable design patterns and best practices:

Inaccurate Measurements: Unintended alterations may skew observed behavior, leading to misrepresentation of the system's actual performance.

Misattribution of Issues: Changes induced by observation may be mistaken for genuine problems, resulting in misallocation of resources to debug non-existent issues.

Performance Degradation: Overly intrusive or poorly designed observability measures can significantly degrade system performance.

Minimize Overhead: Opt for lightweight instrumentation and monitoring tools to mitigate performance impact.

Control and Isolate Measurements: Design monitoring systems to minimize their interference with the observed system, enhancing the accuracy of data collection.

Correlate and Normalize Data: Factor in the influence of monitoring activities when analyzing collected data to ensure more precise interpretations.

Utilize Synthetic Monitoring: Employ simulated scenarios to observe system behavior in a controlled setting, free from real-world interactions.

The Observer Paradox represents a foundational challenge in observability systems, necessitating a deep understanding of its implications and the implementation of effective mitigation strategies. By acknowledging the Observer Paradox and adopting measures to mitigate its effects, one can cultivate an observability system that furnishes valuable insights without compromising the integrity or performance of the monitored system.

Principle of Complementarity

The principle of complementarity encapsulates the notion that diverse data types and monitoring methodologies offer distinct perspectives on the condition and functionality of your system. Each approach boasts its own set of advantages and limitations, and by amalgamating them, you can cultivate a more exhaustive comprehension of your software's dynamics.

Diverse techniques, varied insights:

> **Metrics:** Furnish quantitative insights into critical system resources (CPU, memory, etc.) and performance metrics (response times, error rates), facilitating trend identification and anomaly detection.
>
> **Logs:** Chronicle textual records of system events and operations, facilitating the precise localization of occurrences and issue diagnosis.
>
> **Tracing:** Trace individual requests through the system, unveiling intricate interactions and performance bottlenecks.
>
> **Profiling:** Capture intricate details regarding function calls and resource utilization, aiding in code enhancement and debugging endeavors.

We can succinctly outline the key benefits of complementarity as minimized blind spots, enhanced resolution, and tailored insights.

> **Minimized Blind Spots:** No singular technique comprehensively captures all facets of system behavior. Integrating multiple techniques unveils a broader spectrum of insights.
>
> **Enhanced Resolution:** Different techniques complement each other, deepening the understanding of issues. For instance, metrics may signal a problem, while logs and traces pinpoint its origin.
>
> **Tailored Insights:** Select techniques based on specific needs. Metrics for overall system health, logs for event-specific analysis, and traces for complex request tracing.

We can cite several classic illustrative examples of the principle of complementarity, such as addressing performance concerns, resolving errors, and debugging complex interactions.

> **Addressing Performance Concerns:** Metrics highlight latency spikes; subsequently, logs and traces identify the precise code segment responsible for the slowdown.
>
> **Resolving Errors:** Elevated error rates flagged by metrics prompt further investigation with logs, which pinpoint the exact error messages and affected users.
>
> **Debugging Complex Interactions:** Metrics indicating resource strain prompt an examination with traces, which uncover unexpected service calls contributing to the bottleneck. Also called **Debug First Principle**.

When adopting a mindset grounded in the principle of complementarity, it's crucial to remain mindful of the logical challenges and considerations that may arise.

Data Overload: Managing and analyzing abundant data from diverse sources can be overwhelming.

Complexity: Integrating and correlating data from multiple techniques poses challenges.

Cost Implications: Utilizing various tools and methodologies may increase observability overhead.

By embracing the principle of complementarity, you can harness the strengths of diverse observability techniques to obtain a comprehensive view of your software's condition and performance. Understanding the distinct insights each technique affords and strategically amalgamating them will empower you to adeptly troubleshoot issues, optimize performance, and ensure an enhanced user experience.

Holevo Bound

The Holevo bound establishes a theoretical ceiling on the extractable information from a system, constrained by the finite nature of measurements. It delineates the persistent uncertainty inherent in even impeccably precise measurements, owing to the fundamental limits of information retrieval.

Here are a few notable design patterns and best practices:

Limited Measurements: Real-world observability systems are confined to measuring only a fraction of a system's state due to practical constraints such as sensor expenses and computational capacity.

Concealed States: Elements of the system not directly measured are termed "hidden states."

Quantifying Uncertainty: The Holevo bound quantifies the minimum entropy, or uncertainty, of these hidden states, even with flawless measurements of the observed states.

The Holevo can help to understand implications for observability:

Imperfect Insight: Acknowledging the Holevo bound underscores the impossibility of achieving complete awareness of a system's internal state.

Targeted Data Collection: Understanding this bound aids in prioritizing measurements that yield the most pertinent information tailored to specific requirements.

Advanced Methodologies: Techniques like Bayesian inference and information geometry serve to approach the Holevo bound practically, maximizing information extraction.

We can highlight a range of classic scenarios exemplifying the Holevo bound, including microservices monitoring, rare event diagnosis, and security surveillance.

Microservices Monitoring: Application of the bound facilitates judicious allocation of monitoring resources in distributed systems, concentrating on pivotal services and metrics.

Rare Event Diagnosis: When addressing sporadic issues, comprehension of the Holevo bound facilitates effective troubleshooting by managing expectations and directing efforts appropriately.

Security Surveillance: Utilizing the bound informs strategies for anomaly detection, recognizing the inherent constraints in identifying all potential threats.

However, the Holevo bound encounters challenges in practical implementation:

Ideal Observer Assumption: It operates under the assumption of an ideal observer with flawless measurements, an unattainable scenario in reality.

Ongoing Research: Efforts persist in exploring pragmatic approximations and strategies to circumvent the constraints of the Holevo bound in real-world observability systems.

Understanding the Holevo bound fosters a profound comprehension of the inherent restrictions of observability systems. It empowers informed decision-making regarding measurement tactics and information extraction methodologies.

The Art of Alerting Quietly

The intricacies of effective alerting are at the heart of modern incident response systems. These systems revolutionize incident communication, introducing dynamic on-call schedules, automatic rotations, and the flexibility for team members to cover each other's shifts seamlessly. In scenarios demanding urgency, the system employs aggressive notifications, allowing the setup of secondary on-call engineers for unresponsive primary responders. Further, it extends the reach to senior management or entire teams if initial responses falter. Priority levels, including the capability to limit after-hours alerts to critical issues, enhance the system's adaptability to the ever-evolving technical, business, and social landscapes.

A significant feature of contemporary incident response systems lies in their ability to manage diverse communication channels, especially through mobile apps. These apps empower users to customize notification tones and visual alerts, even bypassing "do not disturb" settings for critical alerts. Prioritizing alerts based on severity levels, with a focus on critical priority events denoting total outages or high impact issues, ensures a streamlined and effective response process.

When examining alerts, the challenge lies in defining time frames and calendars – a delicate balance between identifying abnormalities promptly and avoiding transient issues like software deployments causing fleeting alerts. Alerting levels can be tailored based on various criteria, with revenue impact, customer impact, and functionality at the forefront. Revenue-centric models align with business metrics, understanding the value of each customer transaction. Models based on impacted customers quantify user impact, providing clarity in error analysis. Lastly, functionality-focused models identify critical components vital to the revenue path of a business.

Observability, often overlooked in alerting, is crucial. The system's observability should be monitored, and redundancy in observability tools considered. Classifying observability outages based on redundancy status ensures a swift resolution.

As previously discussed, the spectrum of alerts encompasses varying degrees of severity. It's crucial to recognize that not all alerts carry the same weight. For instance, there's a distinction between "paging" alerts and "ticketing" alerts. The terminology can be nuanced, with some individuals using "alerts" specifically to refer to urgent pages that demand immediate human intervention, even rousing someone from sleep.

The value of "ticketing" alerts is often overlooked. These alerts require attention but not with the same urgency as paging alerts. In the context of large-scale systems, where disruptions are routine and systems are engineered to tolerate a certain level of failure, addressing such alerts can be integrated into regular business hours. For example, replacing a noncritical disk that has malfunctioned can be handled during standard operating times.

Adjustments and pausing alerts are integral to effective alert management. Acknowledging that alerts may not always go as planned, the ability to adjust or temporarily silence alarms is crucial. However, caution is needed to prevent critical issues from being ignored. Silenced alerts, especially from logs, must be handled judiciously to avoid overlooking potential problems. Setting exceptions and adding expiration to paused alerts ensure a balanced approach to alerting in dynamic operational environments.

The integration of alerting and notification aligns with observability (O11y) principles. While monitoring can exist independently, observability necessitates the harmonious integration of well-architected monitoring technologies, tooling, policies, IT Service Management (ITSM), and visibility. Observability serves to bring the internal states of a system into the human realm, addressing fundamental questions of "what," "when," and "why." It empowers a comprehensive understanding of behavioral patterns and the ability to anticipate potential issues. Unlike monitoring, observability is a capability and principle that transcends specific technologies, remaining a constant while monitoring tools and technologies evolve over time.

The timeline of incidents and the notifications cadence play pivotal roles in effective incident management, delineating the progression of unexpected events (Change Failed is also an incident) from initial detection to resolution and subsequent analysis. It commences with the identification of an anomaly or incident within the production, signalling the moment of **incident detection**. Subsequently, the **Triage Assessment** phase comes into effect. If the incident doesn't directly impact SLOs, it automatically generates a trouble ticket in ITSM platforms, such as a Jira or ServiceNow, placed within the SRE downstream Kanban board for tracking.

However, incidents with adverse effects on SLOs trigger the on-call alerting process. This notification process involves several crucial intervals: the **Time to Notify** On-Call Personnel reflects the swiftness with which responsible individuals are alerted to address the incident. Following this, the **Time to Client Notification** measures the duration required to inform relevant stakeholders or clients about the issue, prioritizing transparency and effective communication.

Upon notification, the **Time to Acknowledge** gauges the prompt acknowledgment of the incident by the responsible team members. Subsequent steps include assembling the appropriate team or resources, denoted by the **Time to Assemble**, crucial for a coordinated response effort. Once assembled, the focus shifts to remediation. **Time to Remediation** indicates the time taken to mitigate or resolve the incident and restore normal system functionality.

Post-resolution, the **Time to Close the Incident Ticket** signifies the completion of incident management processes. Meanwhile, the **Time to Root Cause Analysis** (RCA) represents the duration needed to investigate and identify the underlying causes of the incident, facilitating preventive measures. Finally, the **Time to Postmortem Review** (PMR) denotes the interval required for a comprehensive review and blameless analysis of the incident response process, aimed at identifying areas for improvement and implementing preventive measures to mitigate future occurrences.

Typically, there are periodic reviews, either quarterly or annually, to assess these incident management performance KPIs, timelines, and deviations. More frequent reviews are conducted per product or per client as necessary. Together, these elements form a structured framework for incident management, ensuring timely response, resolution, and continuous improvement in system reliability and performance.

In the realm of CNA, the concept of "observability definition" undergoes a profound transformation, especially with the utilization of code instrumentation methodologies. Unlike the conventional definition that merely scrutinizes a system based on its outputs, cloud-native application (CNA) observability delves deeper. It not only examines the outputs and external behaviors of a system but also scrutinizes the internal state using inner signals. This paradigm shift marks a significant departure from the traditional understanding of observability. In this dynamic landscape, the term "observability" assumes a precise linguistic semantics rather than simply inheriting from control theory. Welcome, ladies and gentlemen, to Cloud-Native Application Observability Day, where we embark on a journey to grasp and leverage the true essence of observability in the modern cloud-native era.

Observability Effectiveness

The Event-to-Incident Mapping Principle is a crucial tenet within Information Technology Service Management (ITSM). It establishes that any event with the potential to degrade the quality of service for a system should trigger the creation of an incident. Incidents are specifically tied to events linked to service disruptions or performance issues, facilitating the tracking of outages and downtimes for individual components or configuration items. This tracking contributes to essential metrics such as mean time to detect (**MTTD**), mean time to recover (**MTTR**), and mean time between failures (**MTBF**).

Severity levels are assigned to incidents based on the impact they have on the system. Ranging from Severity-1 (S1) or Priority-1 (P1) to S4 (or P4), incidents are categorized according to their criticality, with S1/P1 representing the most severe levels.

To streamline the alerting process, alerts should originate directly from the monitoring platform rather than the incident ticketing system. However, it is imperative to document alerts as S1 or S2 incident tickets to maintain a record of incident management times and durations.

Alerts and notifications serve distinct purposes within the realm of system monitoring and management. Alerts act as proactive indicators, signalling potential issues or anomalies that demand immediate attention from stakeholders. On the other hand, notifications serve as informative messages, keeping stakeholders apprised of pertinent events and system changes. Both elements are integral to sustaining the reliability, performance, and availability of intricate distributed systems, albeit in different ways.

When establishing priority levels, it is crucial to clearly define the information that both product and engineering teams should comprehend and commit to. The following checklist is routinely employed for this purpose:

- **Priority Level (P1–P5):** Clearly articulate the priority levels to categorize issues, ranging from critical (P1) to lower priority (P5).
- **Definition of Priority:** Provide a straightforward definition of what priority means in a manner that is easily comprehensible for both engineering and product teams.
- **Notification Recipients:** Specify not only who should be notified but also elucidate how these notifications evolve based on the priority level. For instance, leadership may require immediate notification for P1 or P2 events, involving both SRE and development teams.
- **Notification Time Frames:** Define the specific time frames during which notifications are permissible. For example, a P4 issue may be limited to 9 a.m. to 5 p.m. on weekdays. This also establishes expectations for response times – consider scenarios like addressing a development or QA environment issue at 3 a.m.
- **Development Team's Effort Commitment:** Outline the level of effort expected from the development team in resolving the identified issues. While awareness of

an issue is significant, obtaining a commitment from engineers regarding their response provides clarity on resource allocation for issue resolution.

Outages and Downtime Factors

It is crucial to address the evolving meaning of service availability and dispel any misconceptions surrounding certain terms. With advancements in monitoring precision and the setting of service-level objectives (SLOs), service availability is no longer a binary concept (up or down) but rather a scaled status based on performance.

In the past, services were either available or unavailable, and SLOs predominantly focused on availability metrics. Now, with diverse metrics, service performance can be measured, considering how well the system serves users. If performance falls below the minimum threshold, the service should not be considered available.

To clarify these distinctions, consider the following terminology:

- **Available Time:** The total duration for which a service or system was running and available
- **Outage Time:** The total duration for which a service or system was completely unavailable
- **Downtime:** The overall duration for which a service or system was either unavailable or performing below the minimum rate
- **Uptime:** The total time minus the downtime
- **Reliable Time:** The difference between uptime and downtime

The efficacy of the observability principle is quantifiable through metrics such as mean time to detect (MTTD). Prompt identification of anomalies or disruptive occurrences significantly bolsters observability. Another crucial metric is mean time to recover (MTTR), which underscores the importance of swiftly addressing and resolving issues. Consider other aspects such as blind spots in the monitoring system – services, infrastructure elements, or application components not monitored, including overlooked logs and traces.

O11y engineers should meticulously review application diagrams, architectures, and designs to identify monitoring targets. Defining service-level indicators (SLIs) and monitoring metrics is imperative. Enterprise architects consistently underscore the importance of a governance model that guarantees any changes made to the system prompt corresponding adjustments in the monitoring configuration, thereby averting the emergence of new blind spots.

Error Budget and Burn Rate

Implementing alerting based on burn rate represents a more sophisticated approach likely to generate actionable insights. To grasp the significance of this method, let's delve deeper into the concepts of burn rate and error budgets.

As mentioned earlier, the product profile comprises several essential components. These include ownership information, details about the technology stack and deployment strategy utilized, traffic patterns, service-level indicators (SLIs) and service-level objectives (SLOs), error budget policies, operational service hours, and a roster of customers who utilize the product.

Embedded within all service-level objective (SLO) definitions lies the notion of an error budget. When you set an SLO of 99.9%, you are essentially permitting a failure rate of 0.1% (your error budget) within a specified time frame (your SLO window). "Burn rate" measures how rapidly, relative to the SLO, a service consumes this error budget. For instance, if a service has a burn rate of 1, it means that it's depleting the error budget at a pace that exhausts it precisely at the conclusion of the SLO window. In the context of a 99.9% SLO over a 30-day period, maintaining a constant 0.1% error rate consumes the entire error budget, resulting in a burn rate of 1.

Table 4-1. *Burn and Error Rate Chart*

Burn rate	Error rate for a 99.9% SLO	Time to exhaustion
1	0.1%	30 days
2	0.2%	15 days
10	1%	3 days
1000	100%	43 minutes

The pace of consumption will enable us to shrink our monitoring window while ensuring timely and precise alerts. To illustrate, suppose we maintain a constant one-hour alert window and deem a 5% error budget utilization significant for notification. From this, we can deduce the optimal burn rate for triggering alerts.

Never disturb a running system when your error budget is zero.

—maybe from the Bible of Operation

In the context of burn rate–triggered alerts, the duration for an alert to activate is calculated as follows:

$$(1 - SLO / error\_ratio) * size\_of\_alert\_window * burn\_rate$$

Moreover, the portion of the error budget expended when the alert activates is determined by

$$(Burn\_rate * size\_of\_alert\_window) / time\_period$$

For instance, in a 99.9% SLO contract, if 5% of a 30-day error budget is utilized within one hour, a burn rate of 36 is required. Thus, the alerting guideline transforms into the following.

Let R_5 represent the rate of HTTP requests with status codes starting with "5" in the last one hour and R represent the total rate of HTTP requests in the last hour.

$$\frac{\sum R_5}{\sum R} > 0.036$$

When most SREs observe that they are nearing the expiration of their error budget, they often engage in chaos engineering within the production environment while adhering to error budgets. There are numerous methods for understanding and implementing this concept, but my preferred approach is the Wheel of Misfortune Game or Gamification. This involves accumulating points and rewards, culminating in the achievement of a digital badge. Alternatively, you can develop a model like AWS Cloud Quest or `www.principleofchaos.org`. However, it's crucial to ensure that both managers team and colleagues have a thorough understanding of the concept before implementation.

Observability Numberscape

As we have seen in the "Error Budget and Burn Rate" section, percentages serve as a fundamental representation of ratios, expressed as fractions of 100. Essentially, they convey a real number ranging from 0 to 1, denoting a portion within the spectrum of 0% to 100%. This widely adopted method effectively communicates measurements, such as gauges, where the percentage signifies the distance from either empty (0%) to full (100%).

Within the realm of O11y, percentages play a crucial role in assessing service-level indicators (SLIs) to gauge the performance of a service. The following example illustrates this concept more comprehensively in the subsequent section.

Service-level indicators (SLIs) function as percentage-based metrics measuring service performance. Conventional wisdom dictates that an SLI registering at 0% (or 0.00) implies a disastrous performance, while an SLI hitting 100% (or 1.00) signals flawless execution of the specific characteristic.

The formula for calculating SLIs involves dividing the count of favorable events by the total valid events. If the result is not multiplied by 100%, it yields a numerical value between 0 and 1, with precision proportional to the quantity of data points. For instance, with a significant number of samples, two decimal points after the period, like 78.56%, can be employed.

$$\left[SLI = \frac{Good\ Events}{Valid\ Events} \times 100\% \right]$$

Defining a "good event" is a critical aspect of this calculation, representing a combination of the metric and minimal acceptable performance. Consider an SLI for latency in a mobile app, where the metric is the observed latency from the user to the app load balancer in milliseconds. The minimal performance benchmark is set at below 1,000 ms or less than 1 second. Consequently, the SLI quantifies the proportion of requests within the stipulated 1,000 ms threshold measured on the load balancer for the mobile app.

Descriptive statistics are methods used in modern observability platforms to summarize and describe the main features of a M3PLT dataset when treated as a distribution. I've meticulously outlined the key descriptive statistical methods along with practical observability use cases, supplemented with additional mathematical insights in my other works. But if you're looking for a quick refresher, feel free to ask ChatGPT or her siblings for a solid tutorial on the concept. If you're keen to delve deeper into these topics, it's a section worth exploring.

Observability encapsulates the vital ability to consistently derive actionable insights from the telemetry signals emitted by the instrumented systems and synthetic user activities. O11y platform is aimed at optimizing service performance in accordance with predefined Service-Level Agreements (SLAs). It serves as the linchpin for various internal stakeholders, including developers, release and test engineers, Site Reliability Engineers (SREs), infrastructure and platform operation teams, as well as non-engineering personnel, and externally, entities such as regulatory authorities, insurance auditors, key users, and other relevant parties rely heavily on observability reports as the ultimate reference point, considering them as the single source of truth. That's why SREs emphasize, *Observability is the paramount.*

With that said, achieving an acceptable level of observability features in CNAs is crucial. In the following chapters, we will transition from the operational and Site Reliability Engineering (SRE) perspectives to the development realm and address developers. The keyword is instrumentation.

Summary

Congratulations on completing the longest chapter in this book! Throughout its pages, we explored the origins and significance of one of the most misleading buzzwords in the cloud-native market, "observability," from science and technology fields, elucidating why software observability stands apart while sharing similarities with other domains. At its zenith, we delved into telemetry data and signal types such as STELA, USE, RED, and LDTM, and culminated with M3PLT, examining their functionalities and qualities as key indicators of cloud-native observability engineering.

As we draw this chapter to a close, the spotlight shines on the concept of subtle alerting, a pivotal shift in the landscape of SRE workplace dynamics. Through the utilization of AIOps, prioritization techniques, and role-based alerting, we have the potential to transition from an interruption-based working mode to an effective focus-based working mode. This evolution promises to enhance productivity and efficiency, steering our endeavors toward greater success in the realm of observability engineering.

CHAPTER 5

Instrumentation Engineering Fundamentals

> *Many a calm river begins as a turbulent waterfall, yet none hurtles and foams all the way to the sea.*
>
> –Mikhail Lermontov

When considering the stream of telemetry data sources, they often resemble the chaotic rush of a turbulent waterfall, inundating with bursts of data, hurtling and foaming as they cascade down. However, much like the journey of a natural river, this tumultuous influx gradually refines and integrates seamlessly as it flows into the vast sea of the observability backend. This natural progression is expected within the modern cloud-native observability framework.

Software instrumentation involves purposely coding software and services to transmit or expose telemetry data, which is then fed into observability backends via data pipelines, ingestions, and routes. This data serves as the lifeblood of the observability framework. Whether through manual coding methods, semi-automatic processes, or fully automated

Dr. M. Ghane, *Observability Engineering with Cilium*,
https://doi.org/10.1007/979-8-8688-1258-3_5

instrumentation, the goal remains consistent: to identify and channel the torrential flow of data into a coherent stream, navigating the twists and turns of its course toward insightful analysis and understanding.

In the realm of cloud-native observability, this process ensures that the data, once chaotic and overwhelming, becomes a valuable resource, guiding informed decisions and facilitating an inner state of complex systems.

In this chapter, we will build upon the approaches explored in previous chapters, delving deeper into the principles and methods of instrumentation. This exploration is tailored specifically for observability engineers, focusing on the transformative role it plays in modern cloud-native application delivery.

This chapter covers the following topics:

- Methods of software instrumentation
- Introducing visionary and strategic instrumentation tools and technologies

Instrumentation Landscape

To ensure the reliability of software systems, it's essential to prioritize continuous observability. This means not only building the system but also ensuring it functions reliably over time and per FinOps principles. In the majority of production environments, telemetry data and, particularly, logs are typically characterized by their chaotic diversity and unsightliness, rapid consumption of storage space, and seemingly low value – until a critical issue arises, at which point their significance skyrockets. When it comes to cloud-native O11y, at least three key concerns must be addressed:

- **Identifying Data to Collect:** Understanding what data to collect is crucial. Various types of data exist, ranging from metrics, service dependencies mapping, consistent targets metadata models, profiling, logs, and distributed traces (M3PLT) to so-called cloud-native telemetry signals. Each type of data has unique storage requirements. It's essential to optimize storage to avoid unnecessary costs.
- **Collecting the Data:** Different types of data require specific storage and aggregation methods. Recall the three V's of data (volume, variety, and value) of DataOps. For instance, logs can be challenging to parse and store due to their unstructured nature. It's important to consider scalability and multi-tenancy when choosing databases for storing telemetry signals.
- **Taking Action Based on Data:** After collecting data, the next step is to derive meaning from it and take appropriate action. This involves parsing logs, managing storage, and aggregating data in a meaningful way. Tools like Cribl Stack and Grafana Stack are valuable for managing and analyzing telemetry data effectively.

In practical terms, logs stand out as both the most essential and often the messiest data type in understanding system behavior and diagnosing issues. However, managing logs can present significant challenges, from parsing complexities to escalating storage demands and the transient nature of their sources. It's almost similar for other type of telemetry data. Ladies and gentlemen, we're in need of some "good tools." But as Abraham Lincoln once said, "Give me six hours to chop down a tree, and I will spend the first four sharpening the axe." Indeed, tools play a pivotal role, yet their effectiveness hinges on the skill of those utilizing them.

Unboxing the Observability Toolset

Crafting an efficient observability engineering platform demands more than just open source tools; it necessitates reliable and practical solutions. In the vast expanse of contemporary cloud-native observability, certain products and vendors stand out, wielding significant influence in shaping the landscape. I'd like to introduce a selection of these essential tools and delve into why they're invaluable assets for your toolkit. We'll explore some of them further in the next chapters.

In the realm of telemetry data collection and instrumentation, multiple avenues exist to gather dispersed information from different sources. Manual instrumentation or source code level instrumentation involves inserting code during runtime to record essential information in a specific format. This often entails leveraging software development kits (SDKs), libraries, and tools tailored to the programming language in use.

Alternatively, semi-auto instrumentation or binary instrumentation involves modifying the application or infrastructure binary without altering the underlying code. Tools like **Grafana Alloy** complement the OpenTelemetry framework, facilitating seamless data collection across various metrics, logs, and traces. Alloy is a telemetry collector that is 100% OTLP compatible and offers native pipelines for OpenTelemetry and Prometheus telemetry formats, supporting metrics, logs, traces, and profiles. Auto instrumentation or external instrumentation approaches, such as eBPF instrumentation with **Grafana Beyla**, capture signals at the kernel level without modifying code or binaries, offering insights into protocols like HTTP and gRPC. Beyla will be your close friend soon.

Loki is specifically designed by Grafana for log storage, indexing only metadata to reduce storage requirements and enhance query performance. Its compatibility with PromQL and integration with Prometheus Alert Manager make it a valuable tool for log analysis and monitoring in Prometheus-based environments.

Prometheus, with its multidimensional query language (PromQL) and support for push- and pull-based monitoring, addresses many challenges associated with metric data collection and analysis. **Grafana Mimir** complements Prometheus by providing long-term storage and native multi-tenancy, making it suitable for horizontally scalable and reliable deployments.

Cribl Stack provides comprehensive data management and DataOps pipeline optimization capabilities, allowing for effective telemetry data search and storage routing. It offers seamless integration with various backend systems like Splunk, Elastic, and Grafana Loki, enabling efficient log analysis and storage. Cribl has been developed by former Splunk fellows and is designed to facilitate instrumentation for cloud-native applications using Cribl Edge. The Cribl Edge fleet serves as endpoint data collector and management, deployable on Kubernetes as well as other physical or cloud-based nodes. It seamlessly communicates with the Cribl Leader Node, providing comprehensive and structured telemetry events down to the container level within the Cribl stream. These logs and telemetry signals can be efficiently searched using Cribl search or forwarded to various backends such as Splunk, Elastic, and Grafana Loki, or stored directly in AWS S3.

One of the remarkable features of Cribl search is its ability to replay and search across multiple sources, including its edge agent, AWS logs, CDN logs, Lambda, Fargate, API dataset providers, and AWS S3 or Cloudflare, all from a unified dashboard and query interface. By employing Cribl stream as middleware for your data sources and observability backends, you can optimize data (collect, reduce, transform, replay, enrich) and route signals to one or more destinations or replay them using custom or predefined pipelines, processes, and configuration packs. This orchestration reduces overall costs, creates telemetry events as a collection of key-value pairs (fields) out of logs, and mitigates single points of failure. To get started, it's worth noting that nearly 1 TB per day can be processed for free in the Cribl cloud, and you can also benefit from certified training available in the Cribl University.

Distributed traces, the transmutational signal, resemble detailed transaction logs, providing insights into individual transactions rather than broad service or component overviews. Tracing unfolds a narrative of a request's journey through multiple services, illuminating its path and duration. However, the depth of tracing entails trade-offs; it can be resource intensive and demands meticulous setup. **Grafana Tempo** serves as the distributed tracing database, harnessing TraceQL, a tailored query language for tracing data complexities. Unlike traditional metrics and logs, traces excel at delving into transaction paths, making them indispensable for troubleshooting.

Software testing plays a vital role in scenarios where live data is unavailable. Tools like **Grafana k6** enable reliability testing through scripted simulations of user behavior and load scenarios, providing valuable insights into system performance and identifying potential issues before deployment. Synthetic monitoring, facilitated by k6, allows for real-time assessment of system health under controlled conditions. On the frontend, tools like **Grafana Faro** enable real user monitoring through JavaScript integration, offering insights into user experiences, including loading times, interactivity, and visual stability. Conversely, on the backend, OpenTelemetry offers a standardized approach to collecting telemetry signals.

Continuous profiles, the benchmark signal, offer insights into resource consumption over time. Functioning at regular intervals, they blend metrics, logs, and traces, offering both macro and micro perspectives on system utilization events. Nevertheless, traditional profiling methods often strain system resources and present challenges in comparing performance across builds. **Grafana Pyroscope** addresses these concerns by delivering high-performance profiling with minimal overhead. It samples data at intervals, striking a balance between granularity and efficiency. Additionally, Pyroscope's visualization tools, including Flamegraphs and FlameQL, facilitate insightful analysis and comparison of profiles, empowering users to identify performance regressions and optimize resource usage effectively.

Once data is collected, visualization tools like Grafana or Splunk aid in making sense of vast amounts of information, enabling users to create meaningful visualizations and dashboards for analysis and decision-making. Effective visualization becomes indispensable in deriving actionable insights and optimizing system performance.

Assessing the impact on your system and translating that assessment into actionable steps is crucial. Visualization is key; every microservice, state, event, and piece of information can be channelled into Grafana, capable of ingesting various data formats and presenting them in customizable ways. Grafana not only serves as a visualization tool but also enables setting up alerts based on incoming data, facilitating incident response and remediation. **Grafana OnCall**, an open source tool, ensures timely and pertinent responses by managing schedules and automating escalations. Grafana Cloud introduces a complimentary tier known as "Cloud Free," generously providing ample resources. This tier includes access to 10,000 metrics, 50 GB of ingested logs, and 50 GB of ingested traces monthly. Additionally, it offers 500 virtual user hours, ideal for performance testing with Grafana Cloud k6, catering to personal projects or small teams.

Software Instrumentation Pathfinding

Software instrumentation entails intentionally coding software and services to transmit or expose telemetry data, either through manual coding methods or using language-specific SDKs, to feed into observability backends – typically a suite of tools hosted either on-premises or in the cloud. This process, often referred to as manual instrumentation, involves manually incorporating telemetry data gathering into the code base.

Manual instrumentation involves coding telemetry signals into the code base before runtime, offering precise control over the selection and transmission of signals. While efficient in terms of I/O and computing resources, manual instrumentation can be developer mindset dependent, leading to inconsistencies and risks – especially in microservice environments with multiple independent teams. Additionally, code upgrades may necessitate restructuring of observability code, limiting flexibility and compile-time information.

Pure manual instrumentation is increasingly rare today, with framework-specific manual instrumentation being more prevalent. This approach utilizes built-in instrumentation capabilities of frameworks/languages or specialized agents such as Java agents (Dynatrace), ASP.NET Core logging, Spring AOP for tracing, and Python libraries (OpenTelemetry). However, the downside is potential performance degradation due to running agents and libraries at the user space level.

Alternatively, auto-instrumentation tools offer a streamlined approach, automating the process of collecting and sending telemetry data to the observability backend. This doesn't eliminate the need for coding entirely but offloads much of the heavy lifting to pre-existing technologies and tools, requiring developers/SREs to simply connect the dots.

Auto instrumentation often relies on specific runtimes or frameworks to function. If the runtime isn't present, or if it isn't configured correctly, the instrumentation may not work. For example, in languages like Go or Rust, certain packages or libraries may need to be present and properly configured for auto instrumentation to operate.

The significance of instrumentation is amplified in the context of distributed tracing within complex CNAs. Instrumentation primarily serves two functions: context propagation and span mapping. Context propagation ensures that relevant information travels seamlessly across different components or layers of a system, maintaining continuity and coherence in the flow of data and actions. It is typically facilitated transparently using libraries integrated with HTTP clients and servers. Span mapping involves associating discrete units of work, or spans, with their respective context, providing a granular understanding of the execution path and facilitating comprehensive performance analysis and debugging. Notable projects and technologies such as OpenTelemetry APIs/SDKs can be leveraged for this purpose.

Most manual instrumentation methods focus on creating data points and propagating context between services, critical for tracing HTTP requests or message producers and consumers. Auto-instrumentation methods, such as eBPF, offer alternative approaches with potential performance advantages by operating at the kernel level to trace packets.

To maintain data format standardization, one can customize tools like OpenTelemetry and Prometheus, or commercial solutions such as Dynatrace, Datadog, AppDynamics, New Relic, and specific language libraries like Byte Buddy for Java or Pin for C/C++. However, integrating these solutions may come with a trade-off: the observability tax, which can manifest as decreased infrastructure performance and service delays. Many principal observability engineers regard OpenTelemetry (OTel) as a leading solution for manual instrumentation, while solutions like Cilium, based on eBPF, excel in auto instrumentation.

In the upcoming sections, I'll delve into both approaches to provide a comprehensive overview. Understanding the nuances of different instrumentation models and tools enables you to select the most suitable approach for gaining insights into your software's behavior and optimizing its performance efficiently.

If you're considering a balanced approach between manual and auto instrumentation, rest assured, you're not alone. Many engineers are exploring hybrid approaches, which leverage a combination of different models and tools to achieve comprehensive observability with reduced effort and cost.

To achieve this, we'll focus on two key aspects:

1. **Data Quality:** Configure instrumentation carefully to avoid data overload and ensure data quality.

2. **Security Considerations:** Select tools that adhere to security best practices for data handling.

By adopting a hybrid approach and considering these aspects, you can streamline your observability efforts, reduce time to delivery, and enhance flexibility in day-to-day operations and CI/CD tasks.

Many organizations opt for a balanced strategy, incorporating both manual and auto-instrumentation techniques in hybrid approaches. By leveraging a mix of models and tools, these approaches aim to achieve comprehensive observability while managing effort and costs effectively. It's essential to prioritize data quality and security when deploying hybrid approaches, ensuring that instrumentation configurations adhere to industry best practices and facilitate smooth integration into CI/CD pipelines.

In summary, finding the right equilibrium between manual and auto instrumentation enables organizations to attain thorough observability with reduced effort, ultimately optimizing both time-to-delivery and operational efficiency over time.

OpenTelemetry: A Visionary Fit

OpenTelemetry traces its origins back to two distinct yet complementary initiatives: OpenTracing and OpenCensus. Initiated by Ben Sigelman in 2016, OpenTracing sought to establish a consistent API for tracing within distributed systems. Its goal was to empower developers to instrument their code, enabling the capture and visualization of request flows across microservices. In parallel, Google introduced OpenCensus in 2018, which focused on furnishing libraries for gathering application metrics and traces, offering a holistic approach to observability.

As conversations unfolded within the observability community, it became evident that merging these projects held promise for a unified solution. In 2019, the Cloud-Native Computing Foundation (CNCF) announced the merger of OpenTracing and OpenCensus, birthing OpenTelemetry. This consolidation aimed to amalgamate the strengths of both initiatives into a singular, cohesive framework for observability within cloud-native environments.

Subsequent to the merger, the OpenTelemetry project swiftly gained traction, drawing support from key industry players such as Google and Microsoft. Developers rallied around its vision of establishing a standardized, vendor-neutral approach to observability, fostering enhanced interoperability and usability across diverse platforms and programming languages.

In a significant milestone in 2020, OpenTelemetry unveiled its inaugural stable version, OpenTelemetry 1.0. This release laid a robust foundation for developers to instrument their applications for tracing, metrics, and logging, signalling a notable stride in the project's maturation and adoption.

Since then, OpenTelemetry has continued its evolution, regularly introducing new features, enhancements, and integrations. Its modular architecture facilitates seamless customization and extension, enabling developers to tailor observability solutions to their specific requirements. Furthermore, the OpenTelemetry community has experienced steady growth, establishing itself as the second most popular CNCF project, surpassed only by Kubernetes. Contributions pour in, both on the instrumentation and collection fronts, underscoring its collaborative ethos and widespread industry appeal.

OpenTelemetry delineates six distinct types of instruments: Counters, Histograms, UpDownCounters, Asynchronous Gauges, Asynchronous UpDownCounters, and Asynchronous Counters.

- **Counters:** Counters serve as instruments to monitor the cumulative number of occurrences of an event or state within a system. They increment monotonically over time, offering insights into cumulative values like the total number of processed requests.

- **Histograms:** Histograms offer a method to analyze the distribution of values for a specific metric within a system. By categorizing values into predefined buckets or bins, histograms provide visibility into statistical distribution, such as the frequency of various response times in a web service.
- **UpDownCounters:** UpDownCounters, akin to Counters, facilitate both incrementing and decrementing operations. They prove useful for tracking metrics where values fluctuate over time, such as the active connections to a database.
- **Asynchronous Gauges:** Asynchronous Gauges measure the instantaneous value of a metric at a given moment. Providing a snapshot of the metric's current state, they prove valuable for monitoring instantaneous values like CPU utilization or memory usage.
- **Asynchronous UpDownCounters:** Similar to UpDownCounters, Asynchronous UpDownCounters permit both incrementing and decrementing operations but operate asynchronously. They are well-suited for scenarios where metric updates may occur independently or within a distributed environment.
- **Asynchronous Counters:** Operating asynchronously, Asynchronous Counters, like Counters, monitor the total occurrences of an event or state. They are advantageous in scenarios where immediate consistency is unnecessary or when managing high-frequency updates to metrics.

The OTel Specification

While Prometheus inadvertently established a standard, OTel deliberately constructs one: the OTel specification, designed for versatile implementation.

The OTel SDK, also known as client libraries, facilitates the creation of telemetry adaptable to various programming languages. These libraries can automatically generate telemetry or allow manual creation.

Automatic instrumentation is embedded within libraries, offering metrics like HTTP, gRPC tracing, and Express.js metrics upon installation and setup in JavaScript applications. Yet some libraries require configuration for metric generation.

Manual instrumentation employs primitives within client libraries, enabling the generation of specific signals or addition of contextual metadata to emitted metrics, spans, or logs.

Functioning as a middleman for telemetry data, the OpenTelemetry Collector comprises three core components: an ingestion endpoint receiving and translating incoming telemetry into OTel formats (OpenTelemetry Protocol [OTLP] over HTTP, OTLP over gRPC); a processor managing data filtering, batching, and transformation; and an exporter transmitting processed telemetry data to diverse backends.

Additionally, multiple vendor exporters are available based on where telemetry data should be directed. The OpenTelemetry Registry hosts a growing selection of exporter, collector, receiver, and client instrumentation libraries.

OTel: The Promise

OTel serves as a unified standard for instrumenting logs, metrics, and traces to emit telemetry in a standardized format. It pledges simplicity in the telemetry process, supporting multiple vendors and open source software (OSS) without vendor lock-in. Furthermore, it offers extensibility, allowing developers to expand OTel to meet specific requirements.

The widespread support of OTel by popular vendors, libraries, and languages facilitates easier emission of telemetry in OTel format. Another benefit is the ability to correlate signals from various sources, such as logs to metrics, metrics to traces, and even logs and metrics to traces, using a standard specification. Imagine accessing one correlation ID for a failed HTTP request and uncovering all downstream logs, metrics, and traces!

Fully comprehending all OTel components and deploying them effectively in production may pose a steep learning curve, particularly for practitioners accustomed to proprietary observability systems.

Another notable distinction is OTel's push system with a collector, in contrast to Prometheus's pull system.

Being a comprehensive project, OTel exhibits varying levels of maturity depending on the programming language utilized and the types of signals intended for emission. For instance, as of November 2023, the Python trace and metric client libraries are deemed stable, while logs remain in the experimental phase. In contrast, Golang traces are stable, but metrics display a mixed status, and logs are yet to be implemented. For a comprehensive overview of maturity levels, it's recommended to refer to the OpenTelemetry status page. These current limitations in maturity imply that the full adoption of OTel across all telemetry types will necessitate an ongoing effort until stability is achieved across all languages and frameworks supported by your organization.

eBPF-Base Instrumentation: A Strategic Fit

In the upcoming chapter, I'll delve into eBPF's description and history. Here, I'd like to note that eBPF excels precisely where traditional auto-instrumentation methods face limitations. Let's explore how it strategically integrates.

Dynamic, runtime instrumentation: eBPF enhances existing instrumentation by capturing runtime data that may have been previously unavailable. For instance, it enables tracking of network activity or system calls beyond the scope of framework-specific tools.

Targeting performance-sensitive systems, with its minimal overhead, eBPF is ideal for instrumenting applications where maintaining low performance impact is paramount.

Instrumenting third-party libraries and complex systems, by hooking into the kernel, eBPF can instrument even code beyond direct control, providing visibility into external libraries and complex system interactions.

Custom and specific data collection, gathering unique metrics: eBPF allows defining custom probes and programs to capture precise data points beyond standard metrics, facilitating troubleshooting or optimization goals.

eBPF boasts a remarkable attribute: inherent resilience against attempts to compromise the data fidelity of observability systems, particularly by malicious actors seeking to manipulate telemetry data. This robustness is a direct result of eBPF's operation within the kernel space, where it functions as a guardian of system integrity. Consequently, the observability provided by eBPF systems carries an exceptionally high degree of trustworthiness, effectively mitigating the negative effects of both the principle of complementarity and the Observer Paradox.

In the landscape of observability, eBPF closely aligns with the principles of H-infinity control theory. Similar to how H-systems prioritize minimizing the impact of disturbances in control systems, eBPF ensures that observability remains impervious to external interference. This parallel underscore the reliability of eBPF-based observability solutions, positioning them as the gold standard in monitoring and analysis tools.

eBPF's robustness ensures that observability is not merely a passive feature but an active defense mechanism against measurement bias and threats. At its core, the aim is to minimize the observability tax, making it a pivotal element within the arsenal of contemporary observability solutions. eBPF technology serves as a cornerstone, driving the efficiency and effectiveness of modern observability frameworks.

Deep tracing across complex microservice architectures: eBPF excels at tracing requests across distributed services, offering holistic insights into application behavior amidst intricate service interactions.

Introduction to Grafana Beyla

This eBPF-based OSS auto-instrumentation tool simplifies application observability setup. Beyla provides RED (Rate, Errors, Duration) metrics through OpenTelemetry or Prometheus for existing web services, irrespective of the programming language. The Beyla App is primarily written in Golang (90%) with a small portion in C for kernel operations. Its overall resource consumption, or "O11y Tax," is nearly equivalent to that of a non-instrumented app. No application code or configuration changes are needed; simply deploy Beyla alongside the service for monitoring. Here are the key drivers that make Beyla a good starting point:

- **Low Overhead:** eBPF's auto-instrumentation tool boasts minimal overhead, enabling runtime data capture impossible with manual code instrumentation.
- **Dynamic Adjustment:** eBPF allows for dynamic modification of instrumentation points and data collection logic without altering the application code, offering flexibility beyond static methods.
- **OpenTelemetry-eXtendedBPF:** Combines OpenTelemetry framework with eBPF for tracing and metric collection.
- **Kubectl eBPF:** Integrates eBPF capabilities into Kubernetes management for container and pod-level introspection.
- **BCC (Brendan Gregg's Collection of Tools):** Offers pre-built eBPF tools for various network and system analysis tasks.

GRAFANA BEYLA

Recently, Grafana announced that Grafana Beyla is now integrated into Grafana Alloy as the default eBPF-based application auto-instrumentation solution. With this integration, Alloy users can seamlessly capture metrics and traces from running services and connect them to their existing telemetry pipelines. In future versions of Beyla, Grafana plans to expand its capabilities to include additional eBPF-based features, such as network monitoring.

Considerations Before Adopting eBPF

Before diving into eBPF-based production, it's crucial to weigh a few key considerations. Firstly, mastering eBPF programming and kernel mechanics is paramount, as it forms the foundation of leveraging its capabilities effectively. Additionally, navigating the debugging process for eBPF programs can pose challenges, often requiring adeptness in kernel-level debugging. Furthermore, while the eBPF tooling ecosystem is growing, it's essential to acknowledge its current limitations compared to more established observability solutions. These factors underscore the importance of thoughtful deliberation and preparation before adopting eBPF into your infrastructure.

- **Learning Curve:** Acquiring expertise in eBPF programming and kernel mechanics is essential.
- **Debugging Complexity:** Debugging eBPF programs can be challenging, often necessitating kernel-level debugging skills.
- **Limited Tooling Ecosystem:** While rapidly expanding, the eBPF tooling landscape is still evolving compared to mature observability solutions.

In conclusion, eBPF presents exciting opportunities for auto instrumentation, addressing gaps and offering flexibility where traditional methods falter. It's crucial to evaluate specific needs, expertise, and resources before embracing this powerful yet nuanced technology.

Observability Strategy Positioning

As you embark on your observability journey, you'll encounter numerous strategic questions and decisions. However, they can all be distilled down to one overarching question: Who is leading OpenTelemetry implementations, and how extensively can they influence the organization's operations? There's no definitive right or wrong answer to these questions, and the responses will evolve over time. The brief case studies in this chapter shed light on the trade-offs you'll encounter as you strive for optimal observability. For instance, if you're implementing the Collector across your organization's infrastructure, you'll seek the "Goldilocks zone" where cloud-native observability data justifies its cost. However, the business value diminishes if you deviate too much from this optimal zone. Discovering the Goldilocks zone entails capturing the right observability data and retaining the most relevant and effective slices of synthesized observability data.

Context vs. Coverage

eBPF delves into the deepest levels, but OpenTelemetry provides a broader context, presenting an intriguing trade-off. When considering auto instrumentation, eBPF reads OS-level metrics while OpenTelemetry focuses on application-level metrics. Both cover runtimes, libraries, Kafka broker monitoring, and JVM metrics and events at a similar layer. However, eBPF lags behind OpenTelemetry in distributed tracing due to its limited context propagation. OpenTelemetry shines when dealing with interpreted coding languages, offering a nearly plug-and-play solution. Yet, for dynamic observability at kprobes (kernel level) or even static but kernel-level observability without code changes, eBPF excels. It also performs well with uprobes (user level) using USDT, although OpenTelemetry remains more straightforward. OpenTelemetry serves as the benchmark for data format and instrumentation toolkit. For profiling, event and metric reading at the kernel level, and real-time debugging, eBPF emerges as the optimal data source.

eBPF-native observability tools like Cilium have become the cornerstone of auto instrumentation today. eBPF is ubiquitous, being employed across various industry giants such as F5, Cisco, New Relic, VMware, and Elastic, to name a few. With tools like bpftrace, Pyroscope, Parca, Inspektor Gadget, and Grafana Beyla, eBPF offers minimal observability tax compared to other auto-instrumentation methods and SDKs like OTel, which often impose heavier computing loads and require additional code complexity.

Deploying OTel for auto instrumentation can be a significant effort for production teams, especially considering the one-time setup it entails. It is generally recommended for manual instrumentation, storing data in OTel spec format, while eBPF shines in auto-instrumentation scenarios.

When time is of the essence in achieving observability goals, particularly with a deadline like "Fast by Friday," eBPF proves invaluable. However, it's essential to recognize that eBPF is a complex technology. While a kernel-level development team can create custom eBPF tools, working with mature eBPF tools and platforms is advisable for others. Moreover, employing two different eBPF-based tools for the same task simultaneously is not recommended due to potential conflicts and complexities.

Summary

The overarching goal of this book is to close the gap between the theoretical principles of cloud-native observability and their practical implementation. To achieve this, we offer a tangible blueprint, albeit with some subjective viewpoints, illustrating how these concepts can be applied in real-world CNA scenarios. Building upon the foundational knowledge established in previous chapters, we explored the details of instrumentation engineering, which is considered the predecessor to observability in this chapter.

In modern software engineering, observability in complex systems like CNA may be viewed through the lens of abundance and unity.

Abundance in observability refers to the wealth of data produced by a CNA telemetry signal known as M3PLT. This abundance underscores the importance of recognizing and harnessing the richness of available data for analysis.

Unity, meanwhile, highlights the interconnectedness and coherence within complex systems. Despite the abundance of data, there's a unifying thread that binds the elements of a CNA together, including component relationships, mapping, tracing, and emergent properties.

By integrating abundance and unity into cloud-native observability practices, engineers can approach software systems with a mindset that embraces diversity and interconnectedness. Leveraging data abundance allows for comprehensive insights, while understanding system unity aids in grasping holistic system behavior. This integrated approach leads to more effective problem-solving and decision-making in cloud-native software engineering.

CHAPTER 6

Demystifying Cilium's Spellbinding Nature

Once upon a time, in the formidable fortress of the Linux Heroes realm, a group of brilliant engineers set out on a groundbreaking journey. Their mission? To craft a code base that would revolutionize the accessibility of operating system kernels. This masterpiece, known as extended BPF or eBPF, promised to unleash the full potential of the kernel, marking a new era for independent developers' engagement with this vital core.

Join me in this chapter as we embark on a journey through the mesmerizing realms of eBPF, where Kubernetes networking meets efficiency, and traditional barriers are shattered by the transformative magic of cloud-native observability and tracing.

This chapter covers the following topics:

- Story of eBPF
- Genesis of Cilium and Isovalent
- Cilium architecture
- Editions of Cilium

Dr. M. Ghane, *Observability Engineering with Cilium*,
https://doi.org/10.1007/979-8-8688-1258-3_6

Genesis of eBPF

Picture a world where developers could compile and run code in kernel space performance seamlessly, without the shackles of frequent reboots or the burdensome loading of kernel modules. It was a vision that sparkled with promise, an ideal almost too good to be true. Yet, fuelled by unwavering dedication, these engineers were determined to breathe life into this vision.

Their persistence bore fruit when the Linux kernel maintainer, the gatekeeper of the kernel's evolution, not only embraced their audacious vision but also pledged to integrate eBPF into the forthcoming releases. As time unfolded, their dreams crystallized into reality, with major Linux distributions eagerly adopting the new kernel versions. Thus, the world witnessed the dawn of a new era in kernel space development, ushered in by the revolutionary force of eBPF.

As our story unfolds, the protagonist, eBPF, not only revolutionizes the way we observe and trace processes but also becomes the catalyst for a new era of streamlined, resource-conscious observability. The tale is one of innovation, where the hero's tools, like Cilium Hubble and Tetragon, become instrumental in achieving feats previously deemed unattainable.

Legend has it that, in 2011, amidst the flourishing era of Linux, the landscape of networking saw a seismic shift with the emergence of **Software-Defined Networking (SDN)**. However, progress was impeded by Ethernet switching limitations within the Linux kernel and various networking hurdles. It was during this time that the Open vSwitch project emerged, promising solutions to these challenges. Simultaneously, Alexei Starovoitov, then at the helm of a burgeoning startup named PLUMgrid (now holding a prominent position at Facebook), embarked on an alternative approach. He developed a new set of operations aimed at enhancing networking capabilities within the Linux kernel, such as introducing mechanisms for bytecode verification and packet control.

These instruction sets would enable the kernel to perform specific networking tasks more efficiently and with added functionality.

Enter Chris Wright, then spearheading SDN efforts at Red Hat and now serving as its CTO. Admitted the transformative potential of Alexei's innovations, Chris forged a pivotal recommendation that Alexei reimagined these instructions in the vein of BPF (Berkeley Packet Filter) but with a twist - a novel iteration aptly named eBPF (extended BPF). Thus, with the addition of an "e," eBPF was born, ushering in a new era of Linux kernel programmability.

Classic BPF, originally conceptualized by Steven McCanne and Van Jacobson at Lawrence Berkeley Laboratory in the 1990s, laid the foundation for efficient network packet filtering. By introducing a virtual machine, known as the BPF VM, within the kernel, users gained the ability to execute bytecode programs. These programs defined filtering logic, enabling granular control over packet processing based on diverse criteria such as IP addresses, port numbers, and protocols. Importantly, this execution occurred within the kernel itself, obviating the need for resource-intensive context switches between user space and kernel space.

In its nascent stages, eBPF wasn't merely the evolution of classic BPF; rather, it served as a bridge, facilitating the industry's comprehension and potential adoption of what Alexei has been created. By introducing programmability not just in networking but across various kernel subsystems - spanning tracing, observability, security, and performance analysis - eBPF revolutionized kernel-level operations. Computer languages such as C and LLVM-based languages empower developers to craft eBPF programs, which are seamlessly compiled into bytecode by the efficient eBPF runtime within the kernel space.

In reality, eBPF has woven itself into the fabric of your digital life. tcpdump, the omnipresent network monitoring tool, harnesses eBPF's might to deliver unparalleled insights into network traffic. Current eBPF-based Tcpdump version, showcasing a significant enhancement in performance.

The pivotal moment arrived when Brendan Gregg (formerly of Netflix, now at Intel) collaborated with Alexei, advocating that eBPF should extend its focus beyond networking to embrace tracing. With the inclusion of kprobe support by Alexei and Daniel Borkmann (formerly of Red Hat and Cisco, now at Isovalent) and Brendan's development of frontend tools like the BCC toolchain, eBPF surged forward. The famous "merge command" of eBPF into the Linux kernel in 2013 by David Stephen Miller, the primary maintainer of the networking subsystem, heralded a new era of kernelless kernel programming – a paradigm where a virtual machine operates within the kernel space natively, empowering users to execute isolated programs with unparalleled performance, akin to the transformative impact of JavaScript on web browsers.

The rapid adoption of eBPF by industry giants like Netflix and Facebook, followed by its integration into cloud hyperscalers, underscored its efficacy. Facebook's demonstration of eBPF processing 15 million packets per second at DataCenter line rates, with a mere 50 nanoseconds spent per packet, showcased eBPF's prowess. This tenfold performance enhancement compared to existing solutions like IPVS reverberated throughout the industry, illuminating the potential of eBPF and XDP. Today, every packet traversing facebook.com interfaces with eBPF at the XDP layer, exemplifying its ubiquitous role.

eBPF transcends its role as a tracing and observability tool with negligible overhead; it emerges as a formidable asset for security, as evidenced by the Google BPF LSM initiative. Its expansion to the Windows kernel, alongside its presence on macOS and Android platforms, further solidifies its status as an indispensable technology.

Understanding the profound impact of eBPF within a cloud-native framework necessitates a deep dive into the deliberate isolation we've crafted for our applications. Through containers and Kubernetes pods, we've empowered these applications to function independently. However, this isolation poses a challenge when it comes to instrumenting them for common functionalities like logging, tracing, or security. Rather than tackling each application individually, the quest is for a unified platform capable of seamlessly instrumenting them all at once. Enter eBPF.

Situated within the kernel, eBPF offers a pivotal solution. By enabling instrumentation at the kernel level, it furnishes us with an array of potent tools capable of monitoring and influencing system-wide operations. This capability revolutionizes the life of SREs. No longer burdened with concerns about provisioning observability or networking capabilities, SRE and developers can harness the power of eBPF to embed these functionalities directly into the kernel. In essence, eBPF represents a transformative force within the cloud-native landscape, reshaping the very fabric of infrastructure software.

eBPF licensing is governed by the license of the Linux kernel, which is the GNU General Public License version 2 (GPLv2).

Birth of Cilium

The inception of the **Cilium** project owes much to the visionary efforts of Thomas Graf, a luminary figure whose contributions span across Red Hat, Cisco, and Isovalent. Alongside three other pioneering individuals, including Daniel Borkmann, co-maintainer of eBPF in the Linux kernel, Graf played a pivotal role in crafting the Cilium project. Their collective zeal to democratize advanced networking technologies catalyzed the birth of Cilium on December 16, 2015, introducing a transformative networking layer characterized by innate security, scalability, and cloud-native prowess.

At its core, Cilium addressed the pressing challenges of Kubernetes by transcending the limitations and idiosyncrasies of the Linux network stack. Unlike its predecessors reliant on conventional approaches like iptables or IPVS, Cilium boldly embraced eBPF as the linchpin of cloud-native networking. Its mission? To render eBPF integration seamless for both application developers and SREs, heralding a paradigm shift in the orchestration landscape.

As Kubernetes burgeoned into the de facto standard for container orchestration, Cilium emerged as a pivotal component of the ecosystem, streamlining fundamental tasks such as Container Network Interface configuration and inter-pod connectivity. The inaugural Cilium Design Summit underscored the pivotal role of observability, laying the groundwork for its ascent.

Formally embraced by the Cloud-Native Computing Foundation on October 13, 2021, as an incubation-level project, Cilium swiftly ascended to graduation status a year later, a testament to its rapid evolution and unwavering relevance within the CNCF fold.

Cilium As Networking Hero

Cilium's eBPF-driven data plane orchestrates a sleek Layer 3 network infrastructure capable of spanning diverse clusters, whether via native routing or overlay mechanisms, facilitated by the Cilium Cluster Mesh. It boasts Layer 7 protocol awareness, empowering granular enforcement of network policies across the entire OSI spectrum, including Fully Qualified Domain Names (FQDNs), underpinned by an identity-centric security model divorced from traditional network paradigms.

Moreover, Cilium's feature-rich repertoire encompasses distributed load balancing, supplanting conventional kube-proxy with XDP and socket-based load-balancing strategies, fortified by efficient hash tables within the eBPF realm. The platform's prowess extends to advanced functionalities like integrated ingress and egress gateways, bandwidth management, stand-alone load balancing, and service mesh capabilities. Service meshes, as we will delve into later, act as an infrastructure layer facilitating communication between microservices, ensuring smooth traffic flow, and enhancing security. While other key players like Calico and Istio have also embraced eBPF, Cilium stands out as the brainchild of the very creators of eBPF itself. This intimate connection grants Cilium a unique understanding of eBPF's capabilities, enabling it to fully leverage its potential.

Uniquely architected for IPv6 and identity-based networking, Cilium pioneers support for cutting-edge kernel features such as BBR TCP congestion control and BIG TCP within the Kubernetes domain, reaffirming its status as a vanguard of innovation.

Cilium As Observability Hero

Enter Hubble, the beacon of observability and UI facet of Cilium, seamlessly integrated within the CNI framework. Hubble unveils a panoramic vista of network packet flows, elucidates policy decisions governing traffic ingress and egress, and illuminates service communication dynamics within Kubernetes via intuitive service maps. Its data export prowess to Prometheus, OpenTelemetry, Grafana, and Fluentd enables nuanced analysis of Layer 3/4 and Layer 7 metrics, enriching operational insights.

Cilium As Security Hero

Tetragon stands sentinel as Cilium's bastion of security observability and runtime enforcement, leveraging eBPF's prowess to imbue Kubernetes environments with granular policy enforcement and real-time monitoring capabilities. It furnishes users with unparalleled visibility into process lifecycles, orchestrating synchronous monitoring, filtering, and enforcement within the kernel domain.

Rounding out Cilium's arsenal is eBPF-go, a versatile, pure-Go library engineered to interface seamlessly with the eBPF subsystem in the Linux kernel. Emphasizing reliability, compatibility, and minimal external dependencies, eBPF-go stands as a testament to Cilium's commitment to empowering developers with robust tooling for eBPF integration, widely embraced in production environments.

Last but certainly not least, PWru (Packet, where are you?) stands as a pioneering tool in the realm of network packet tracing within the Linux kernel, leveraging the power of eBPF with sophisticated filtering capabilities. Designed to delve deep into kernel intricacies, it serves as a vital resource for diagnosing and resolving network connectivity issues. Through the attachment of eBPF debugging programs to key Linux kernel functions responsible for packet processing, PWru offers users an unparalleled insight into the inner workings of packet handling, surpassing the capabilities of traditional tools like tcpdump and Wireshark.

Furthermore, PWru goes beyond mere packet inspection by providing comprehensive metadata such as network namespace, processing timestamps, and internal kernel packet representation fields. This wealth of information empowers users to unravel complex network scenarios with precision and clarity.

Backing the innovative strides of Cilium is Isovalent, a commercial entity founded in 2018 by luminaries Thomas Graf and Dan Wendlandt, known for their contributions to Open vSwitch and VMware. With the proliferation of eBPF-enabled kernels and the widespread adoption of Cilium, Isovalent quickly rose to prominence within the cloud-native ecosystem. Recognized as the de facto Kubernetes Container Network Interface (CNI) solution, where offers robust network policies, segmentation, and transparent encryption.

In a strategic move, Grafana Labs forged a partnership with the Cilium project, further solidifying its position in the market. Today, Cilium sets new standards with its offering of a sidecar-free service mesh empowered by eBPF 2.0 and mTLS for enhanced network security. Introducing features like SPIFFE integration and the Cilium mesh, it extends its capabilities to facilitate multi- and hybrid-cloud networking, serving as a versatile cloud networking transit gateway.

Cilium operates under the Apache License 2.0, a renowned open source software license endorsed by the Open Source Initiative (OSI) for its liberal terms. This license empowers users with extensive freedoms, permitting them to utilize, adapt, distribute, and sublicense the software for both commercial and noncommercial endeavors, sans significant constraints. Key facets of the Apache License 2.0 encompass

- **Permissive Licensing:** Users enjoy broad permissions, enabling seamless modification, distribution, and sublicensing of the software with minimal encumbrances.
- **Patent Grant:** Contributors furnish a patent license, assuring users of unhindered utilization of the software without apprehension of patent disputes.
- **No Warranty:** The license disclaims warranties, presenting the software "as is," devoid of any assurances or fitness guarantees for specific purposes.
- **Attribution:** Users must uphold copyright notices, license declarations, and disclaimers when redistributing the software.
- **Trademark Use:** Provisions in the license govern the utilization of trademarks affiliated with the software.

When conducting a thorough evaluation of a company, it is imperative to meticulously outline its investor base and legal framework. Take Isovalent, for example, which has secured investments from esteemed venture capital firms such as Andreessen Horowitz, affectionately known as A16z. This powerhouse's portfolio includes industry giants like GitHub, Facebook, Coinbase, PagerDuty, Nicira, Okta, Slack, and Skype. Furthermore, Isovalent has garnered support from Thomvest Ventures, recognized for its adept nurturing of startups such as ThousandEyes. Noteworthy investments also hail from M12, Microsoft's Venture Fund; Cisco; Grafana Labs; and Google Ventures (GV), with a nod to the likely involvement of descendants from the leading Big Three asset managers, namely, BlackRock, Vanguard, and State Street. Isovalent Cilium Enterprise Edition is an enterprise-grade, hardened distribution of open source projects Cilium, Hubble, and Tetragon, built and supported by the Cilium creators. In terms of legal structure, Isovalent operates as a Private Limited Company (Ltd) in the United Kingdom.

The widespread adoption of Cilium within the cloud service provider landscape is nothing short of remarkable. It's not a secret that major players like Google with Anthos and GKE Dataplane V2, Microsoft's AKS and Amazon AWS that leveraged Cilium CNI anywhere with EKS, to embrace its robust networking, observability, and security features. This trend extends across other industry leaders such as Alibaba Cloud and DigitalOcean (DOKS), underscoring Cilium's pivotal role in fortifying Kubernetes platforms despite any geographic or political limitations.

Beyond the realm of cloud services, Cilium has found enthusiastic adoption among Telcos like T-Systems International, renowned SaaS providers such as GitLab and SAP, and technology stalwarts like SUSE Rancher Labs, Canonical, and F5. Even manufacturing giants like Daimler Truck AG recognize the value of Cilium in their cloud-native ecosystems.

Moreover, a myriad of medium-sized enterprises, academic institutions, AI and MLOps research centers, and media organizations rely on Cilium for their networking and security needs, not to mention the extensive roster of enterprises, including but not limited to Adobe, Bell Canada, ByteDance, Capital One, Datadog, IKEA, Schuberg Philis, and Sky, who entrust Cilium to power their production environments.

This is just the tip of the iceberg. With the proliferation of eBPF-based products and their clients, coupled with the publicly undisclosed technology stacks of numerous other enterprises, Cilium stands poised to dominate a significant portion of the cloud-native market. Truly impressive, wouldn't you agree?

The trajectory of Isovalent took a significant turn with Cisco's announcement of its intent to acquire the company, following its successful acquisition of Splunk. This M&A process, initiated in 2024, underscores the value and potential of Isovalent in the cloud-native observability and security landscape. Despite these developments, Isovalent remains committed to its open source roots, offering both enterprise and community editions of the Cilium project under the auspices of the Cloud-Native Computing Foundation (CNCF).

Today, Isovalent, bolstered by the endorsement and smart money of Cisco, stands at the pinnacle of strength, primed to spearhead innovation, and set new standards of excellence in the domain of microservices and cloud-native network infrastructure. With this robust partnership, we anticipate a surge in forthcoming collaborations, envisioning deeper integrations of Cilium with leading platforms like Splunk, alongside other security and observability-centric products within the extensive Cisco portfolio.

Summary

Congratulations! You've reached the culmination of the first part of the book and embarked on the second leg of our journey into the realm of Cilium engineering and functionality. Today, eBPF stands as a pillar of the modern Linux kernel, enabling developers to seamlessly create advanced, secured, and low performance tax tools integrated into the kernel space. Operating akin to a virtual machine within the host OS or like JavaScript within a web browser, eBPF represents a significant leap forward, preserving BPF's foundation while introducing transformative functionality. Its seamless integration within cloud-native ecosystems makes it essential for contemporary infrastructure, aligning with CNA 1.0 principles through event-driven architecture. This capability is particularly valuable in containerized environments, ensuring efficient execution within the kernel space's strict isolation. eBPF's efficiency stems from its lightning-fast event-driven mechanism, surpassing traditional user-space tools. Yet its power also demands responsible usage, with ongoing refinement of security measures by the Linux community and eBPF foundation. Notably, eBPF empowers exceptional security measures, swiftly neutralizing threats like those addressed by Tetragon, enhancing cloud-native environment integrity. Cilium, among the leaders in harnessing eBPF, pioneers integrated eBPF-native products for Kubernetes service mesh, observability, and runtime security enforcement. In observability and tracing, eBPF's brilliance outshines traditional methods, offering unparalleled efficiency and tools like Cilium Tetragon and Hubble. These products enhance system performance by up to 40%, guiding the way to operational excellence.

CHAPTER 7

Delineating Cilium Core Architecture

The genesis of the eBPF and Cilium project emerged from a simple yet ambitious vision: to craft a robust CNI agent tailored for Kubernetes, integrating observability and security features, while sidestepping the constraints of iptables through native eBPF utilization. Seamlessly integrating into the L3 network of Kubernetes, Cilium delineates policies and identity-based networking, aspiring to relegate cloud-native networking to the realm of mundane concerns, freeing developers, architects, and SRE teams from its daily grip. At the helm of this endeavor is Thomas Graf, the driving force behind Cilium and CTO of Isovalent, advocating for its security, simplicity, and scalability not solely within Kubernetes clusters, but across VM networks, serverless architectures, private clouds, and multi-cloud environments. His vision positions Cilium as the cornerstone of cloud-native infrastructure. *Did they attain their ambitious objective?*

Conventionally, major players such as Google GCP and Microsoft Azure, alongside with other hyperscalers, are spearheading a paradigm shift. Nowadays, the Cisco Systems–backed Cilium project harbors the potential to ascend as the frontline across these layers independently, equipped with all-encompassing capabilities to redefine the landscape. *Why do these prestigious enterprises repose their confidence in Cilium?*

Dr. M. Ghane, *Observability Engineering with Cilium*,
https://doi.org/10.1007/979-8-8688-1258-3_7

In this chapter, I will delve deeply into these topics to illuminate aforementioned questions:

- Cilium anatomy and functionality
- Competitor's landscape
- The art of winning hearts to Cilium
- Cilium certification

Recap of eBPF

Before delving into the intricacies of Cilium architecture, let's revisit the valuable insights gained from our exploration of eBPF in preceding chapters.

Implementing eBPF programs within container-based applications and services has ushered in a new era of manageability, security, and performance enhancement.

In the contemporary landscape of CNA platforms such as Kubernetes, where a singular kernel powers diverse workloads, the utilization of eBPF programs emerges as indispensable. These programs offer unparalleled control and observability across the entire infrastructure, seamlessly and efficiently.

eBPF serves as a catalyst for accelerated innovation within the Linux kernel, fundamentally altering the landscape of developer interactions and the enhancement of kernel functionalities.

This dynamic technology empowers users with the ability to craft and execute compact, secure programs directly within the Linux kernel. These programs cater to diverse needs, ranging from real-time monitoring to robust security enforcement and performance optimization.

FUTURISTIC INSIGHT

Key cloud hyperscalers leverage Cilium assuming the mantle of **default CNI**, with Istio in **Ambient Mode** for Kubernetes container east-west traffic and policy management. Augmented by **Envoy** proxy for API gateway functionalities and **SPIFFE/SPIRE** for workload identity, this integrated technology stack, christened CAKES by Solo.io, epitomizes the predominant trend in cloud infrastructures. Following **Cisco's** contribution and investment in Isovalent, Cilium EE now has the potential to become a leading player in the cloud hyperscaler arena. This strategic partnership positions Cilium EE to achieve significant advancements and secure a prominent role in the industry in the near future. It's crucial to note that the **Istio** version embraced by hyperscalers diverges from the Community edition.

Cilium Architecture

Cilium represents a cutting-edge network security and observability solution tailored specifically for Kubernetes environments, with potential for extension to various other cloud-native platforms and beyond. In this chapter, our focus remains on Kubernetes for clarity and coherence. Leveraging the robust capabilities of eBPF technology within the Linux kernel, Cilium facilitates the seamless integration of dynamic security measures, enhanced visibility, and precise networking controls directly into the kernel space. Central to Cilium's architecture are four fundamental components: the Cilium agent, the intuitive Cilium client command-line tool, the efficient Cilium operator, and the indispensable Cilium CNI plug-in.

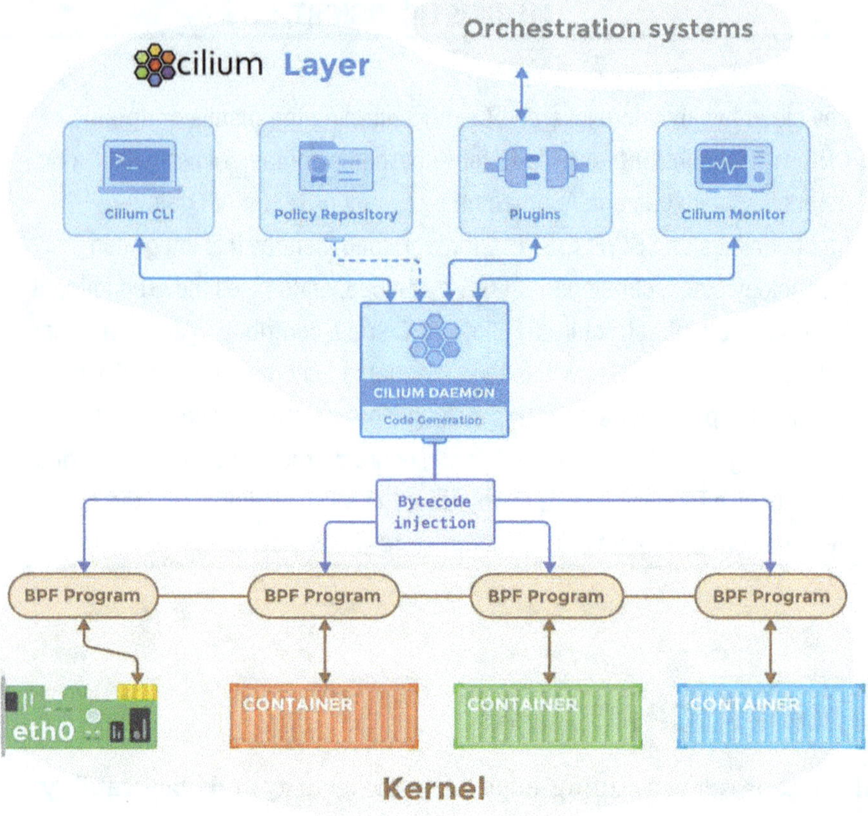

Figure 7-1. *Cilium Architecture Diagram*

The architecture of Cilium consists of a few primary components.

Agent

The Cilium Agent, running across all nodes within the cluster, undertakes the task of configuring networking, load balancing, policies, and monitoring through Kubernetes or APIs. Leveraging eBPF, it seamlessly embeds security and networking protocols into the Linux kernel of each node. For Windows hosts, the same procedure extends to integrating them into the Windows kernel.

Operator

The Cilium Operator oversees essential cluster tasks but isn't directly involved in network policy determinations. Its absence may result in IP Address Management delays and kvstore unhealthiness or instability, necessitating agent restarts.

Command-Line Interface (CLI)

The Cilium Command-Line Interface (CLI), packaged alongside the agent, allows for the inspection and control of the local agent's status, providing convenient access to eBPF maps.

CNI Plug-in

The Cilium Kubernetes CNI (Container Network Interface) plug-in springs into action when Kubernetes orchestrates pod scheduling or termination on a node. Operating from a centralized perspective, the operator efficiently manages cluster tasks collectively rather than individually per node. During pod scheduling or termination, Kubernetes calls upon the CNI plug-in, which in turn engages with the node's Cilium API to configure essential data paths for networking, load balancing, and network policies.

Cilium boasts a robust architecture engineered for scalability, adeptly navigating complex network topologies. Its repertoire includes a suite of features, ranging from multi-cluster and multi-cloud capabilities to advanced load balancing, transparent encryption, and comprehensive network security functionalities. Powered by eBPF at its core, Cilium stands out for its ability to deliver high-performance and low-latency networking and security solutions tailored for modern distributed systems.

How Cilium Works

In prior discussions, we introduced Cilium as a seamless integration in DataCenter refresh initiatives and an instrumental network tool designed specifically for CNA platforms like Kubernetes clusters, offering robust security measures in a cloud-native environment. At its core, Cilium functions by intercepting and scrutinizing network traffic amid Kubernetes pods, utilizing this data to enact and uphold security protocols.

When packets traverse between pods, Cilium's data plane steps in to inspect their origins and destinations. Through a meticulous evaluation process, it determines the packet's eligibility for transmission, guided by a predefined set of security policies set by the cluster administrator. These policies can encompass various criteria, including pod identities, labels, annotations, and the nature of the transmitted data.

Central to Cilium's efficacy is its utilization of eBPF, a virtual machine facilitating the execution of intricate security policies directly within the Linux kernel. This methodology allows Cilium to enforce policies seamlessly, without necessitating alterations to application code or network configurations.

Beyond security enforcement, Cilium introduces a suite of advanced networking capabilities to bolster the performance and resilience of Kubernetes clusters. Notably, it enables load balancing and traffic routing between pods, alongside offering comprehensive network traffic monitoring and tracing utilities.

In contrast, Cilium's service mesh architecture harnesses eBPF programs seamlessly integrated into the Linux kernel, enabling transparent policy enforcement and granular insight into network activities. This empowers Cilium to enforce identity-centric policies, fostering secure service communication, while facilitating comprehensive network flow analysis for enhanced security and observability.

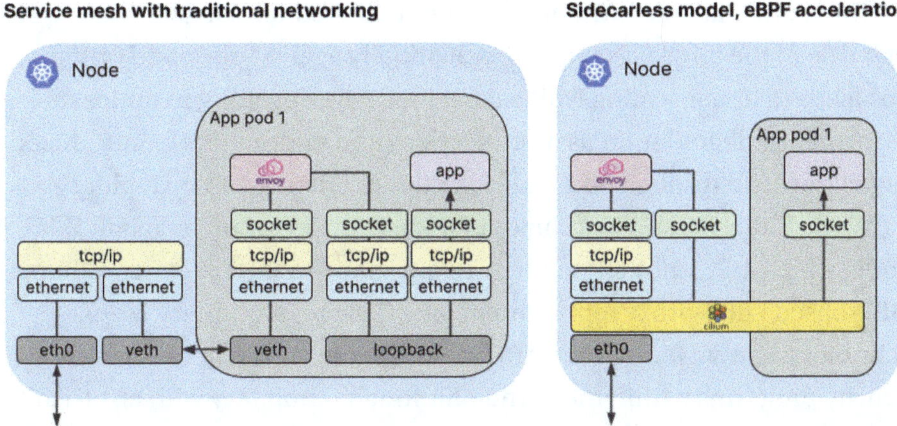

Figure 7-2. *Traditional Service Mesh vs. Cilium Sidecarless Concept*

In the traditional networking domain, performance hinges on various factors such as configuration intricacies, network protocol choices, the quality of network interface cards, and the underlying hardware infrastructure. While these factors remain significant in Kubernetes environments, engineers encounter a critical decision as their Kubernetes deployments expand: whether to employ kube-proxy.

By default, kube-proxy is deployed on each node, facilitating smooth network traffic flow from services to their designated pods. It abstracts the underlying pod IPs upon the creation of new services or endpoints, enabling communication among services via the service's virtual IP address. Despite its name, kube-proxy doesn't operate as a conventional proxy. Instead, it synchronizes rules within the underlying operating system's packet filtering by monitoring the Kubernetes control plane. It governs essential network rules for traffic routing, including Network Address Translation (NAT) when necessary, ensuring packets reach their intended destinations. However, kube-proxy's reliance on the aged iptables technology, dating back 25 years, proves insufficient for Kubernetes' dynamic nature.

The main challenge with iptables lies in its sequential algorithm, where each rule in the table is evaluated individually against observed traffic. This leads to linear scaling with each added rule, resulting in noticeable performance degradation as more services and endpoints are introduced. Packet traversal through each rule introduces latency and instability.

While Kubernetes users can opt for kube-proxy's more efficient IPVS mode, which still relies on netfilter, an alternative solution exists: Cilium's eBPF-based kube-proxy replacement. eBPF is a revolutionary Linux technology known for its ability to safely execute virtual networking and security programs within the kernel. Although familiarity with eBPF isn't mandatory for installing and operating Cilium, a basic understanding can prove advantageous.

Cilium's kube-proxy replacement harnesses efficient eBPF hash tables, utilizing eBPF maps as the kernel's mechanism for data storage and retrieval. The benefits of Cilium's eBPF kube-proxy replacement become particularly evident at scale. While iptables struggles with latency amid a growing number of microservices, the efficiency of eBPF is highlighted in the performance benchmarking graphic provided below.

Why Opt for Cilium?

Cilium is not the only CNI nor CNA security nor observability toolset in the market. It's not even the only provider of eBPF-based solutions. Many others provide almost similar services even with eBPF. To name a few in container networking, we have the Calico project from Tigera and the CNIs offered by hyperscalers. As service mesh, I can name Istio (both OSS and commercial version) and Linkerd. When looking for Ingress, again Nginx and Istio or as load balancer, F5 and AVI and for multi-cloud as can name Aviatrix. My initial question was this: why do so many organizations choose Cilium for their Kubernetes environments? **Form3** selected Cilium to avoid cloud vendor lock-in, while **Tietoevry** adopted it for more advanced network policies, improved DNS capabilities, and to reduce tool sprawl. **PostFinance** turned to Cilium to build a scalable Kubernetes platform, and **Capital One** leveraged it to develop a secure and maintainable Private platform-as-a-service (PaaS). **Ascend** dramatically reduced their network debugging time from 4–16 hours down to just 20 seconds by adopting Cilium. **Seznam** replaced their F5 load balancer with Cilium's standalone Layer 4 load balancer, and **VSHN** implemented it to reduce their Kubernetes support burden.

Cilium stands out amid a sea of alternatives in the realms of Container Network Interface (CNI), CNA platforms, and observability solutions. However, it doesn't hold a monopoly in this domain nor is it the sole provider of an eBPF-based solution. Numerous other options offer similar functionalities, leveraging the power of eBPF technology. Notable contenders include the Calico project by Tigera and the CNIs offered by hyperscalers. In the realm of service mesh, both the open source and commercial versions of Istio are noteworthy mentions. Nginx and Istio are prominent players in the Ingress arena, while previously F5 and AVI dominate the load balancer space. Aviatrix stands out for multi-cloud deployments.

In the realm of cloud-native infrastructure, Cilium emerges as a remarkably versatile solution, presenting a plethora of advantages. Tailored to tackle diverse use cases ranging from fortifying network security to orchestrating service mesh intricacies and beyond, Cilium stands as a formidable force. Identifying a singular competitor capable of rivalling Cilium's expansive capabilities proves to be a challenging endeavor.

Nonetheless, within the landscape of cloud-native infrastructure, alternatives exist, each endeavoring to deliver analogous functionalities. Certain contenders may specialize in specific domains such as network security or service mesh administration, yet they often fall short of providing the holistic solution embodied by Cilium.

Ultimately, Cilium's distinguishing factor lies in its capacity to furnish a cohesive and comprehensive approach to cloud-native infrastructure, setting it apart from the competition. Let's delve deeper into some of the key alternative CNI and service mesh solutions in next sections.

Networking/CNI

In the realm of networking CNI solutions, two notable contenders stand out: Calico and Cilium. However, distinct characteristics set Cilium apart from its competitors.

Cilium was purposefully crafted with Kubernetes at its core, ensuring seamless integration and optimized utilization of Kubernetes' unique capabilities. Unlike Calico, which originated in the realm of OpenStack and was later adapted for Kubernetes, Cilium's foundation ensures it fully harnesses Kubernetes' strengths.

A fundamental divergence lies in the technological underpinning; Cilium harnesses the power of eBPF technology from its inception. This empowers Cilium to outperform traditional networking approaches in terms of performance and scalability. While Calico has integrated eBPF support subsequently, it lacks the native integration that characterizes Cilium's architecture, consequently offering a less comprehensive networking solution.

Moreover, Cilium's versatility extends beyond mere network security and policy management, addressing a broader spectrum of critical use cases across cloud-native infrastructures.

In summary, although Calico enjoys a prominent position in the networking CNI landscape, organizations seeking to optimize their networking infrastructure in the cloud-native era would find Cilium's Kubernetes-centric approach and utilization of eBPF technology a superior choice.

Service Mesh

In the realm of service mesh solutions, both Cilium and Solo.io stand out for their robust features tailored for managing and securing microservice environments. However, distinctive nuances set Cilium apart, rendering it the superior choice for organizations seeking to optimize their service mesh infrastructure.

Firstly, a fundamental divergence lies in the technology employed for service mesh management. While Solo.io relies on the widely adopted Istio framework, Cilium adopts a unique approach, integrating its own service mesh capabilities seamlessly. This distinctive approach enables Cilium to deliver a more streamlined and resource-efficient solution, eliminating the need for additional sidecars that often introduce latency and resource overheads, thereby mitigating costs, especially in cloud environments.

Moreover, the disparity extends to the complexity involved in setting up and managing their respective solutions. Istio, while powerful, can pose challenges in configuration and administration, particularly for newcomers to the service mesh landscape. In contrast, Cilium's integrated service mesh capabilities are intricately woven into the Container Network Interface (CNI), ensuring smoother integration and operation. This convergence of CNI and service mesh technologies foretells a future of simplified, unified infrastructure management.

FUTURISTIC INSIGHT

The brainpower driving Istio originates from Tetrate, a private company headquartered in California. Backed by influential investors such as Dell Technologies Capital, Intel Capital, 8VC, and Samsung NEXT, Tetrate has solidified its position in the technological landscape. Looking ahead to 2025, it wouldn't be unexpected for Cilium, supported by industry giant **Cisco**, to make significant strides in acquiring technology stacks from other leading vendors.

Notably, while Solo.io utilizes Cilium for networking functionalities in layers 2 to 4, their current lack of contribution to the open source community raises concerns regarding their influence over Cilium's evolution and direction.

In summary, while Solo.io presents a formidable contender in the service mesh arena, Cilium's innate service mesh capabilities, streamlined workflows, and deep Kubernetes integration position it as the optimal choice for organizations striving to enhance their service mesh infrastructure. With its emphasis on simplicity, efficiency, and performance, Cilium emerges as the ideal solution, offering a smoother pathway to elevated service mesh capabilities.

In the realm of authentication and encryption (mTLS), Solo.io is often lauded for its focus. However, it's crucial to recognize that implementing a full-service mesh solely for this purpose could be likened to using a chainsaw for butter. The solution may prove overly complex for the task at hand. In contrast, Cilium offers a simpler, more efficient approach to addressing these needs, minimizing complexity and overhead while delivering effective security measures.

Cloud-Native Observability

Networking complexities within Kubernetes (K8s) often lead to potential blind spots. Cilium addresses these challenges with two connectivity approaches for linking pods across different nodes within the same cluster: encapsulation/overlay routing and native/direct routing. It's important to note that in hybrid or multi-cloud clusters, shared labels, annotations, and policies are absent, necessitating a solution like Cilium mesh.

The default and widely used mode is "encapsulation," where a network overlay – typically VXLAN but also GENEVE – is established within the cluster, creating tunnels between all nodes. Cilium facilitates BGP peering sessions over IPv4 or IPv6, enabling the advertisement of LoadBalancer

Service IPs or PodCIDR ranges to the broader network. Typically, peering sessions are set up with a Top-of-Rack (ToR) device. Cilium supports essential BGP features such as MD5-based session authentication, timer customization, communities, local preferences, and graceful restart. The Cilium CLI simplifies verification of established peering sessions and advertised routes.

Alternatively, if BGP isn't preferred or BGP-capable devices are unavailable, networks can be advertised locally over Layer 2 using Address Resolution Protocol (ARP). Known as "Layer 2 (L2) Announcements," this method ensures that local clients are aware of the MAC address corresponding to a specific IP. It's commonly employed in small environments or home labs, as BGP's flexibility and scalability are better suited for data center networks.

Users of CNAs frequently encounter hurdles when it comes to observability. The complexity of distributed systems poses a significant challenge in achieving comprehensive observability for clients. From network to application layers, there are notable visibility gaps that hinder a full understanding of application behaviors. Furthermore, the lack of detailed contextual data within observability tools prolongs the troubleshooting process, impacting timely issue resolution. Identifying performance bottlenecks within distributed architectures remains another common challenge, potentially causing operational inefficiencies.

Cilium and Hubble have a variety of competitors and alternative tools, which can be divided into two main categories. The first category comprises cloud-native observability tools and platforms emphasizing distributed tracing, observability, and monitoring. Examples include popular service meshes like Istio and Solo.io. The second category consists of vendors specializing in application performance monitoring (APM) and network performance monitoring (NPM), such as Dynatrace, Datadog, and AppDynamics.

Cilium boasts a robust value proposition built upon three core elements. Firstly, it offers unified observability, which encompasses a comprehensive view from the network to the application layer (L4–L7), all within a single platform. This consolidation of insights streamlines monitoring efforts and enhances operational efficiency. Secondly, Cilium provides rich contextual data by integrating network and runtime insights. This enriched data context empowers users with a deeper understanding of system dynamics, facilitating more informed decision-making. Lastly, Cilium facilitates streamlined troubleshooting by furnishing actionable insights, thereby reducing downtime and bolstering service reliability.

These value propositions translate into tangible benefits and outcomes for clients. By reducing mean time to detect (MTTD) and mean time to resolution (MTTR) for issues within cloud-native environments, Cilium enhances operational efficiency and minimizes disruptions. Furthermore, its comprehensive visibility into application and network performance enables organizations to make data-driven decisions, leading to faster issue resolution and optimized application performance.

Cilium's key differentiators further enhance its value proposition. Firstly, its ability to operate without necessitating changes to existing applications ensures seamless adoption and integration. Secondly, by providing a holistic view across network, application, and runtime layers, Cilium promotes complete system health awareness.

Additionally, its integration of insights for security and operations teams ensures a well-rounded understanding of system dynamics. Lastly, Cilium's utilization of eBPF technology enables high-performance observability with minimal resource impact, optimizing system performance.

Cilium CE or EE?

A valid inquiry facing any of the CNCF products that has another edition with commercial support is when and why to go for the Enterprise edition EE and when for the Community edition CE. The simple answer is if you have enough time and skilled human resources to build your platform on top of the Community edition, you are very welcome to participate here. You can build a custom platform that meets all your unique needs and values to do everything yourself by asking at public Slack channels where you get best-effort help from the community.

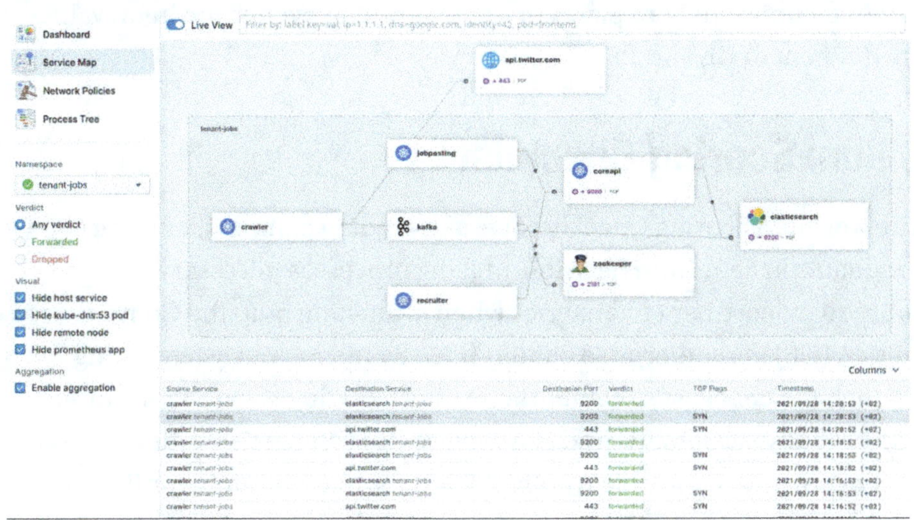

Figure 7-3. *Cilium Dashboard*

If you are short of skilled kernel developers and time, you can go for EE where you could get direct access to eBPF and Cilium maintainers and implement your solution in a short time frame. With EE, you would get 24/7 support with 30-minute response times.

It's important to note that Cilium EE is a separate distribution than the CE, meaning that the Community version is only tested by the community whereas Enterprise incorporates community testing into hardened enterprise releases. This also means that bug fixes are not always backported to the CE. Cilium EE has many specific Enterprise features that are not available in the Community version, but sometimes it's the other way around as well. A feature might be available in CE and may not be available in Enterprise yet, so if you implement the community feature and upgrade to Enterprise in a few months, perhaps it will not be fully supported by your Enterprise contract yet. This also means that you would have a technical debt to pay later on. I know that even some helm values are different in CE and EE.

Cilium Scoring Checklist

The weighted Scoring Checklist acts as a guiding compass, offering invaluable insights into decision-making processes necessary for subsequent cost-benefit analyses when evaluating both the Community edition (CE) and Enterprise edition (EE). By meticulously navigating through the checklist's segments covering workflows, tooling, security, observability, scalability, and challenges, you can precisely identify areas of concern and determine whether solutions like Cilium CE or EE could offer support. To quantify your assessment, assign a score ranging from 0 to 10 to each query, multiplying it by its respective normalized weight. Should the cumulative score exceed 75, it strongly advises considering Cilium as the center of gravity of your cloud-native infrastructure transformation.

Challenges	Point	Weight	Score
Do your Kubernetes workloads include critical operations where minimizing downtime and expediting incident resolution are paramount?			
Does your environment encompass over 50 Kubernetes nodes in total across production, development, and testing?			
Are you obligated to uphold secure network isolation and comply with regulatory standards such as PCI DSS, FedRAMP, or Germany's BSI Act?			
Are you intrigued by advanced networking and security features like service mesh and API-aware network monitoring?			
Have you encountered hurdles in scaling conventional networking and security solutions due to cost or rigid configurations tailored for cloud-native environments?			
Are you open to investing in Cilium CE's advanced capabilities and services to fortify the success of your Kubernetes platform, or do you prefer the assurance of commercial support?			
What methodologies do you presently employ for monitoring your Kubernetes applications, and are you content with the depth of insights they provide?			
Have you faced any obstacles in troubleshooting issues within your Kubernetes environment?			
How do you presently oversee and uphold application performance and availability in your Kubernetes environment?			

(*continued*)

Challenges	Point	Weight	Score
How many distinct tools do you currently utilize for monitoring, logging, and tracing within your Kubernetes clusters?			
Are you leveraging a service mesh for network observability? How has the inclusion of sidecars impacted your system's intricacy and resource utilization?			
Can you outline your process for soliciting monitoring data from SRE teams? Is this workflow streamlined and effective?			
Could you guide me through your current infrastructure configuration? How many distinct tools and platforms are under your management?			
Within your multi-cloud or hybrid cloud approach, have you encountered hurdles in maintaining uniformity across diverse environments?			
What portion of your team's time is dedicated to the management and configuration of your assortment of tools and systems?			
How does your team stay abreast of the learning curve associated with each tool employed?			
How assured are you in your current security stance, particularly concerning zero-trust security principles and your capacity to swiftly respond to incidents?			
What's the tally of distinct tools you're currently employing for network control, observability, and security enforcement? What obstacles have you faced in their integration and management?			

(continued)

Challenges	Point	Weight	Score
Could you describe the intricacy of your existing network and security infrastructure within your Kubernetes environment?			
Are you implementing a multi-cloud or hybrid cloud strategy, and if so, how do you handle network policies and security across these diverse environments?			
What are the primary challenges you're grappling with in your current Kubernetes networking and security configuration?			
Do you operate within a multi-cloud or hybrid cloud setting, and if yes, what obstacles do you encounter in maintaining uniform networking and security standards across these platforms?			
Have you encountered any performance bottlenecks or scalability hurdles as your Kubernetes environment has expanded?			
Are you utilizing a service mesh? How do you manage the intricacies it introduces?			
Total Score			

To encapsulate, the business benefits stemming from the adoption of Cilium can be delineated into four key domains: cost reduction, operational efficiency, streamlined complexity, and fortified security protocols. Through proficient utilization, Cilium facilitates automation of up to 90% of Day 2 operational tasks across various cloud platforms. It furnishes a comprehensive security augmentation by enhancing observability and facilitating troubleshooting, thereby fortifying both runtime and network security and fortifying defenses against potential threats while ensuring adherence to regulatory standards. This enhanced security stance not only aids businesses in conforming to industry regulations such as FedRAMP/PCI but also aligns with standards like BSI or advanced controls of ISO 27001, effectively mitigating risks associated with noncompliance.

Cilium EE Licensing Model

It's understandable if you're currently contemplating whether to opt for Cilium Enterprise edition or Community edition. The concise answer? It depends. The comprehensive answer involves conducting assessments, as detailed in first few chapters of this book, focusing on your team, company, and product. Gauge the maturity levels across technical and cultural dimensions, and assess human resource availability, Linux kernel, eBPF and Golang skill sets, and the outsourcing inclinations of your C-level managers. Consider client risk appetites and conduct structured cost-benefit analyses.

By undertaking these evaluations, you'll gain clarity on what suits your needs best at present. Repeat this process during major change management cadences. For instance, if you operate within a well-matured cloud organization and KMM service oriented with extensive experience in outsourcing non-core business functions and manage over 80 nodes across multi-environment Kubernetes clusters spanning hyperscalers and on-premises DataCenters – serving mission-critical CNAs to financial institutes – consider embarking on a Cilium EE Proof of Concept/Value journey. Your DevOps teams, platform teams, SREs, and IT operations will undoubtedly benefit from leveraging the advanced features of Cilium EE.

The first task is to craft a detailed story including personas illustrating your current troubleshooting challenges, instances of team finger-pointing, major outages encountered, and the efficacy and efficiency of your current issue identification and resolution methods. Highlight challenges related to obtaining visibility into CNAs, resolving performance issues, and meeting client security compliance requirements, and the need for comprehensive observability to contextualize network traffic.

Following this, proceed to articulate your conditions of satisfaction, detailing your expectations for an acceptable solution. Outline functional features, nonfunctional features, and MoSCoW initiatives. "MoSCoW" stands for "Must-Have, Should-Have, Could-Have, Won't-Have," representing the four priority levels of requirements or features in descending order of importance. Subsequently, formulate an Acceptance Test Plan delineating the pilot testbed and quantitative metrics essential for measuring success.

Once you've garnered internal approval, engage Cilium EE sales engineers to illuminate cost and best fit licensing models. Isovalent offers Cilium EE on a per-worker nodes CPU core licensing model, devoid of limitations concerning the number of pods or service policies. This approach proves equitable, particularly if a majority of your worker nodes reside within cloud providers' infrastructure. Given Isovalent's team active presence, you can negotiate licensing terms and fees to establish a mutually beneficial arrangement.

The Art of Winning Hearts to Cilium

Suppose you've relished diving into this book, embracing its approach to representing cloud-native observability with Cilium, immersing yourself in the intriguing Cilium Lab scenarios, or honing your skills with Cilium in your sandbox environment, recognizing its potential to significantly enhance your company's or clients' production clusters. Remembering our exploration in first few chapters, discovering the **right** technical solution is just the beginning of the journey. Cultivating the appropriate strategy, plan, and **culture** and assembling the right **team** is equally crucial. But where does one begin? The answer lies in education.

Drawing from insights in cognitive science, particularly the well-known status quo bias and loss aversion bias, education emerges as the transformative catalyst. The status quo bias elucidates the inclination for individuals to cling to the current mode of operation over potential FMO alternatives. Even when presented with objectively superior options, people often resist change due to factors such as familiarity, comfort, newer task, job security, and apprehension about potential negative outcomes. Consequently, they may hesitate to embrace new technologies or ideas unless they can familiarize themselves with them within a safe, blameless environment.

Loss aversion bias underscores individuals' strong preference for avoiding losses rather than acquiring equivalent gains. This innate tendency leads people to prioritize safeguarding what they already possess over pursuing potential gains of equal value. When evaluating new technologies or concepts, individuals tend to focus on potential risks or drawbacks, sometimes overlooking the future advantages and benefits. This phenomenon is particularly noticeable among some of senior engineers and team leads, who may exhibit a greater aversion to change compared to their younger, more enthusiastic counterparts.

Many principal SRE engineers initiate their approach with a 45-minute internal workshop focused on discussing the core values and anticipated outcomes. Subsequently, they recommend delving into relevant literature and exploring Isovalent Labs. Consider scheduling another session dedicated to collectively navigating through intriguing lab setups. It's imperative not to overlook any potential risks or concerns; therefore, addressing them in accordance with established risk management methodologies is essential.

Commence with a small-scale pilot testbed to showcase the practicality and efficacy of eBPF and Cilium. Identifying a cadre of internal enthusiasts who are eager to pioneer new initiatives can be invaluable; collaborating with them initially while concurrently disseminating educational materials and knowledge to others within the organization is advisable.

Encouraging participation in industry events such as KubeCon, CNCF gatherings, or other cloud-native seminars can provide valuable insights into prevailing industrial trends and foster momentum within the team.

Additionally, to garner buy-in from C-level decision-makers, it's prudent to supplement initiatives with a comprehensive Proof of Concept (PoC) report, cost-benefit analysis, and considerations of client and market compliance requirements, among other pertinent factors.

You're likely acquainted with essential tools such as web proxies, Layer 7 load balancers, and SSL VPN gateways. These components are integral for load balancing, routing, and managing HTTP/HTTPS traffic within your network environment. In Kubernetes, this pivotal function is known as "Ingress," initially supported by the Kubernetes Ingress API and more recently enhanced by the Kubernetes Gateway API. Ingress facilitates the exposure of HTTP and HTTPS routes from external sources to services within the cluster, with traffic routing governed by defined rules within the Ingress resource.

The Gateway API represents a notable advancement beyond the path-based routing capability of the Ingress API, offering a broad spectrum of routing functionalities. These include traffic splitting, URL redirection, path rewriting, mirroring, HTTP request/response manipulation, and TLS termination and passthrough, among others, which were previously achievable only through custom annotations with Ingress.

For effective Ingress operation, the cluster must have an Ingress controller running, and here Cilium stands out as the sole Container Network Interface (CNI) that can also function as an Ingress controller.

In the realm of outbound traffic management from Kubernetes clusters, ensuring security and effective traffic governance is paramount. Integrating traditional firewalls from vendors like Palo Alto Networks, Check Point, or Cisco presents challenges due to their limited understanding of Kubernetes objects such as namespaces or labels. When packets exit the cluster, their source IP addresses are typically masqueraded or source NATed to that of the originating node, rendering the true origin of traffic unknown to the firewall. CNI solutions like Cilium offer a remedy with Egress Gateway, serving as Kubernetes-Aware Source NAT to direct traffic from specific namespace pods to exit via a designated interface and be NATed with a predefined IP address. This setup empowers firewalls to enforce rules accurately, albeit introducing a potential single point of failure with the egress node.

Cilium EE addresses this limitation with Egress Gateway High Availability (HA) functionality, supporting multiple egress nodes. These nodes act as gateways, distributing traffic in a round-robin manner and offering fallback options in case of egress node failures.

In monitoring and visualizing network flows within Kubernetes, Hubble emerges as the go-to tool bundled with Cilium, akin to a fusion of NetFlow and Wireshark. Powered by eBPF, Hubble hooks into the network, extracting networking data with its own CLI and UI. While the open source edition of Cilium includes a standard version of Hubble, the enterprise edition of Cilium elevates this with an advanced enterprise edition of Hubble. This version boasts multi-tenant self-service access, historical flow and analytics data, and a built-in network policy editor. Cilium EE offers an advanced enterprise Hubble view, simplifying and expediting network policy generation.

In summary, education serves as the linchpin for overcoming these biases and fostering an environment conducive to innovation and growth. By providing opportunities for learning and experimentation within a safe framework, organizations can empower their teams to embrace change and leverage emerging technologies to drive success.

What to Share in the First Workshop Session?

Starting the workshop with pertinent questions about your current Kubernetes mode of operation issues, particularly focusing on networking, security, and observability, can pave the way for discussions about reported outages, breaches in SLI (service-level indicator), or recent error budget depletions from notable service providers or within your own company. Describe transparently how improved observability and security tools could have mitigated or prevented such incidents.

Cilium emerges as a robust solution, offering multi-tenant connectivity data and metrics. It provides both real-time and historical perspectives without imposing any disruptions on applications, deployments, or clusters. Its user-friendly CLI and UI interfaces ensure accessibility for developers and operators alike. Furthermore, Cilium facilitates seamless structured events and telemetry data exportation to popular visualization tools like Splunk, Grafana, and Prometheus. This integration empowers thorough analysis of Kubernetes environments, aiding in swift issue resolution while maintaining operational continuity.

By leveraging Cilium, enterprises can significantly enhance their incident response capabilities, minimize downtime, and attain deeper insights into application performance. This, in turn, translates to an elevated customer experience, reinforcing the value of investing in robust observability and security solutions.

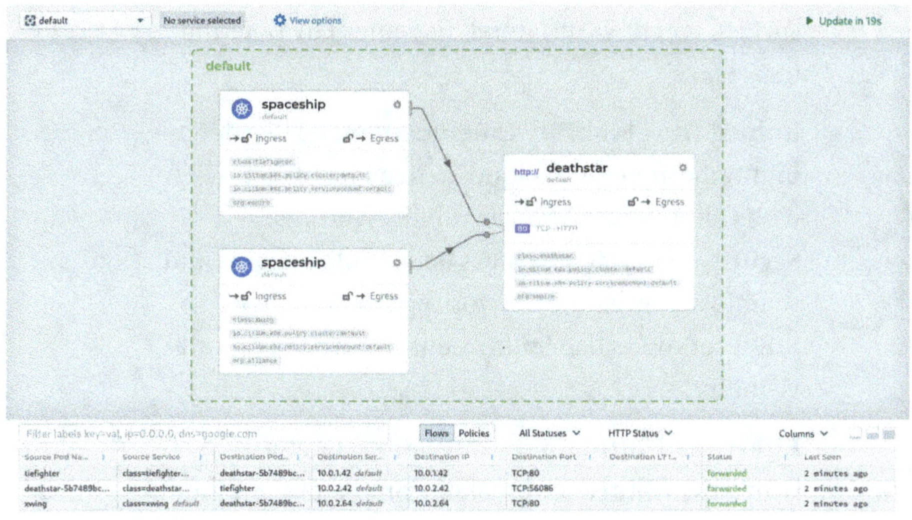

Figure 7-4. *Hubble Dashboard*

Preparing for your workshop with your SRE department or Platform Engineering team, let's delineate the exceptional features of your session:

Cutting-Edge Technological Foundation: Cilium distinguishes itself through its pioneering utilization of eBPF technology, meticulously developed from scratch. This state-of-the-art technology facilitates rapid innovation within the Linux kernel, delivering unmatched speed and adaptability.

Revolutionary Network Security: Cilium reimagines network security by embracing zero-trust segmentation, transcending conventional approaches. Through the establishment of micro-perimeters and adoption of a need-to-know policy model, Cilium dramatically diminishes the attack surface and thwarts lateral movement by potential threats.

Robust Observability Enhancements: Dive deep into Kubernetes and cloud-native infrastructure with Cilium's robust observability features. Security teams can harness actionable insights and seamlessly integrate network activity into leading SIEM solutions like Splunk, enhancing operational visibility.

Effortless Multi-cloud Integration: Engineered with a distributed and scalable architecture, Cilium effortlessly manages policy enforcement across diverse clusters and clouds. This streamlined approach, facilitated by Multi-cluster Networking, simplifies the management of complex environments.

Simplified Service Mesh Deployment: Cilium Enterprise revolutionizes service mesh by eliminating cumbersome sidecars, streamlining deployment, driving cost savings, and enhancing security through the separation of identity from encryption.

Advanced Authentication and Encryption: Cilium Service Mesh distinguishes itself by discarding sidecars, offering a streamlined deployment process. Furthermore, its decoupling of identity from mTLS encryption ensures heightened security and flexibility, bolstering infrastructure resilience.

Fine-Grained Network Policy Controls: Operating at the application layer, Cilium provides fine-grained security policies tailored to each application. This level of control furnishes unparalleled visibility into application-level traffic, crucial for modern microservice environments.

Efficient Load Balancing: Bid farewell to legacy solutions as Cilium redefines load balancing in Kubernetes environments. By replacing outdated netfilter and iptables-based approaches, Cilium ensures efficient and scalable load balancing within clusters.

Comprehensive Threat Detection and Response: Harness Cilium's advanced capabilities for rapid threat identification and response. Seamlessly integrate with any SIEM solution for comprehensive network and runtime visibility, empowering informed decision-making, and threat mitigation.

Tool Consolidation: Cilium offers a holistic approach to combat tool sprawl within Kubernetes ecosystems by integrating networking, security, and observability functionalities into a single platform. Leveraging Cilium's capabilities significantly diminishes reliance on disparate tools, simplifying operations and optimizing efficiency across Kubernetes deployments.

Key benefits of leveraging Cilium include

Unified Telemetry: Centralizing network and security telemetry into a unified dashboard streamlines monitoring and analysis, enhancing visibility and control.

Application-Layer Observability: Cilium empowers users with granular observability and management tools at the application layer, obviating the need for complex service mesh architectures.

Lightweight Load Balancing: Cilium's innovative North/South load balancer supplants bulky routing and firewall appliances, offering a more agile and efficient solution for traffic management within Kubernetes environments.

With these outstanding features, your workshop is positioned to provide invaluable insights and practical strategies for optimizing your team's operations and enhancing security posture.

Cilium Certifications

In the realm of DataCenter refresh initiatives, Cilium serves as a critical enabler for seamless integration between legacy Cisco-based networks and modern Kubernetes environments. Its role is pivotal in ensuring a smooth transition process that upholds operational continuity, bridging the gap between traditional infrastructure and CNA 1.0 platforms.

Cilium's native support for Border Gateway Protocol (BGP) simplifies the connection between traditional networks and Kubernetes environments. This feature facilitates effortless communication between Cisco infrastructure and Kubernetes platforms, streamlining connectivity and bolstering overall performance. Additionally, Cilium seamlessly integrates with Cisco's Application Centric Infrastructure (ACI), further enhancing connectivity and enforcing uniform policy management across all infrastructure components.

With its integration into traditional network security frameworks, Cilium enhances conventional firewall functionalities by enabling egress gateways. This innovative approach allows traditional firewalls to adapt to the context of Kubernetes environments, thereby elevating overall security measures and ensuring robust protection against potential threats.

Cilium empowers platform and application teams by providing increased autonomy and self-service capabilities. Tools like Hubble enable platform teams to efficiently monitor and troubleshoot network traffic within clusters or namespaces, promoting operational independence while alleviating the burden on network teams. Moreover, Cilium facilitates self-managed load balancing, granting Kubernetes teams greater control and flexibility over their networking requirements. Rich observability data provided by Cilium equips application teams with actionable insights for proactive network performance management and optimization, fostering collaboration and efficiency across teams.

In the domain of load-balancing solutions, Cilium offers a cost-effective alternative to traditional hardware-based approaches. By replacing expensive load balancers with its software-driven approach, partners can deliver more competitive pricing without compromising on performance. Cilium's software-based load balancing offers advantages such as enhanced performance, GitOps-driven self-service capabilities, automation for reduced operational burden, and scalability to accommodate evolving business needs.

In the rapidly evolving landscape of technology, it's common for technologists and engineers to seek validation of their expertise through field certifications. Industry giants like Cisco and Microsoft have established robust training paths and certification programs to support professionals at various levels. Now, even hyperscalers are following suit.

One such example is the collaboration between the Linux Foundation Training and the Cloud-Native Computing Foundation (CNCF) to offer an associate-level certification for users of Cilium. The Cilium Certified Associate (CCA) exam serves as a benchmark, confirming foundational knowledge in connecting, securing, and observing Kubernetes clusters using Cilium. Developed by a consortium of subject matter experts (SMEs) from esteemed companies including Isovalent, Cisco, Microsoft, Solo.io, and Datadog, among others, the CCA exam is tailored for individuals seeking to deploy Cilium in their environments.

Targeted at platform or cloud engineers with interests spanning networking, security, and observability, the CCA certification necessitates a comprehensive understanding of key concepts and competencies. To excel in the exam, candidates must grasp vital topics such as the role of eBPF in Cilium, Cilium architecture, network policies, service mesh implementations, and network observability using Hubble.

Preparing for the CCA certification entails familiarizing oneself with the exam scope and domains, delving into materials ranging from official documentation to supplementary resources. This book serves as an asset in your preparation journey, complementing other relevant literature and online sources. Additionally, leverage technical labs available in the Isovalent resource library for hands-on learning experiences.

In essence, the CCA certification not only validates your proficiency in Cilium but also enhances your expertise in navigating modern networking, security, and observability challenges within Kubernetes environments. Embrace the opportunity to elevate your skill set and propel your career forward in the dynamic realm of cloud-native technologies.

Summary

Beyond merely providing a CNI plug-in for Kubernetes or enhancing multi-cloud service mesh capabilities, Cilium sets its sights on a loftier goal: becoming the gravitational center of CNAs. Led by the visionary Thomas Graf and the vibrant Cilium community, our exploration delves into the intricate architecture and components of Cilium, unravelling its symbiotic relationship with the Linux kernel, Kubernetes components, and pod traffic management. We traverse the landscapes of both the Community and Enterprise editions of Cilium, juxtaposing them against competitors within the dynamic cloud-native ecosystem, both present and future. Brace yourself for the unveiling of captivating Cilium use cases in the upcoming chapter.

CHAPTER 8

Portraying Cilium Use Cases

A groundbreaking CNA solution generally need you to redefines your production level networking, observability, and security. Unlike conventional approaches, Cilium offers a unified platform that seamlessly integrates these critical functions, ensuring a holistic and efficient operational experience.

Delve into its myriad functionalities, as we explore nine distinct networking use cases, complemented by three robust security and an intriguing array of four observability use cases. A common observability challenge with sidecars lies in their ephemeral and short lifespan similar to the main container. In this chapter, we introduce scenarios and deployment methods like the innovative sidecarless service mesh architecture, a hallmark feature distinguished by its capacity to eliminate unnecessary complexity and streamline deployment processes. This pioneering approach competes directly with Istio's Ambient Mode, which, despite its advancements, grapples with stability and security concerns.

In this chapter, I'll delve into the practical applications of Cilium within the context of CNA 1.0. We'll explore its diverse utility across three main domains:

- **Networking:** Unveiling how Cilium revolutionizes network management and connectivity within the CNA framework

Dr. M. Ghane, *Observability Engineering with Cilium*,
https://doi.org/10.1007/979-8-8688-1258-3_8

- **Security:** Exposing the robust security features and capabilities Cilium brings to the table, safeguarding runtime, traffics, and data transaction
- **Observability:** Shedding light on how Cilium enhances visibility and insights into container and service-level operations, empowering effective monitoring and troubleshooting

Cilium Networking Use Cases

Given Cilium's origin as a networking tool, it's no wonder that it offers nine compelling use cases in the realm of cloud-native networking:

Service Load Balancing: Cilium's XDP and eBPF-powered load balancing ensures high performance with minimal overhead, offering a cost-effective alternative to traditional hardware solutions.

High-Performance Cloud-Native Networking CNI: Cilium's optimized control and data planes support large-scale cloud environments, delivering efficient load balancing and full IPv6 support.

Multi-cluster Connectivity: Cilium's Cluster Mesh facilitates seamless cross-cluster communication, enhancing reliability and fault tolerance while simplifying service discovery and deployment.

Optimal Bandwidth Management: Cilium's Bandwidth Manager and support for BBR ensure efficient network traffic management and performance optimization, offering significant latency reduction and throughput improvement.

Kube-proxy Replacement: Cilium replaces kube-proxy with a purpose-built solution, leveraging eBPF for efficient load balancing and incremental updates, ensuring compatibility and seamless transition.

BGP Integration: Cilium harnesses BGP for scalable and secure routing solutions, seamlessly integrating into existing network infrastructures for efficient traffic management.

Egress Gateway: Cilium's Egress Gateway enhances network security and traffic control, providing stable connectivity and fine-grained routing control for outbound traffic from Kubernetes environments.

Cilium Service Mesh: By embedding the mesh layer directly into the kernel using eBPF, Cilium eliminates the need for sidecar proxies, ensuring efficient and scalable networking across various protocols.

Gateway API: Cilium's implementation of the Gateway API extends the capabilities of the Kubernetes Ingress API, offering advanced routing functionalities and role-oriented access control for streamlined traffic engineering within Kubernetes environments.

Service Load Balancing

Configuring and managing load balancing within your cluster can prove challenging due to the intricate nature of establishing connectivity and synchronization between clusters and the external environment.

Traditional hardware load balancers often come with exorbitant costs, while software alternatives may fail to meet the performance standards required. Moreover, the implementation of External-to-Pod (North-South) LB typically demands supplementary tooling, further complicating matters and adding to both expenses and operational overhead.

However, the advent of XDP and eBPF-powered scalable load balancing and Ingress, as exemplified by Cilium, offers a transformative solution. Cilium leverages these cutting-edge technologies to allure traffic with BGP and accelerate its flow through the utilization of XDP and eBPF. Together, these advancements culminate in a highly resilient and secure implementation of load balancing. Operating at the kernel layer, Cilium and eBPF enable intelligent decision-making concerning workload connections, whether within the same node or across clusters. Leveraging eBPF and XDP, Cilium facilitates substantial enhancements in both latency and performance. Notably, Cilium's stand-alone load balancer emerges as a pinnacle of efficiency, delivering remarkable throughput gains while minimizing CPU overhead.

The Cilium stand-alone Layer 4 Load Balancer is finely tuned for the scale and dynamism characteristic of cloud-native environments. By adopting Cilium as a replacement for costly legacy hardware, organizations can unleash the full potential of Direct Server Return (DSR) and Maglev for managing north/south traffic within on-premises environments, all without necessitating Kubernetes oversight of network border management.

Cloud-Native Networking CNI

Cilium is tailored for large-scale cloud environments with dynamic workloads, boasting an optimized control plane capable of supporting up to 5K nodes. Its data plane harnesses the power of eBPF for efficient load-balancing and extends full support to IPv6.

While there exists a myriad of CNIs for Kubernetes, their features, scalability, and performance widely differ. Many rely on legacy technologies like iptables, ill-equipped to handle the scale and fluidity of Kubernetes environments, resulting in heightened latency and diminished throughput. Moreover, most CNIs offer limited support, primarily focusing on L3/L4 Kubernetes network policy. The prevalence of custom CNIs from various cloud providers further compounds operational complexities, especially for users navigating multi-cloud environments.

Cilium stands apart with its meticulously crafted control and data planes, purpose-built for the demands of large-scale, dynamic cloud-native environments. Its control plane operates seamlessly within Kubernetes clusters housing thousands of nodes and hundreds of thousands of pods. Leveraging eBPF, Cilium's data plane ensures efficient load balancing and facilitates incremental updates, sidestepping the pitfalls of unwieldy iptables rulesets.

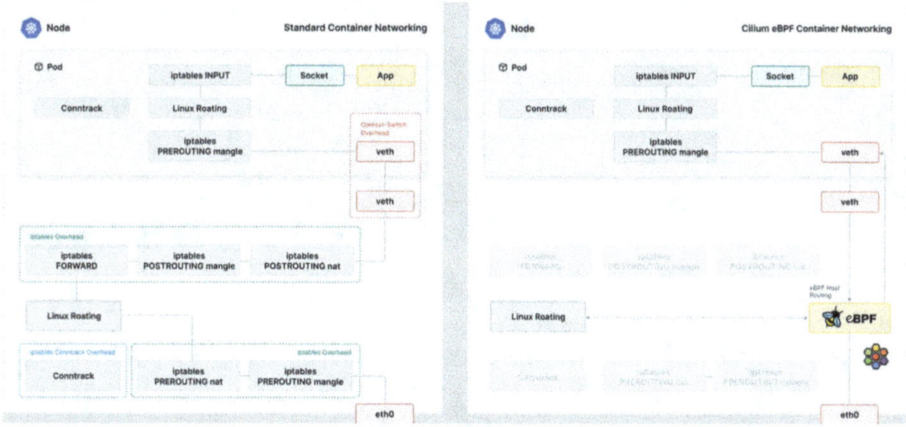

Figure 8-1. Standard Container vs. Cilium-Backed Container Schematic Diagram

Cilium's scalability knows no bounds. Whether managing a handful of nodes or orchestrating a cluster of thousands, Cilium rises to the occasion. Powered by eBPF, its networking infrastructure is finely tuned for large-scale operations, eliminating concerns of network bottlenecks as your operations expand.

Yet Cilium isn't solely focused on performance, it also champions robust security features. Introducing identity-based security, surpassing traditional IP address-based/static port-basedACLs, Cilium empowers fine-grained policy enforcement. This granular control over communication reduces the attack surface, bolstering the security posture of your cloud-native applications.

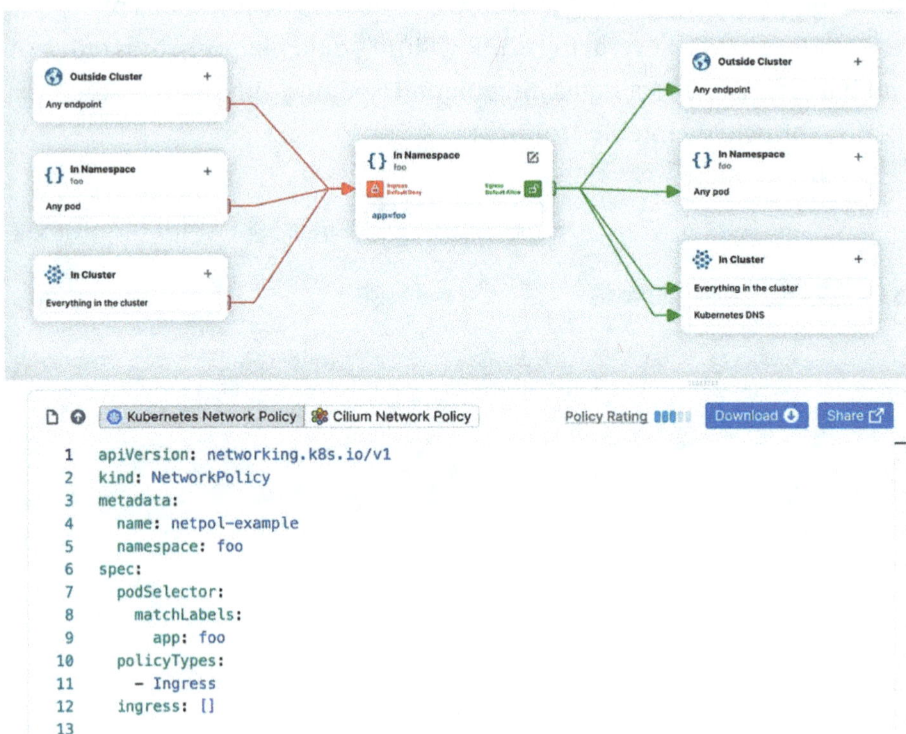

Figure 8-2. *Service Mapping*

Multi-cluster connectivity establishes a unified zone of connectivity across clusters, streamlining load balancing, observability, and security between nodes spanning multiple clusters.

Multi-cluster Kubernetes setups are often embraced for reasons like fault isolation, scalability, and geographical distribution. However, this approach introduces networking complexities. Traditional networking models falter in areas such as service discovery, network segmentation, policy enforcement, and load balancing across clusters. Moreover, managing security protocols and policies across disparate environments poses a daunting challenge due to the distributed nature of services.

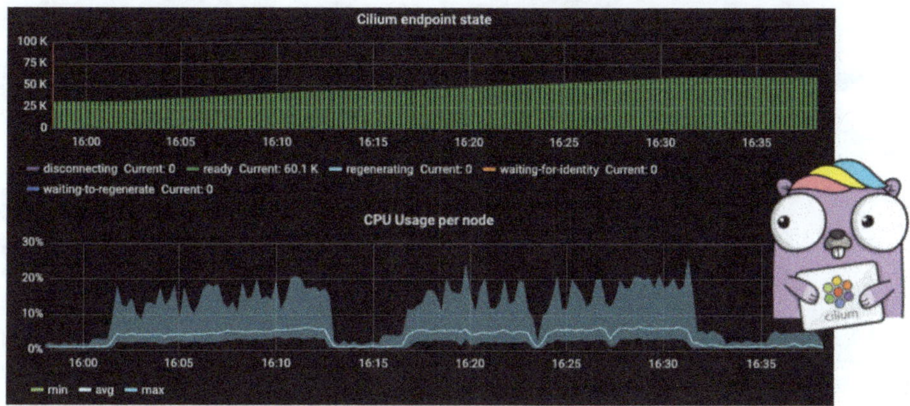

Figure 8-3. *Cilium Signals*

In a world where agility, scalability, and security are paramount, Cilium emerges as the definitive choice for Kubernetes networking. With its unparalleled performance, scalability, and security features, Cilium empowers organizations to harness the full potential of cloud-native computing, paving the way for seamless innovation and growth.

Cluster Mesh

Introducing Cilium Cluster Mesh, a groundbreaking solution empowering seamless network integration across multiple Kubernetes clusters. With Cilium as the common network interface across all clusters, Cluster Mesh fosters an interconnected environment where pods can effortlessly discover and utilize services from any cluster within the mesh. Regardless of the Kubernetes distribution or geographical location, Cluster Mesh unifies disparate clusters into a cohesive network, amplifying your infrastructure's capabilities.

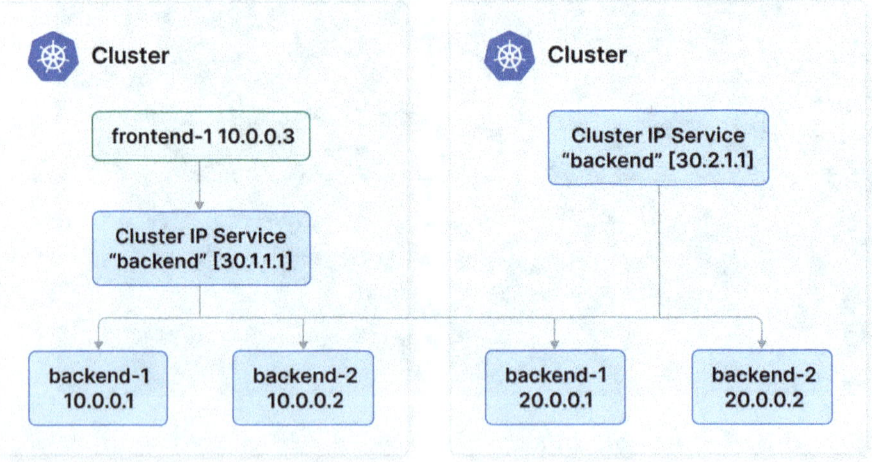

Figure 8-4. *Cluster IP Service Diagram*

Cluster Mesh elevates service reliability and fault tolerance to new heights. It facilitates the operation of Kubernetes clusters across diverse regions or availability zones, enabling seamless failover in the face of resource unavailability, misconfigurations, or scheduled upgrades. Your services remain resilient and accessible, ensuring uninterrupted operations.

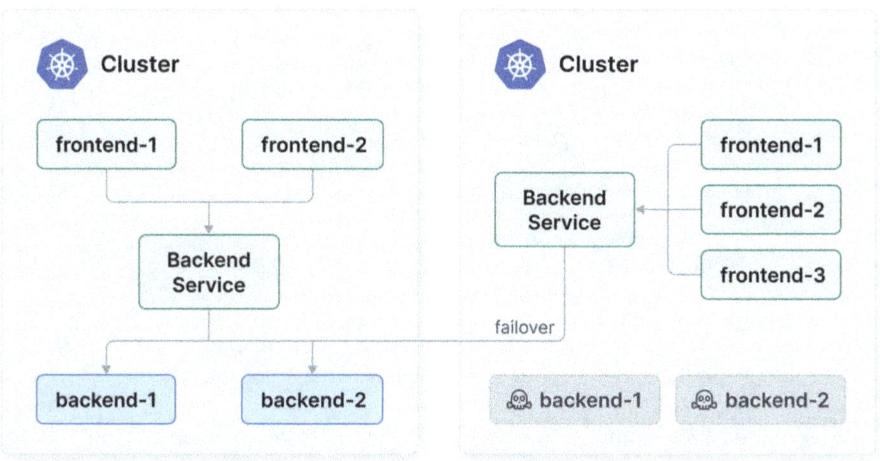

Figure 8-5. *Cluster Failover*

Automating service discovery across Kubernetes clusters, Cluster Mesh streamlines cross-cluster communication. Leveraging standard Kubernetes services, it amalgamates services with identical names and namespaces into a unified global service. This simplifies application deployment and interaction, transcending cluster boundaries effortlessly.

Experience native Pod IP routing performance across multiple Kubernetes clusters with Cluster Mesh. By leveraging tunnelling or direct routing, it eliminates the need for gateways or proxies, fostering seamless inter-cluster communication and optimizing your microservice architecture's efficiency.

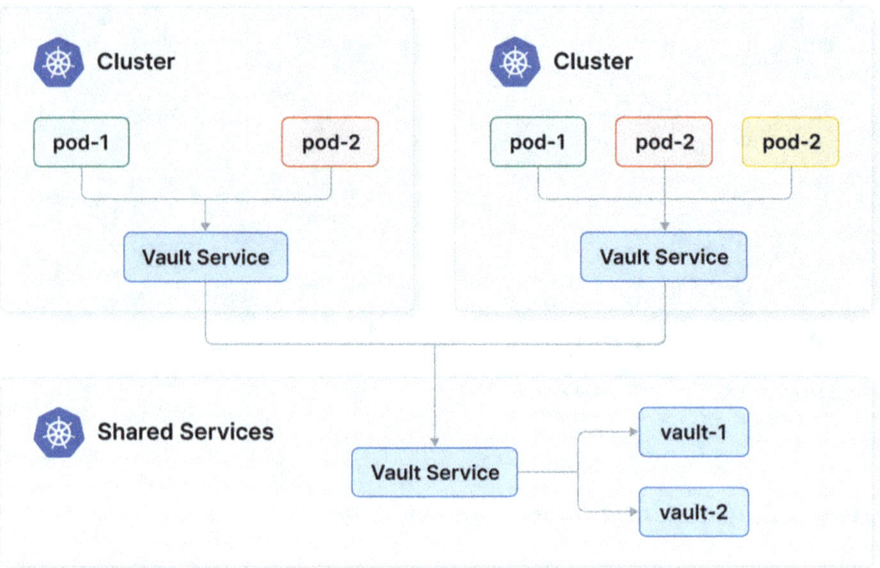

Figure 8-6. *K8s Vault Service*

Cluster Mesh facilitates the sharing of essential services such as secrets management, logging, monitoring, and DNS across all clusters, minimizing operational overhead and ensuring management simplicity while maintaining tenant cluster isolation.

Extending Cilium's Layer 3–7 network policy enforcement to every cluster within the mesh, Cluster Mesh ensures consistent security measures across your entire Kubernetes deployment, regardless of scale.

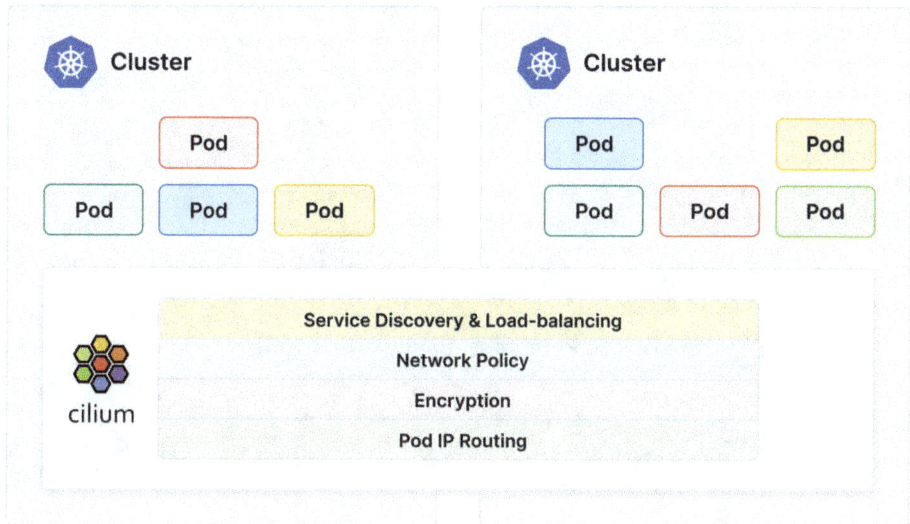

Figure 8-7. *Cilium Cluster*

While Kubernetes lacks native traffic control capabilities, Cluster Mesh addresses this gap by offering essential traffic rate-limiting features. Unlike Kubernetes' experimental Bandwidth Rate-Limiting, Cluster Mesh provides robust traffic management without compromising latency, ensuring optimal resource utilization and user experience even across diverse network environments.

Cilium's Bandwidth Manager

Cilium's Bandwidth Manager simplifies rate-limiting per pod with just a single line of YAML configuration. Compared to other solutions, this innovative feature offers a remarkable 4x reduction in latency, ensuring a seamless network experience without compromising performance. Engineered for multi-queue and multi-core NICs, the Bandwidth Manager is a versatile tool for optimizing network traffic.

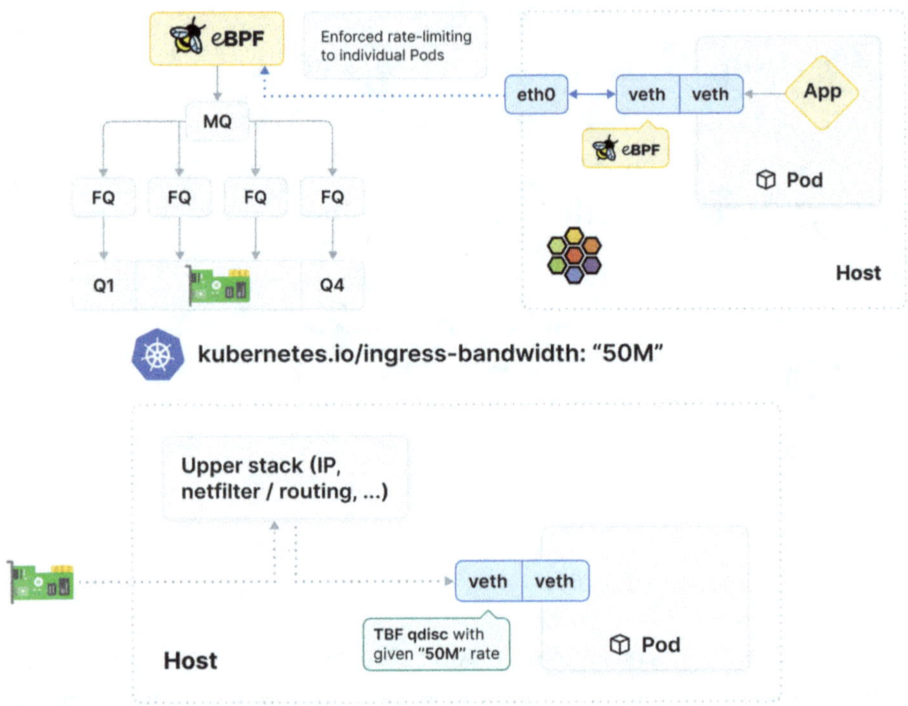

***Figure 8-8.** Layer 2 Frames with and without eBPF*

One standout feature of Cilium is its support for BBR, a congestion control algorithm developed by Google. By integrating BBR, Cilium becomes the pioneer platform to do so, offering users access to unparalleled performance enhancements. Google's testing has demonstrated up to a staggering 2,700x improvement in throughput with BBR, positioning it as an indispensable tool for optimizing network performance. Cilium's implementation of BBR delivers exceptional improvements in both throughput and latency, particularly benefiting external-facing applications, thereby elevating the overall user experience.

BBR

BBR, which stands for Bottleneck Bandwidth and Round-trip propagation time, is a sophisticated congestion control algorithm developed by Google. Unlike traditional TCP congestion control algorithms that primarily focus on packet loss as a signal of congestion, BBR takes a different approach. It aims to optimize network throughput by dynamically adjusting the sending rate of data packets based on two key metrics: bottleneck bandwidth and round-trip propagation time.

Bottleneck bandwidth: This refers to the maximum data rate that can traverse a network path without causing congestion. BBR continuously estimates the available bandwidth by monitoring the rate at which data packets are delivered at the bottleneck link.

Round-trip propagation time (RTT): RTT is the time it takes for a data packet to travel from the sender to the receiver and back. BBR measures the RTT to gauge the network's latency characteristics.

By dynamically adjusting the sending rate based on these metrics, BBR aims to achieve high throughput and low latency, even in challenging network conditions. It does so by effectively utilizing available bandwidth while minimizing queuing delays.

Moreover, Cilium introduces BIG TCP, a groundbreaking feature that pushes the boundaries of packet sizes beyond the traditional 64KB limit. Leveraging IPv6's Hop-by-Hop header, BIG TCP enables the specification of payload lengths of up to 512KB. This capability proves invaluable for organizations building high-speed networks operating at 100Gbps and beyond. Notably, BIG TCP eliminates the need for modifying the MTU on network devices, offering a seamless implementation process compared to alternatives like Jumbo Frames. With BIG TCP, Cilium empowers users to harness maximum network performance potential, enhancing node efficiency and overall network throughput.

Liberating Kubernetes from kube-proxy and iptables

iptables and netfilter stand as the bedrock technologies underpinning kube-proxy, facilitating the implementation of the service abstraction. These technologies boast a rich legacy cultivated over two decades of development, rooted in conventional networking environments that typically exhibit more static characteristics compared to the dynamic nature of contemporary Kubernetes clusters. However, as cloud-native paradigms continue to evolve, their suitability for the task at hand wanes, particularly concerning performance, reliability, scalability, and operational efficiency.

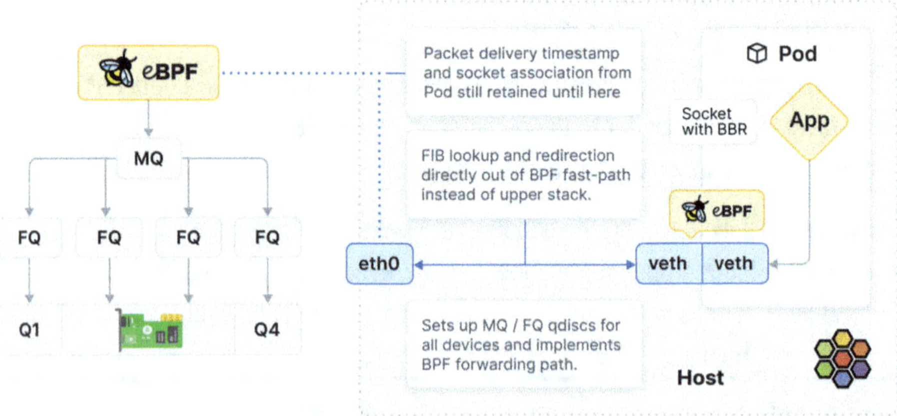

Figure 8-9. *Overlay Network*

In response to the evolving needs of modern cloud-native ecosystems, Cilium emerges as a revolutionary alternative. Its control and data planes are purpose-built to thrive in highly dynamic environments, where hundreds or even thousands of containers can be spawned and decommissioned within seconds. Cilium's control plane is finely tuned, capable of orchestrating Kubernetes clusters comprising up to 5,000 nodes and 100,000 pods with unparalleled efficiency. Leveraging eBPF, Cilium's data plane ensures efficient load balancing and incremental updates, sidestepping the complexities associated with unwieldy iptables rulesets.

Transitioning from kube-proxy to Cilium presents itself as a seamless endeavor, particularly for those already utilizing kube-proxy as a DaemonSet. Cilium seamlessly integrates into the Kubernetes ecosystem, offering a Kubernetes-native implementation fully compatible with the Kubernetes API. Existing applications and configurations can seamlessly transition to Cilium without any disruptions.

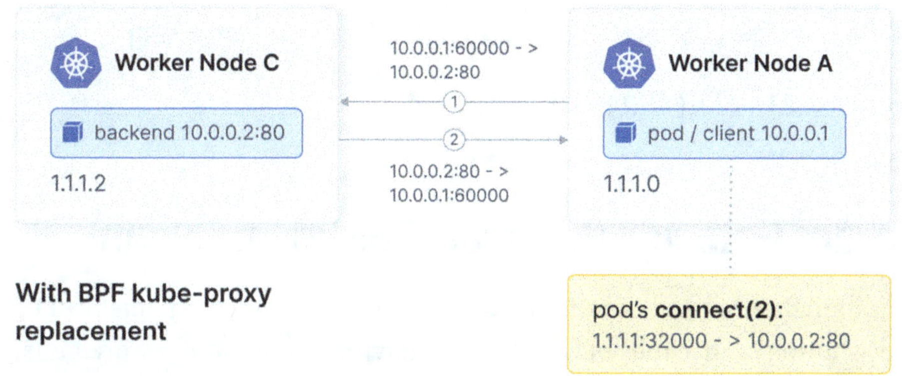

Figure 8-10. *Pod Networking*

Moreover, Cilium's kube-proxy replacement boasts advanced configuration options tailored to suit diverse requirements. Features such as client source IP preservation guarantee the integrity of service connections, while Maglev Consistent Hashing elevates load balancing and resilience to new heights. With support for Direct Server Return (DSR) and Hybrid DSR/SNAT modes, traffic routing can be optimized to enhance overall performance significantly.

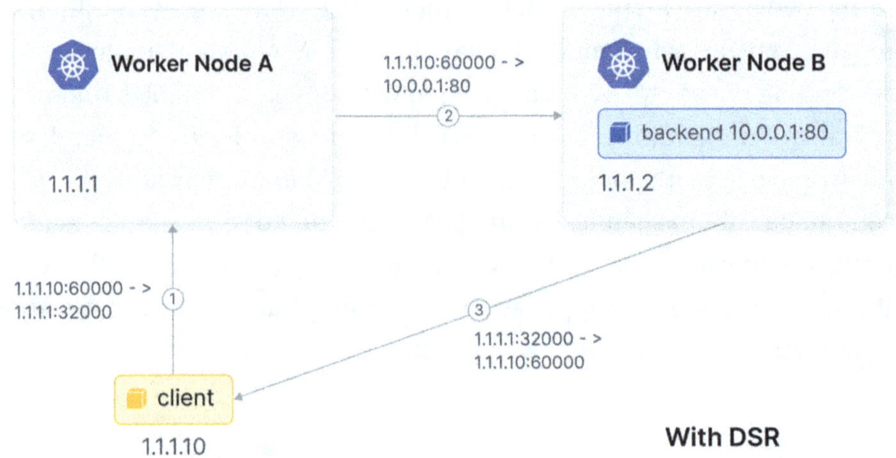

Figure 8-11. *DSR Diagram*

Border Gateway Protocol (BGP) with Cilium

Traditional IP routing can often feel rigid and unyielding, especially in the ever-shifting landscapes of cloud-native environments where workloads are in a constant state of flux. In contrast, BGP boasts an innate capacity to navigate intricate network topologies and routing intricacies, rendering it exceptionally well-suited for the dynamic and decentralized essence of contemporary cloud-native setups.

By harnessing the formidable prowess of BGP – the very backbone of the Internet – Cilium magnifies its potential to furnish your cloud environments with routing solutions that are not just swift and scalable but also fortified with robust security measures. Seamlessly meshing with your pre-existing infrastructure, Cilium's BGP implementation serves as an ideal companion for a spectrum of deployments, ranging from hybrid to multi-cloud to edge scenarios. Equipped with advanced traffic engineering capabilities, it furnishes you with meticulous control over your network flows, thereby fine-tuning both the performance and security of your network ecosystem.

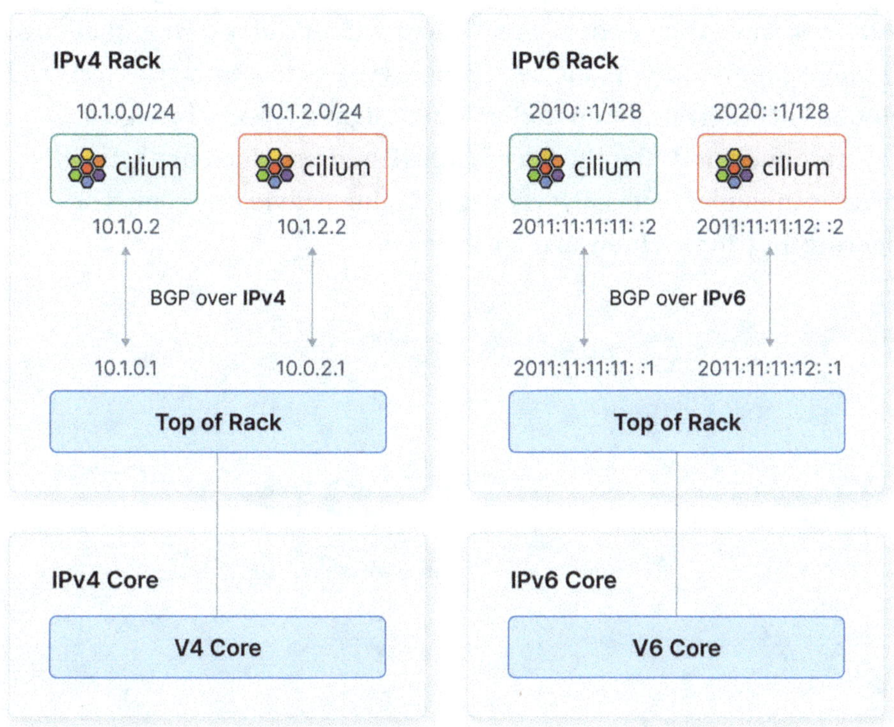

Figure 8-12. *BGP over IPv4 and IPv6*

Cilium's BGP integration is meticulously crafted to be effortlessly assimilated into your current networking framework, ensuring that regardless of where your applications are hosted, Cilium stands ready to orchestrate efficient BGP routing for all your workloads. Given that BGP is already a cornerstone in many network infrastructures, Cilium seamlessly integrates into the existing fabric, allowing Kubernetes pods to seamlessly commune with other facets of your network architecture.

Egress Gateway

In Kubernetes environments, pods typically boast ever-changing IP addresses, while even node IPs undergo frequent shifts, posing challenges for stable connectivity. To tackle this, egress gateways emerge as a crucial solution, steering outbound traffic from designated pods through a predetermined node flaunting a reliable IP address. Such predictability proves invaluable, especially when interfacing with legacy setups or adhering to stringent firewall regulations.

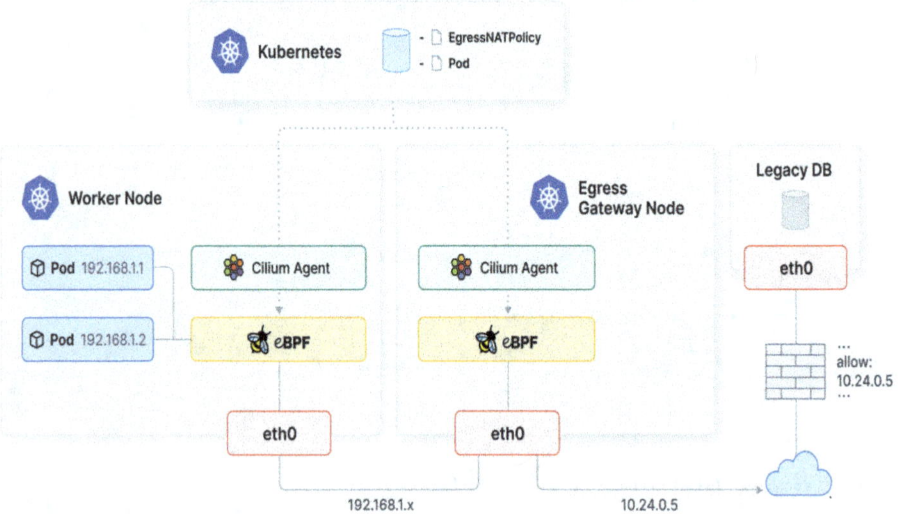

Figure 8-13. *Egress Gateway*

Enter the Egress Gateway with Cilium, a transformative force in Kubernetes networking. It deftly navigates dynamic IP hurdles, seamlessly integrates with legacy infrastructures, and fortifies network security. By affording meticulous traffic routing control, it empowers administrators to channel pod traffic via steadfast, predictable IPs. This capability fosters nuanced traffic management, robust monitoring, and filtering, all the while streamlining interoperability with systems mandating identifiable source IPs.

With the egress gateway, administrators wield fine-grained authority over which pods' traffic traverses the gateway node. Achieved through the application of egress gateway policies leveraging label selectors, this selective routing proves pivotal in enforcing security protocols, orchestrating network segmentation, and optimizing network expenditures.

In the realm of multi-tenant Kubernetes clusters, diverse workloads necessitate interactions with varied external systems, each with its unique network prerequisites. Herein lies the prowess of egress gateways, facilitating the tailoring of routing rules specific to workloads, thereby accommodating diverse network demands.

Cilium Service Mesh

Traditional service meshes pose significant challenges, including complexity in managing IP and port-based network policies, performance overhead from proxy-based architectures, limited visibility into service-to-service communication, interoperability issues with existing infrastructure, scalability challenges with increasing service and traffic volumes, and operational resource overhead.

Cilium Service Mesh revolutionizes conventional service mesh frameworks by embedding the mesh layer directly into the kernel using eBPF, eliminating the need for sidecar proxies. It efficiently manages connectivity at both networking and application protocol layers, seamlessly handling various protocols like IP, TCP, UDP, HTTP, Kafka, gRPC, and DNS.

At its core, Cilium leverages eBPF, an innovative technology integrated into the Linux kernel. By harnessing the power of eBPF, Cilium ensures lightning-fast, efficient, and scalable networking, bypassing the performance limitations of traditional proxies and facilitating direct, streamlined communication between services.

Cilium Service Mesh empowers users with a spectrum of control plane options, enabling them to strike the perfect balance between complexity and functionality. From simpler alternatives like Ingress and Gateway API to more feature-rich options like Istio, and even leveraging the full capabilities of Envoy through the Envoy CRD, users can tailor their control plane to suit their specific needs.

With Cilium Service Mesh, users gain unprecedented flexibility, allowing them to choose between running a service mesh with or without sidecars, depending on their unique requirements and constraints. This adaptability significantly reduces the complexity and overhead associated with sidecars, offering users a seamless and efficient service mesh solution.

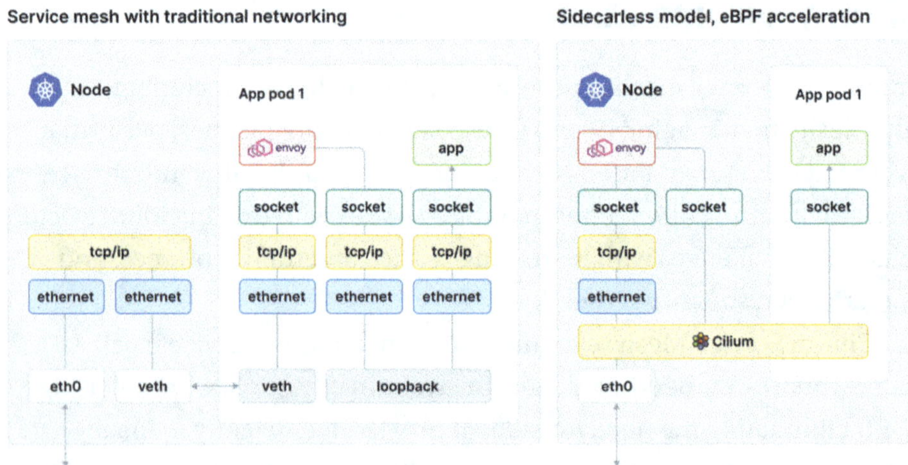

Figure 8-14. *Cilium Mesh*

Gateway API

The Gateway API addresses the limitations inherent in the Kubernetes Ingress API, a traditional tool used for routing traffic into Kubernetes clusters. While the Ingress API offers basic routing capabilities based on path and host rules, it falls short in supporting advanced routing features, restricts traffic to HTTP and HTTPS protocols, lacks clear separation of user/operator concerns, and can introduce inconsistencies through vendor-specific annotations. Gateway API effectively overcomes these challenges, offering a more robust, extensible, and role-oriented approach to traffic engineering within Kubernetes environments.

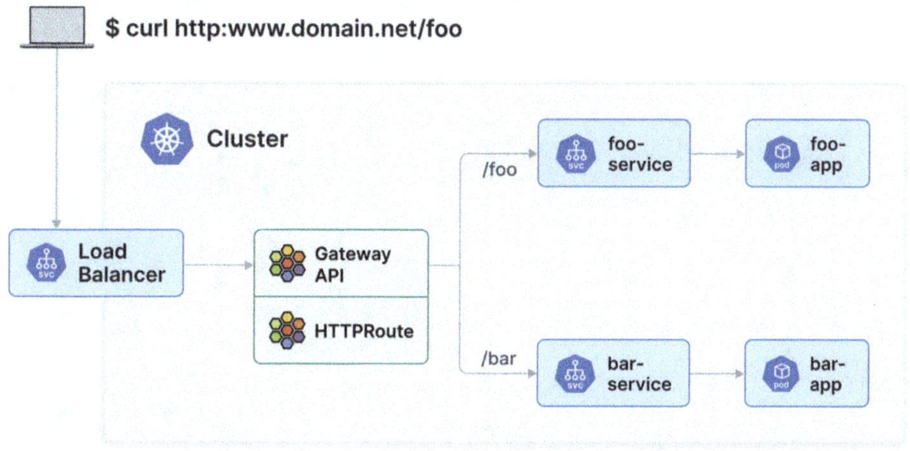

Figure 8-15. *Cilium Loadbalancer*

Cilium's implementation of the Gateway API not only conforms fully to the Kubernetes Ingress standard but also extends its capabilities beyond the constraints of the Ingress API. It empowers users with advanced routing functionalities including traffic splitting, header modification, and URL rewriting. Moreover, it broadens protocol support beyond HTTP and HTTPS to encompass TCP, UDP, and gRPC, enabling more flexible and sophisticated routing strategies.

Tailored to the needs of different operational roles such as infrastructure providers, cluster operators, and application developers, Cilium's Gateway API implementation divides the Ingress API into distinct Gateway API objects. This modular approach allows for precise assignment of access and privileges based on individual responsibilities.

For instance, while application developers may create Route objects within designated namespaces, they are restricted from modifying Gateway configurations or editing Route objects in other namespaces.

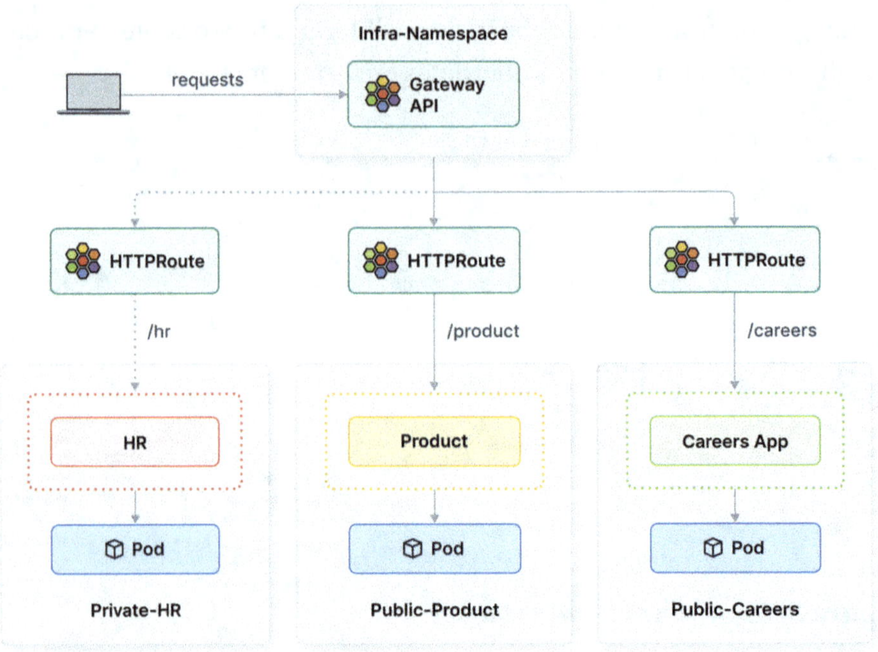

Figure 8-16. *Cilium API Gateway*

Cilium's overarching goal is to streamline operations by consolidating various cloud-native networking, observability, and security tools. In addition to native support for the Gateway API, Cilium offers features such as a sidecarless service mesh, transparent encryption, network policies, and integrated observability through Hubble. This unified approach simplifies the tasks of cluster operators, who can manage and upgrade their Kubernetes networking infrastructure with a single tool, addressing a multitude of networking needs efficiently.

Cilium Security Use Cases

Transparent Encryption: Cilium offers transparent encryption features designed to safeguard data during transmission by leveraging efficient IPsec functionalities integrated into the Linux kernel. With just a single configuration adjustment, it ensures encrypted communication among all workloads within or across Kubernetes clusters, without necessitating any alterations to applications or the need for proxying.

Security Forensics: Cilium's Hubble facilitates comprehensive security forensics in Kubernetes by furnishing identity-aware network flow logs alongside process context, facilitating thorough long-term auditing.

Advanced Network Policy: Cilium provides a range of sophisticated network policy options for Kubernetes, including basic, DNS-aware, and application-aware policies, in addition to cluster-wide network policy enforcement and host-layer firewalling.

Transparent Encryption

Numerous compliance frameworks mandate encryption, a feature not inherently present in Kubernetes for pod-to-pod communication. Addressing this gap typically involves either integrating encryption directly into applications or adopting a service mesh solution. However, both approaches present challenges: application integration demands intricate knowledge of both application and security domains, while service mesh implementations often entail considerable complexity in management and operation.

Cilium offers a streamlined remedy by facilitating encryption for all node-to-node traffic with a single toggle, eliminating the need for application modifications or additional proxies. It boasts features such as automatic key rotation with overlapping keys, efficient data path encryption via in-kernel IPsec or WireGuard, and the ability to encrypt all types of traffic, including nonstandard protocols like UDP. By configuring all nodes across clusters with a shared key, communication between nodes is automatically encrypted.

Identity-Based Policies at Scale

Kubernetes network policies offer a focused approach to establishing security protocols at the L3/L4 level with a focus on applications. One of the primary hurdles lies in effectively enforcing these policies in scenarios where traditional IP regulations are insufficient. With the dynamic allocation of IPs in modern systems, reliance solely on TCP/UDP ports and IP addresses for scaling security measures becomes challenging.

Cilium addresses this challenge by implementing Kubernetes network policies at the L3/L4 level while also extending functionality to include L7 policies. These L7 policies enable granular API-level security for commonly used protocols such as HTTP, Kafka, and gRPC. Cilium decouples security from network addressing using workload identity derived from labels and metadata, allowing for more flexible and efficient scaling without constant security rule updates.

Cilium offers a user-friendly network policy editor interface designed to simplify the process of crafting network policies, reducing the mental strain associated with YAML syntax and formatting. Implementing network policies often presents challenges, as nuances in the policy specification - such as default allow/deny behaviors, namespacing, wildcarding, and rule combinations - can lead to misconfigurations.

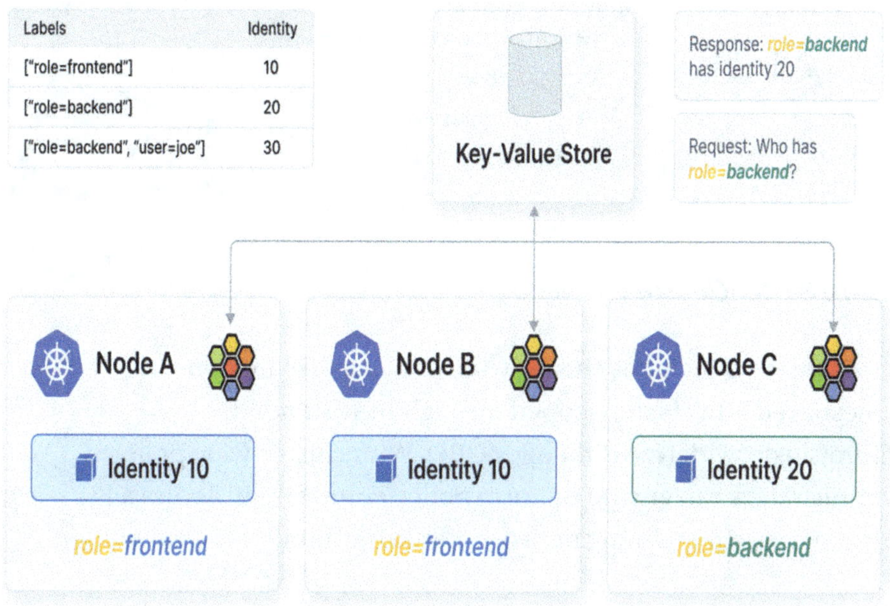

Figure 8-17. *Cluster Namespacing*

With Cluster Mesh, Cilium extends its capabilities to enforce network policies across multiple clusters. This multi-cluster implementation ensures that the familiar policy enforcement mechanisms remain consistent, seamlessly scaling to cover the complexities of inter-cluster communication.

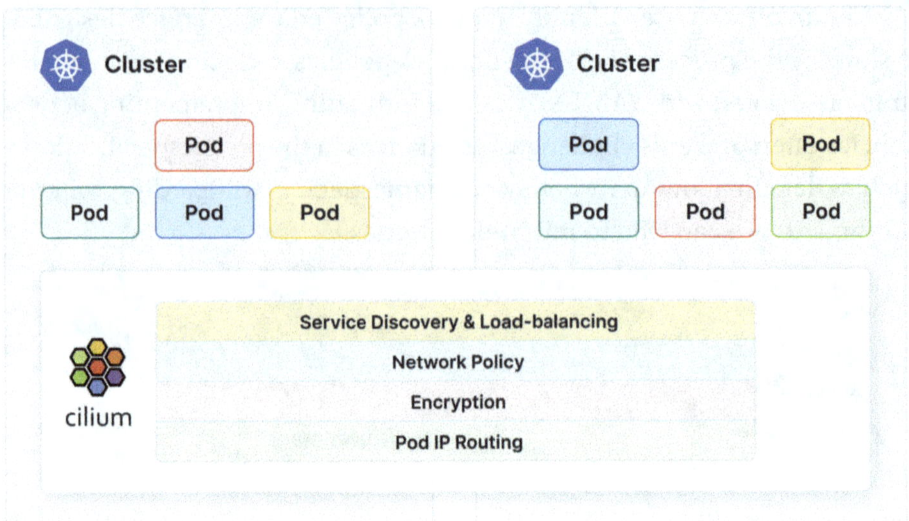

Figure 8-18. *Cilium Cluster*

Cilium also includes cluster-wide policies that are non-namespaced and cluster-scoped through the extended CiliumClusterwideNetworkPolicy CRD. With cluster-wide policies, administrators can ensure uniform policy enforcement across all namespaces, streamlining network administration.

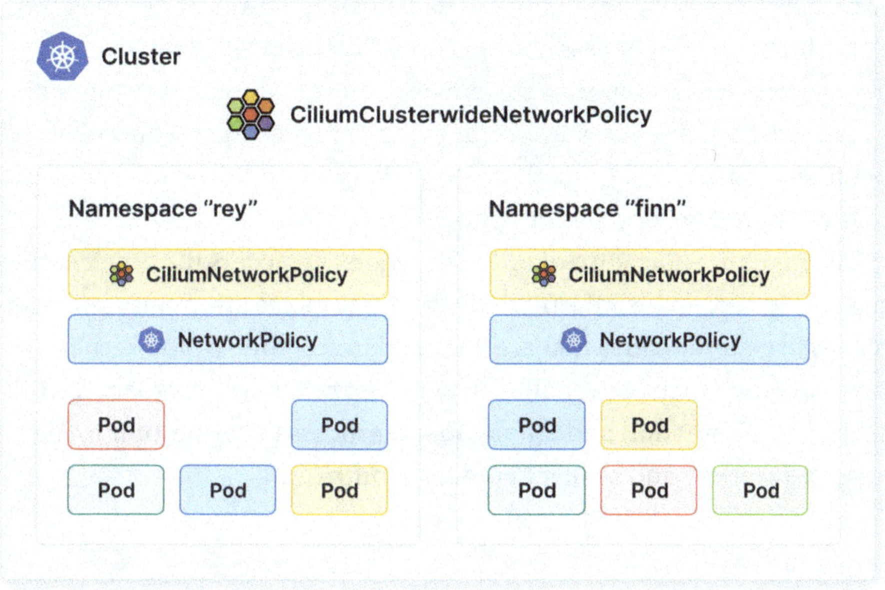

Figure 8-19. *Cilium Network Policy*

Runtime Enforcement

Cloud-native environments are often characterized by their dynamic and distributed nature, necessitating a robust security strategy that covers both detection and prevention. Traditional methods of observing and filtering events in user space can be resource intensive and may result in blind spots in security monitoring, leaving systems vulnerable to potential attacks.

Tetragon addresses these challenges by offering transparent security observability and real-time runtime enforcement utilizing eBPF-based technology. This innovative approach ensures deep visibility into system activity without necessitating alterations to the application itself. By leveraging in-kernel filtering and aggregation logic embedded within the eBPF-based kernel-level collector, Tetragon operates with minimal overhead.

One of Tetragon's key features is its embedded runtime enforcement layer, which provides access control capabilities across various enforcement levels, including system call control. Moreover, Tetragon is designed to be Kubernetes-aware, allowing it to recognize Kubernetes identities such as namespaces and pods. This capability enables tailored security event detection for individual workloads.

Through the utilization of eBPF, Tetragon can access the Linux kernel state and integrate this information with Kubernetes awareness and user policies to generate rules that are enforced in real time by the kernel. This enables a range of capabilities including process namespace and capabilities annotation and enforcement, process file descriptor to file name association, and socket to process control.

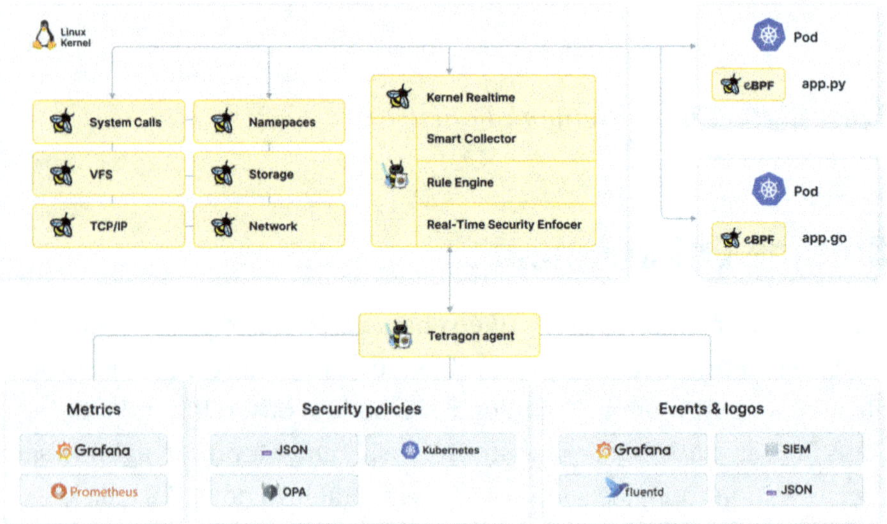

Figure 8-20. *Tetragon Agent Diagram*

Cilium Observability Use Cases

Identity-Aware Visibility: Cilium utilizes eBPF technology to offer comprehensive observability within Kubernetes environments. Through its Hubble framework, Cilium delivers an array of tools including APIs, CLI, and a user-friendly graphical interface, enabling seamless troubleshooting of application and connectivity issues. This solution possesses inherent knowledge of Kubernetes labels and DNS identities, ensuring precise identification and resolution of issues.

Advanced Self-Service Observability: Leveraging eBPF, Cilium empowers efficient visibility into Layer 7 proxies such as Envoy, as well as various applications and protocols including HTTP, gRPC, and Kafka. By capturing process context at the kernel layer, Cilium's approach ensures a deeper understanding of system dynamics. This wealth of data is accessible through Cilium's Hubble framework, which additionally offers TLS-interception capabilities for HTTPS traffic analysis.

Network Metrics and Policy Troubleshooting: Cilium delivers Prometheus-compatible network flow metrics at both Layer 3/4 and Layer 7, enriched with contextual identity information. This enables teams to swiftly detect and investigate network and application behaviors and anomalies. Furthermore, the flow and metric data provided by Cilium include insights into traffic permitted or denied by network policies, streamlining the troubleshooting process for policy-related issues.

Service Map

When troubleshooting cloud-native environments, challenges may arise across various layers such as the network, environment setup, or dependencies. It can be tough to ascertain if DNS is functioning correctly or if an application failure stems from policy-related issues. Detecting recent policy-related changes or pinpointing potential blockages in essential traffic flow between service components can be particularly daunting. Additionally, sifting through logs for insights can prove to be both cumbersome and time-consuming.

Hubble presents a suite of monitoring solutions encompassing service dependencies and communication mapping, network surveillance, application oversight, and security monitoring. Leveraging eBPF technology, Hubble enables programmable visibility, facilitating a dynamic approach that minimizes resource overhead while delivering comprehensive insights.

A mere glance at kubectl get pods does not provide insights into inter-service dependencies or connections with external APIs or databases. Hubble streamlines the process by automatically discovering service dependencies within Kubernetes Clusters at L3/L4 and L7 levels. This enables intuitive visualization and filtering of data flows through a service map, simplifying the management of service dependencies.

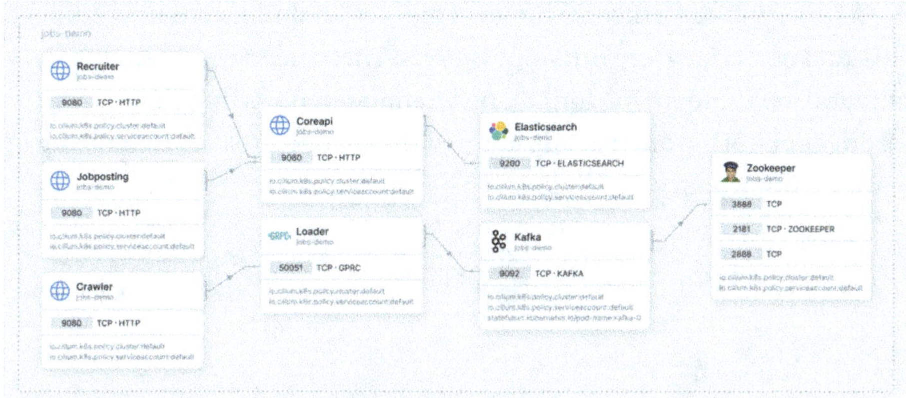

Figure 8-21. *Cilium Service Map*

Metrics and Tracing Export

Metrics alone may lack context for effective issue diagnosis. Configuring metrics exporters and integrating them with monitoring systems can be error-prone and manual. Inadequate, inconsistent, or incorrect metrics can be misleading, resulting in incorrect conclusions about the application state. Troubleshooting often requires correlating metrics with traces for a comprehensive system understanding.

Cilium offers a Metrics and Tracing export feature designed to seamlessly integrate into your monitoring strategy, empowering users to monitor, analyze, and optimize their Kubernetes environments effortlessly. By harnessing Prometheus metrics and combining them with Hubble's network behavior insights, Cilium provides users with deep visibility into their applications and network while streamlining setup and configuration. Additionally, Cilium seamlessly integrates with leading tracing systems such as Jaeger, Zipkin, and OpenTelemetry, ensuring distributed tracing capabilities are readily available. Engineered to manage high data volumes efficiently, Cilium prioritizes performance without compromise.

Cilium captures a diverse range of metrics, including latency, request rates, and error rates for your applications. These metrics adhere to a standardized Prometheus format, facilitating seamless integration with existing monitoring and visualization tools, enabling real-time tracking of network performance.

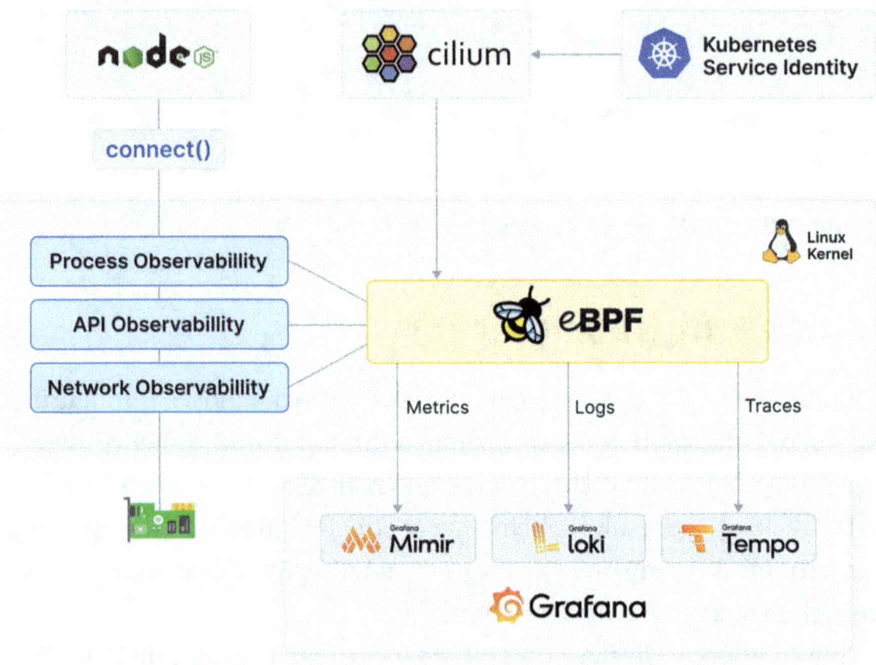

Figure 8-22. *eBPF Orchestration*

Identity-Aware L3/L4/DNS Network Flow Logs

Traditional network flow logs often lack the requisite level of detail and contextual information crucial for effectively monitoring and resolving network challenges within intricate environments, thereby complicating the task of tracing traffic to specific workloads. This not only prolongs debugging efforts but also hampers the identification of the origin and extent of security breaches.

By furnishing real-time visibility into network flows, augmented with enriched metadata, including identity-based insights pertaining to Kubernetes workloads, Cilium streamlines the process of monitoring and troubleshooting network traffic within Kubernetes clusters. This facilitates the seamless tracing of traffic to individual workloads, thereby simplifying the monitoring, troubleshooting, and resolution of network issues. Additionally, it empowers operators to swiftly detect and respond to security incidents.

Cilium enriches network flow logs by incorporating additional details regarding the identity of Kubernetes workloads generating or receiving the traffic. This identity data is derived from Kubernetes labels, annotations associated with the workloads, and any other pertinent metadata accessible through the Kubernetes API server.

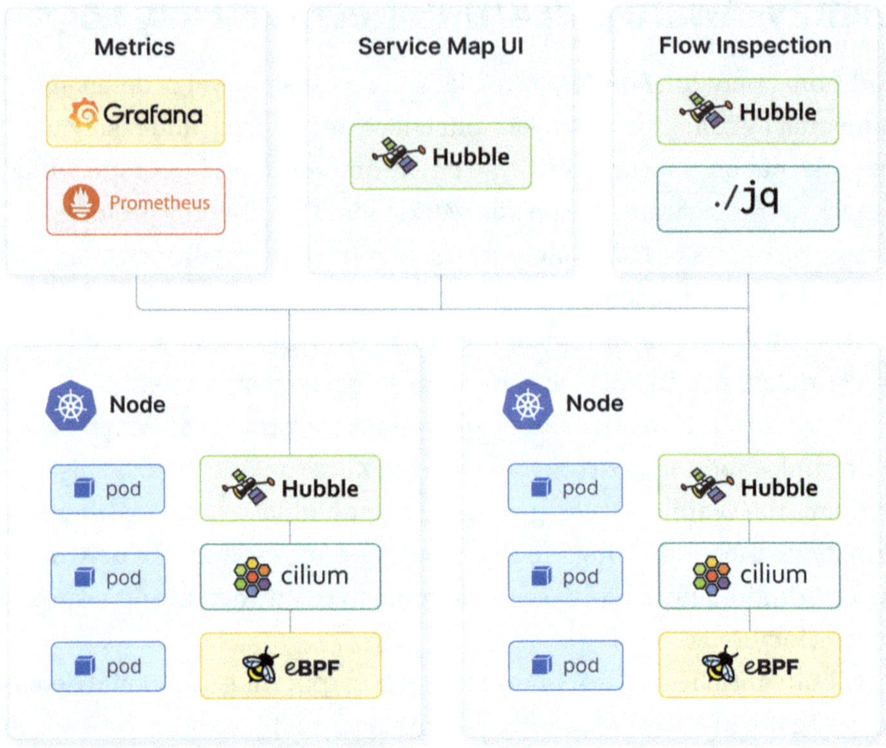

Figure 8-23. *Cilium Observability*

Network Protocol Visibility

Traditional network observability tools typically offer visibility at the packet level, which may not suffice in environments characterized by intricate communication patterns and diverse application protocols, such as cloud-native setups. Troubleshooting network issues in such contexts can pose challenges, underscoring the importance of gaining protocol-level visibility to ensure effective observability and security.

Cilium stands out with its protocol-aware visibility, providing application owners with profound insights into their workload's communications at the protocol level. This entails Cilium's native comprehension of various application protocols - including TLS, gRPC, Kafka, DNS, HTTP, and others like SCTP - enabling meticulous observability of API-specific endpoints and DNS identities for external endpoints.

Hubble emerges as an eBPF-based observability platform tailored for Kubernetes environments. It harnesses the capabilities of the Cilium CNI and eBPF technology to furnish granular visibility into network traffic and application behavior, all without necessitating alterations to applications themselves. Through Hubble, administrators can adeptly troubleshoot complex network issues interactively and devise custom metrics to leverage eBPF's capabilities, all without delving into kernel code intricacies.

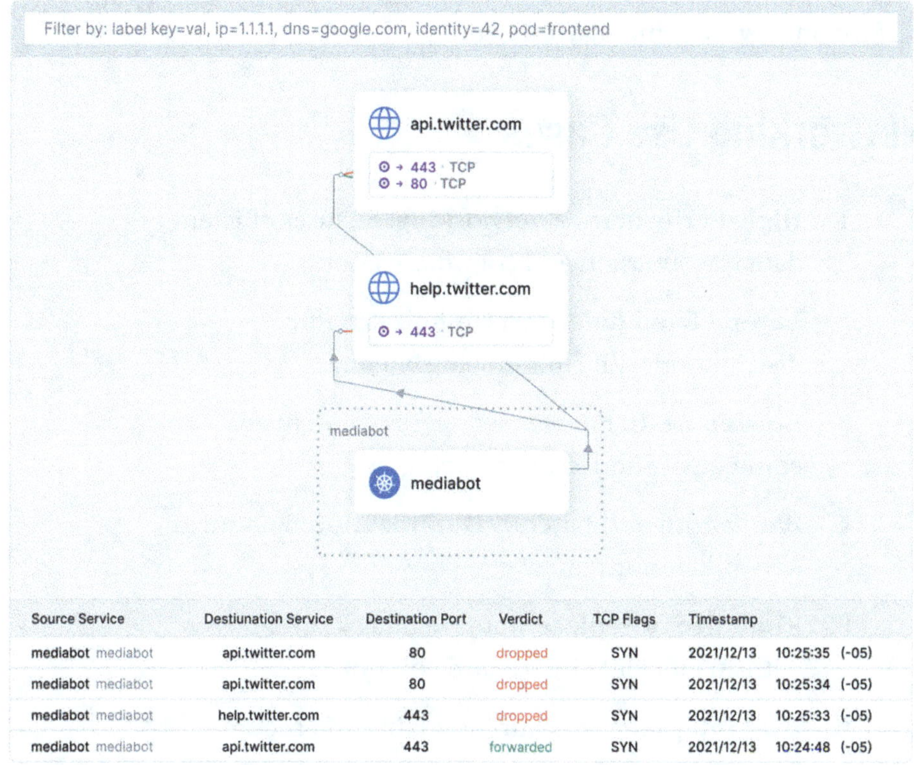

Figure 8-24. *Hubble Service Map*

Summary

With its unparalleled support for multi-/hybrid cloud environments, Cilium transcends traditional boundaries, enabling organizations to navigate diverse infrastructures effortlessly. Cilium proves to be a multifaceted instrument, offering a spectrum of applications for ensuring network security and seamless connectivity within 12-factor containers and cloud-native environments even beyond of Kubernetes. This chapter delves deep into the multifaceted capabilities of Cilium networking, security posture enhancing, and observability within Kubernetes environments use cases. It begins by addressing the challenges of traditional load-balancing solutions, emphasizing the transformative power of Cilium's XDP and eBPF-driven approach in delivering high performance with minimal overhead.

Networking Use Cases

1. **High-Performance Networking:** Ensures efficient data transmission and communication
2. **Layer 4 Load Balancer:** Optimizes traffic distribution while minimizing latency
3. **Cluster Mesh:** Enables seamless cross-cluster connectivity and load balancing
4. **Bandwidth and Latency Optimization:** Enhances network performance
5. **Kube-proxy Replacement:** Replaces kube-proxy with an efficient eBPF-based solution
6. **BGP Integration:** Ensures scalable and secure routing across clusters

7. **Egress Gateway:** Provides stable outbound traffic routing and enhances security
8. **Service Mesh:** Simplifies service-to-service communication without sidecar proxies
9. **Gateway API:** Offers advanced routing functionalities and role-based access control

Security Use Cases

1. **Transparent Encryption:** Safeguards data transmission through transparent encryption
2. **Security Forensics:** Enables comprehensive security auditing and runtime-level forensics
3. **Advanced Network Policy:** Provides robust network policy enforcement

Observability Use Cases

1. **Identity-aware Visibility:** Facilitates seamless troubleshooting and precise issue identification
2. **Advanced Self-Service Observability:** Offers efficient visibility into various protocols and system dynamics
3. **Network Metrics and Policy Troubleshooting:** Enables swift detection and investigation of network and application behaviors

This narrative underscores Cilium's commitment to simplifying Kubernetes networking while simultaneously enhancing performance, observability, scalability, and security, making it an indispensable tool for modern CNA deployments.

CHAPTER 9

Observing the Unseen with Cilium and Grafana

The analogy likening data to oil has become a familiar trope. Yet, if data truly resembles the coveted resource, how do we extract its value and refine it into something precious? Much akin to raw ore containing sought-after elements like gold amid impurities, raw data necessitates purification. How then do we distill the vast volume of data we accumulate?

When operating applications within a platform such as Kubernetes, paramount importance lies in achieving robust observability and gaining deep, meaningful insights from M3PLT telemetry data types. Nevertheless, for numerous organizations, updating existing applications to furnish the requisite observability remains a formidable challenge.

We explore how Cilium Tetragon and Hubble facilitate direct network observability right from the kernel of your platform. Through practical examples encompassing bandwidth, latency, and DNS monitoring, we traverse from host and pod perspectives to the binaries within containers.

Within this chapter, you'll gain insights into how Cilium can furnish golden metrics for an existing application, both with and without tracing functionality. Additionally, we'll elucidate how Grafana dashboards provided by Cilium can empower you to discern the behavior of your application.

Dr. M. Ghane, *Observability Engineering with Cilium*,
https://doi.org/10.1007/979-8-8688-1258-3_9

Key themes addressed in this chapter include

- The pivotal roles of Cilium in observability engineering scenarios
- Functionalities of Cilium Hubble and Tetragon

Cilium Observability Ensemble: Hubble and Tetragon

Hubble, the observability component integrated with Cilium, is designed to expose underlying network flows between workloads and other identities. It caters not only to SRE teams but also to application teams, offering easily digestible insights into networking aspects. Yet some platform owners require greater granularity, especially for specialized use cases like multicast, SR-IOV, or Segment Routing IPv6.

Tetragon provides host-based visibility via eBPF, featuring intelligent in-kernel filtering and aggregation logic for minimal overhead. Tetragon achieves profound visibility without necessitating additional hardware, applications, or platform modifications. It was initially developed as part of Cilium EE and evolved into a stand-alone subproject within the Cilium CE. This close integration means Tetragon can be deployed independently or alongside Cilium in Kubernetes and host-based environments, catering to diverse user needs. We'll explore these enterprise features, enhancing kernel-level visibility into system protocols and real-world troubleshooting scenarios.

Picture the scene: Your CIO strides over to your desk, a look of frustration etched on face, and laments, "We pour millions into software, hardware, and cloud investments, yet we're still in the dark about the activities of our overlay network and the processes driving these connections!" After a moment of contemplation, you respond with a knowing smile, introducing Cilium Tetragon and Hubble to address CIO concerns.

The Mechanics of Tetragon

Tetragon facilitates deep kernel observability by applying high-level eBPF policies through the Tetragon agent. These policies operate at the kernel level, continually monitoring events of interest. Upon detecting a security-relevant event, the eBPF policy triggers predefined actions, ranging from event reporting to aggregation of metrics or proactive event prevention.

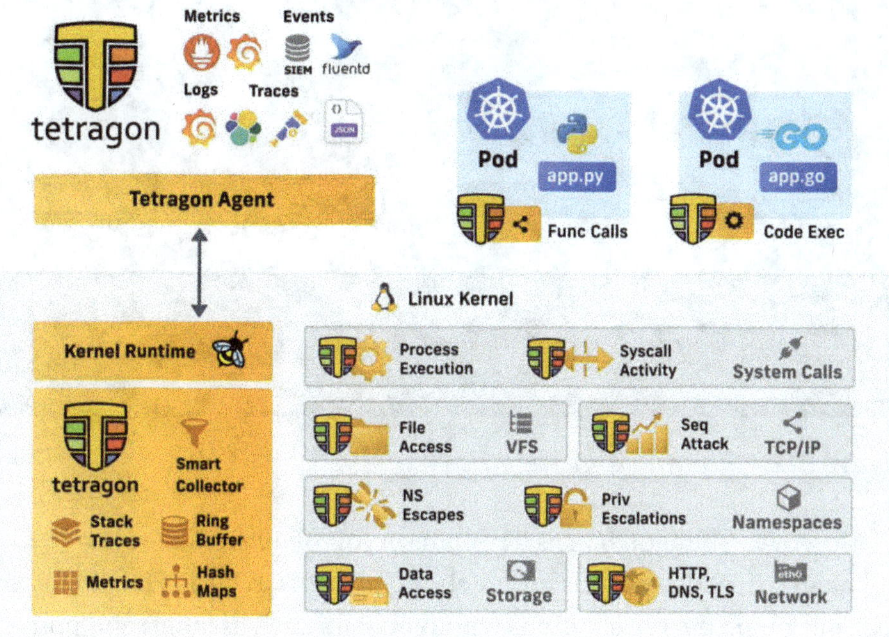

Figure 9-1. *Tetragon Architecture*

Tetragon stands out with its array of key advantages. Firstly, it excels in associating network and process data, offering granular insights into network events at the process and binary levels. This holistic perspective provides a comprehensive understanding of network activities, crucial for effective monitoring and troubleshooting.

A notable feature of Tetragon lies in its minimal overhead, achieved through the utilization of eBPF filtering. By leveraging this technology, Tetragon ensures meaningful observability while keeping CPU and memory consumption at a minimum. This efficiency is particularly valuable in high-performance computing environments where resource utilization optimization is paramount.

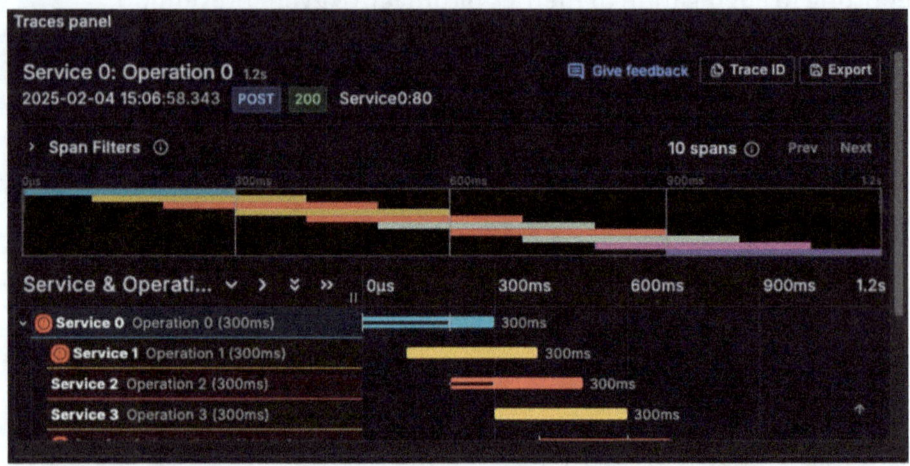

Figure 9-2. *Filtering and Tagging*

Moreover, Tetragon boasts a deep reservoir of network data. It proficiently decodes various protocols including TCP, UDP, TLS, HTTP, and DNS, enriching the observations with metadata such as labels and pod names in Kubernetes environments. This comprehensive coverage enables thorough analysis and facilitates informed decision-making.

One of Tetragon's most compelling attributes is its ease of installation and adoption. No application or code changes are required, streamlining the integration process. Additionally, existing observability solutions like Grafana and Splunk seamlessly visualize Tetragon's data, ensuring a smooth transition and integration with existing workflows.

In the forthcoming walkthrough, our focus is on Tetragon's eBPF-powered network observability capabilities, emphasizing its protocol parsing features. This section provides a step-by-step guide to configuring event collection, whether on a stand-alone host or within a Kubernetes cluster. By delving into Tetragon's functionalities, readers will gain a practical understanding of its capabilities and how to leverage them effectively for enhanced network observability.

Next is an example policy YAML enabling Tetragon to parse relevant protocol (TCP, UDP, DNS) events and interface events.

```
apiVersion: cilium.io/v1alpha1
kind: TracingPolicy
metadata:
  name: network-tracing
spec:
  parser:
    dns:
      enable: true
    interface:
      enable: true
      packet: true
    tcp:
      enable: true
      statsInterval: 20
    udp:
      cgroup: true
      enable: true
      statsInterval: 20
```

In addition to network event insights, Tetragon's observability includes information related to the listen system call, facilitating passive network analysis directly from eBPF events, without the need for active scans like NMAP.

After applying the above policy, events such as process_connect, process_close, process_accept, and process_listen will be generated for TCP and UDP sockets. Additionally, the DNS parser translates machine addresses into human-readable FQDNs, enhancing understanding of network communications.

With deeper observability from the kernel level, we can explore some use cases using event data alongside Tetragon's Network Observability dashboards. These dashboards are categorized into sections like overview, transmit/receive by Kubernetes workload/node and binary, and drops by workload/node and binary. These sections offer insights across TCP/UDP latency and throughput, HTTP golden signals, and host binaries, ensuring a comprehensive view of network characteristics. As you navigate through the panels of the dashboard, you'll encounter a standardized set of panels present in most Tetragon network dashboards, ensuring consistency for streamlined troubleshooting:

- Transmit by K8s workload and binary
- Receive by K8s workload and binary
- Retransmits and drops by K8s workload and binary
- Transmit by node and binary
- Receive by node and binary
- Retransmits and drops by node and binary
- Transmit by Remote DNS Name
- Receive by Remote DNS Name
- Retransmits and drops by Remote DNS Name

In the next section, I will describe how "TCP Throughput - Socket" dashboard can help us to pin the top talkers applications in a CNA 1.0 environment.

Identifying Bandwidth-Intensive Applications

The “TCP Throughput - Socket” dashboard provides comprehensive metrics and insights into TCP traffic transmission and reception across your platform. Utilize filters to pinpoint specific traffic of interest, whether by namespace, workload, pod, node, binary, or remote DNS name.

The dashboard’s initial panel presents an overview of bytes and segments sent and received, with line graphs facilitating pattern recognition. Monitoring both TCP segments and bytes is crucial, as it offers insights into network health and potential performance issues.

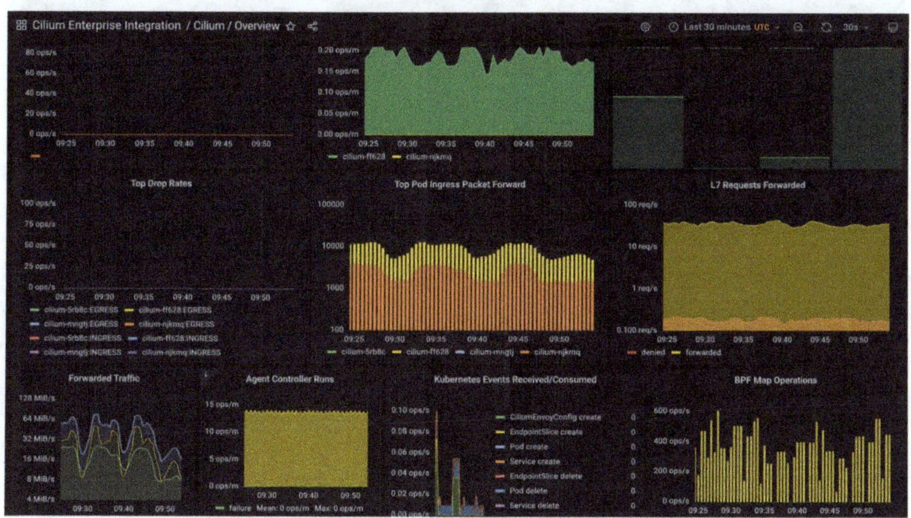

Figure 9-3. *Sample Tetragon Signals*

By analyzing TCP traffic patterns, SRE team can identify bandwidth-intensive applications, ensuring efficient resource allocation and cost management, especially in cloud environments where egress traffic often incurs additional costs.

The dashboard also provides insights into retransmits and drops, shedding light on potential issues within the network or applications, ranging from resource exhaustion to external factors like DNS issues.

A derivative of this TCP Throughput dashboard is one tailored for filtering pod-to-pod communications. By configuring filters for specific application workloads, the dashboard displays network metrics between the designated pods.

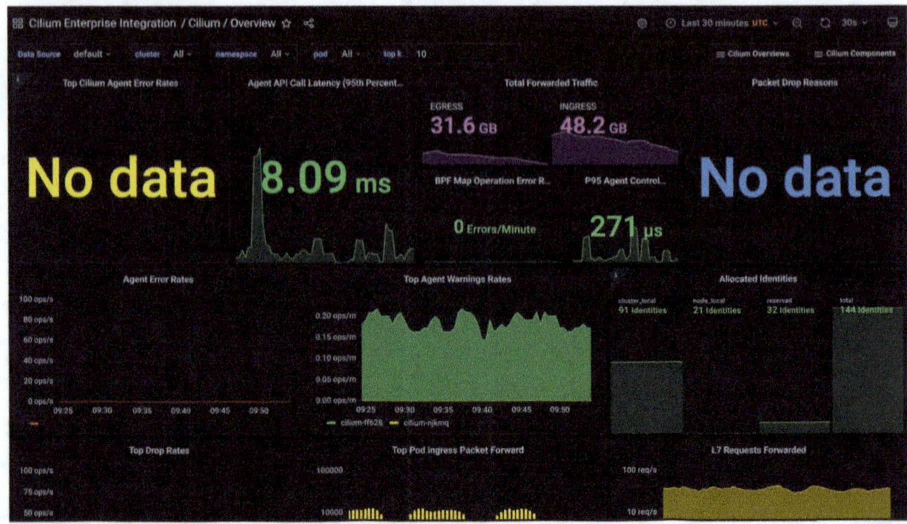

Figure 9-4. Sample Tetragon Tracing

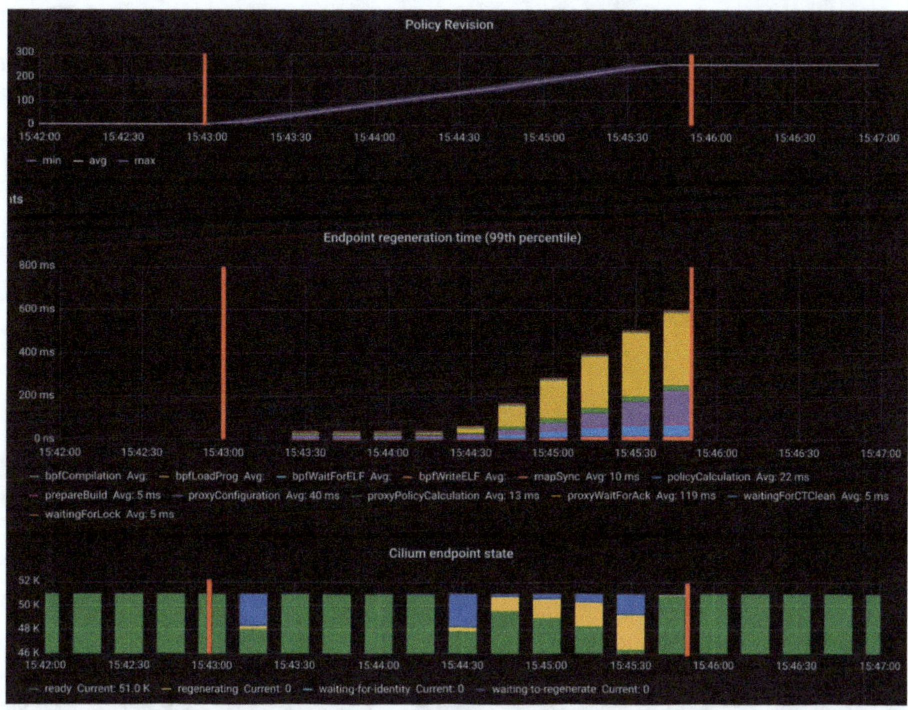

***Figure 9-5.** Sample Tetragon Signals*

For each breakdown showcased here, we've covered TCP metrics, with corresponding dashboards available for UDP traffic as well.

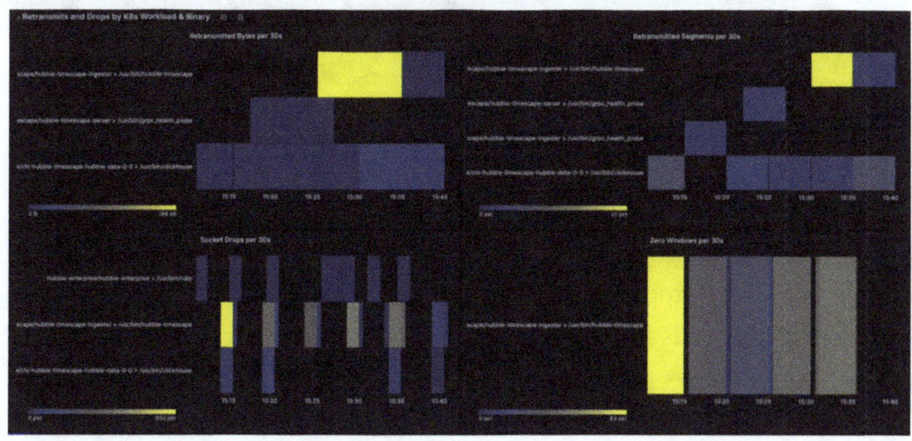

***Figure 9-6.** Sample TCP Signals*

Now, let's address another common challenge: latency. Using the "TCP Latency - Socket" dashboard, we can delve into TCP metrics gathered from Kubernetes hosts and pods.

Identifying Latency-Intensive Applications

Introducing the "TCP Latency - Socket" dashboard, a powerful tool for delving into latency dynamics within Kubernetes environments. By leveraging Smoothed Round Trip Time (SRTT), this dashboard provides invaluable insights into application communication round trips, meticulously smoothing out anomalies for a clearer understanding of latency nuances.

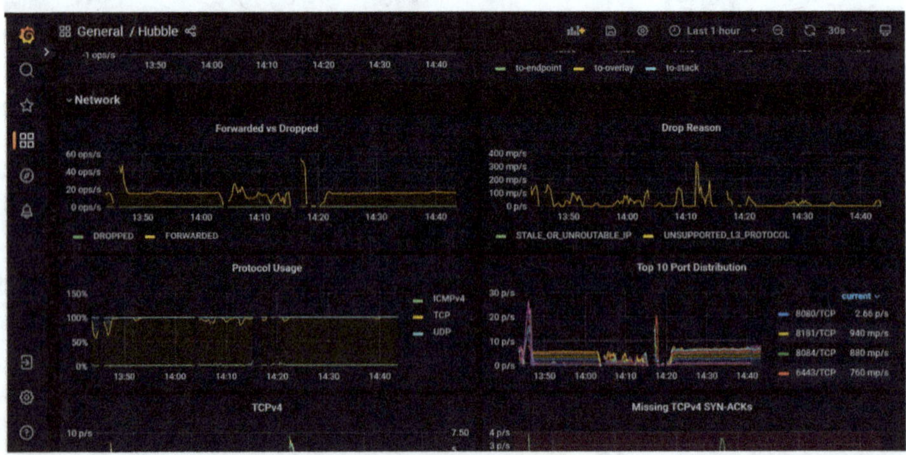

Figure 9-7. *Sample SRTT Dashboard*

Within this dashboard, administrators encounter a detailed histogram illustrating packet latency distribution, alongside a dynamic heatmap plotting latency trends over time. These visualizations serve as indispensable aids for discerning latency patterns and pinpointing potential bottlenecks that may hinder application performance.

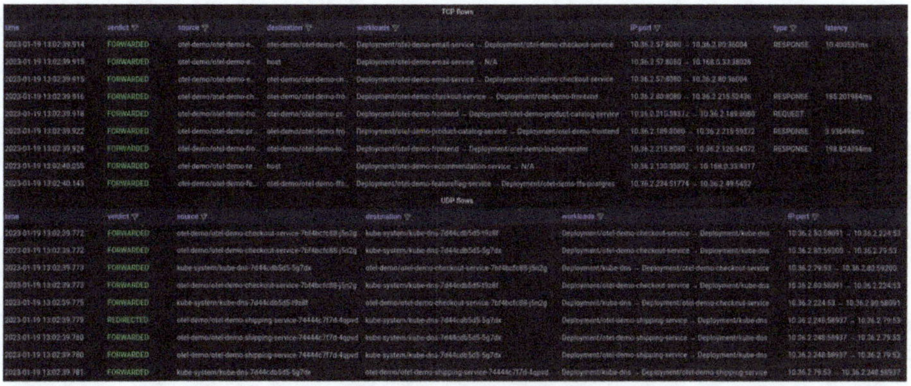

Figure 9-8. *Sample of SRTT Signals level of details*

Further exploration within specific namespaces unveils deeper insights into latency-sensitive applications. The "SRTT Quantiles by K8s Workload & Binary" panel facilitates the identification of latency outliers, offering actionable guidance for optimizing application performance with precision.

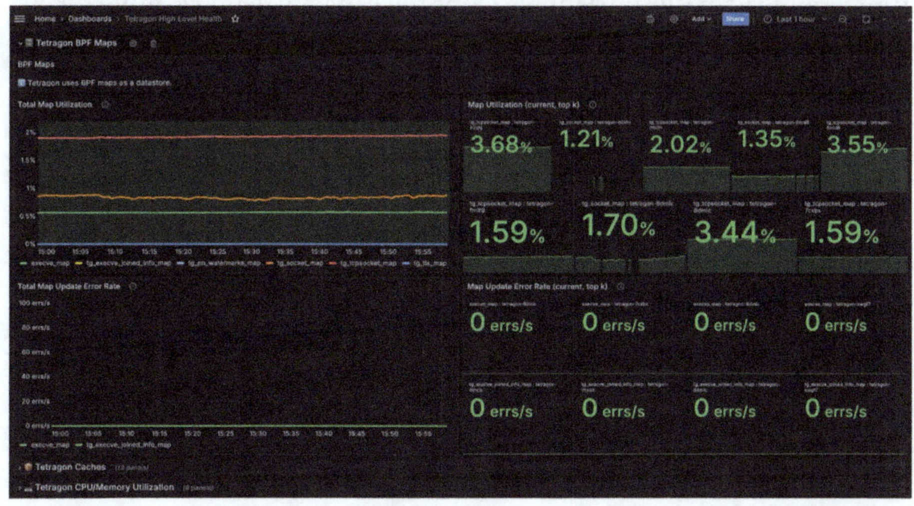

Figure 9-9. *Sample DNS Traffic Signals*

Transitioning to another crucial aspect of network observability – DNS resolution challenges in Kubernetes environments – Tetragon's Network Observability dashboards come to the fore. Through targeted filtering of requests to remote DNS names, administrators can swiftly identify latency issues and rectify potential errors in DNS resolution, ensuring seamless operation of critical services.

With Tetragon's comprehensive suite of tools, achieving unparalleled network observability becomes a reality. Whether navigating Kubernetes environments or managing stand-alone hosts, Tetragon empowers users with deep insights into network metrics, enabling proactive optimization and efficient troubleshooting.

The Mechanics of Hubble

Hubble stands as a fully distributed networking and security observability platform, engineered to leverage the power of Cilium and eBPF technology. By integrating with Cilium, Hubble gains the capacity to utilize eBPF for unparalleled visibility into network operations. This approach ensures that all visibility is programmable, enabling a dynamic methodology that minimizes overhead while offering in-depth insights tailored to user requirements. Hubble has been meticulously crafted to harness the capabilities of eBPF, marking a significant advancement in network observability.

At its core, Hubble is open source and has been contributed, along with Cilium, to the CNCF. Additionally, Hubble is enriched with Cilium EE components, which we will delve into further in subsequent discussions.

The "Hubble server" runs on each node and embedded into the Cilium agent in order to achieve high performance and low overhead.

The "Hubble Relay" is there to provide full network visibility across the entire cluster or across clusters. When the Hubble Relay is deployed,

Hubble provides full network visibility by providing a Hubble API which scopes the entire cluster or even multiple clusters in a *ClusterMesh* scenario.

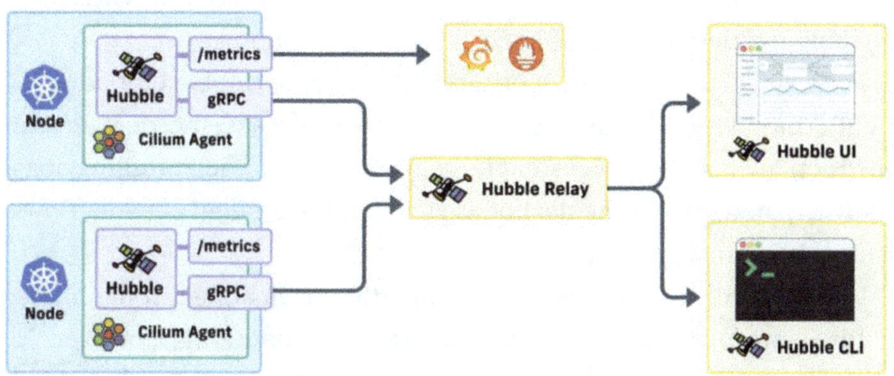

Figure 9-10. *Conceptual diagram of Hubble Architecture*

Why Hubble?

Amid the plethora of monitoring and observability systems available, the necessity for Hubble arises from its unique capabilities. Traditional network analysis tools like Wireshark or tcpdump lack contextual understanding of traffic, especially within cloud-native environments. Hubble bridges this gap by infusing Kubernetes context - including labels, pods, namespaces, and network policy verdicts - into network packets. Aptly termed as the "tcpdump" or "Wireshark" of cloud-native environments, Hubble operates not only at Layers 3/4 but also extends its reach to Layer 7 protocols.

Source Pod	Destination Pod	Destination Port	Traffic Direction	Verdict	Timestamp
otel-demo-loadgenerator-8fd98c8b56-lkvx8	otel-demo-frontend-7ffc85fcf5-zjrn5	8080	ingress	forwarded	2023/05/12 09:56:03 (+01)
otel-demo-loadgenerator-8fd98c8b56-lkvx8	otel-demo-frontend-7ffc85fcf5-zjrn5	8080	ingress	forwarded	2023/05/12 09:55:51 (+01)
otel-demo-loadgenerator-8fd98c8b56-lkvx8	otel-demo-frontend-7ffc85fcf5-zjrn5	8080	ingress	forwarded	2023/05/12 09:55:49 (+01)
otel-demo-recommendationservice-76b9d6559d-md9zh	otel-demo-productcatalogservice-75e468ddc4-kfx7b	8080	egress	forwarded	2023/05/12 09:55:48 (+01)
otel-demo-cartservice-75c975bb7c-zdrjd	otel-demo-redis-fb8c54789-fdz4n	6379	ingress	forwarded	2023/05/12 09:55:46 (+01)
otel-demo-cartservice-75c975bb7c-zdrjd	otel-demo-redis-fb8c54789-fdz4n	6379	egress	forwarded	2023/05/12 09:55:46 (+01)
otel-demo-loadgenerator-8fd98c8b56-lkvx8	otel-demo-frontend-7ffc85fcf5-zjrn5	8080	ingress	forwarded	2023/05/12 09:55:46 (+01)
otel-demo-adservice-7fdd7664d9-bxlxn	otel-demo-featureflagservice-5bdb6c6f59-4w88j	50053	ingress	forwarded	2023/05/12 09:55:44 (+01)

Hubble offers deep visibility into Layer 7 protocols such as HTTP, DNS, and Kafka, with the ability to granularly monitor traffic types like gRPC, which utilizes HTTP for transport. For HTTP, Hubble furnishes comprehensive insights into request methods, status, headers, URLs, and protocols and derives metrics such as request duration.

Following the cloud-native observability pillars, Hubble embodies an eBPF-based M3PLT observability tool, encompassing metrics, service dependency mapping, consistent targets metadata model, profiling, logs, and distributed traces. The dashboard showcases detailed network flows that Hubble can aggregate.

With its extensive data capture capabilities, navigating through the wealth of information collected by Hubble can be daunting. However, filters offer a solution, enabling users to home in on specific traffic based on various criteria such as pod, port, service, namespace, label, IP address, HTTP methods, or status codes.

Hubble comprises several components, including the Hubble server and relay. Data consumption is facilitated through CLI-based and UI-based methods, with gRPC service options to utilize Prometheus, Grafana Alloy, or Grafana Beyla for visualization.

Hubble finds utility in diverse scenarios, empowering SREs and application teams to troubleshoot complex environments effectively. Numerous organizations, as evidenced by public case studies, have embraced Hubble to enhance their networking capabilities and security posture.

While Hubble offers groundbreaking observability, it's essential to acknowledge minor performance costs and limitations, such as all-or-nothing data collection behavior and latency introduced by Layer 7 visibility.

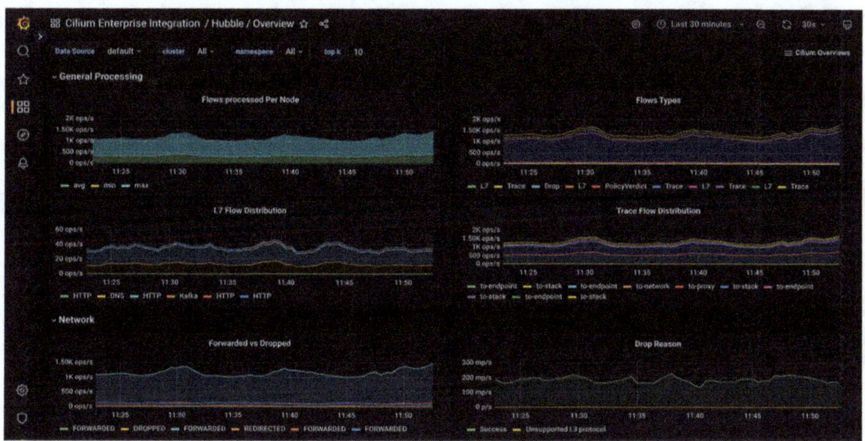

***Figure 9-11.** Hubble Visibility*

Leveraging Cilium's support for Kubernetes network policies, Hubble facilitates the creation of granular policies, easing the transition to a zero-trust model. The Enterprise edition further streamlines this process with a built-in Network Policy editor, enabling dynamic policy creation based on live environment data.

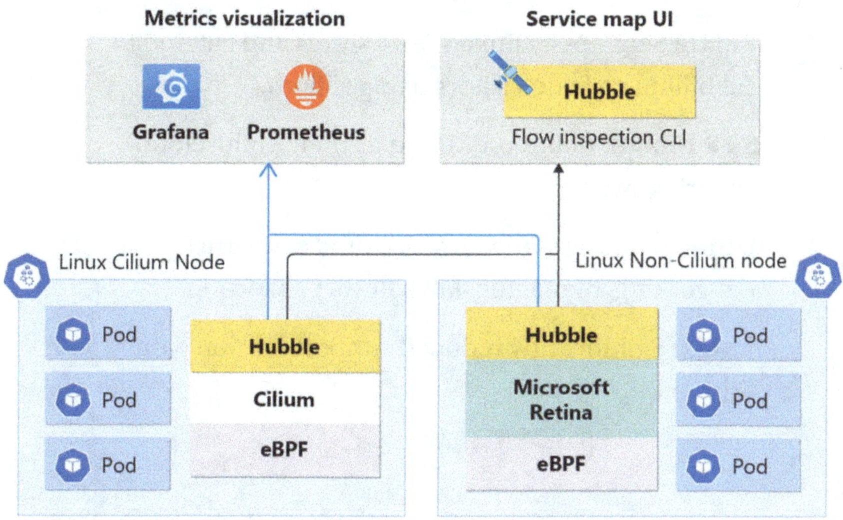

***Figure 9-12.** Hubble Dashboard*

Who Utilizes Hubble?

A glance at the Cilium CE version, user list readily reveals that a vast majority of Cilium users harness the power of Hubble. For specific instances, delve into the following narratives:

Nexxiot: Achieved zero network outage with over 100,000 devices deployed in the field.

Form3: Cilium facilitates cluster connections across multiple clouds for seamless failover.

Hetzner: Witnessed a significant surge in requests per second (RPS) and throughput while concurrently reducing CPU usage for ingress.

PostFinance: Overcame iptables challenges pertaining to scale, observability, and latency.

Publishing Company: Safeguarded over 100,000 requests per second (RPS) within a multi-tenant environment.

Retail: Seamlessly linked 390+ stores and catered to 4.3 billion website visitors using Cilium.

S&P Global: Relies on Cilium as their multi-cloud superhighway.

Utmost: Successfully implemented zero-trust networking, managing 4,000 flows per second.

VSHN: Significantly reduced support burden with Cilium EE.

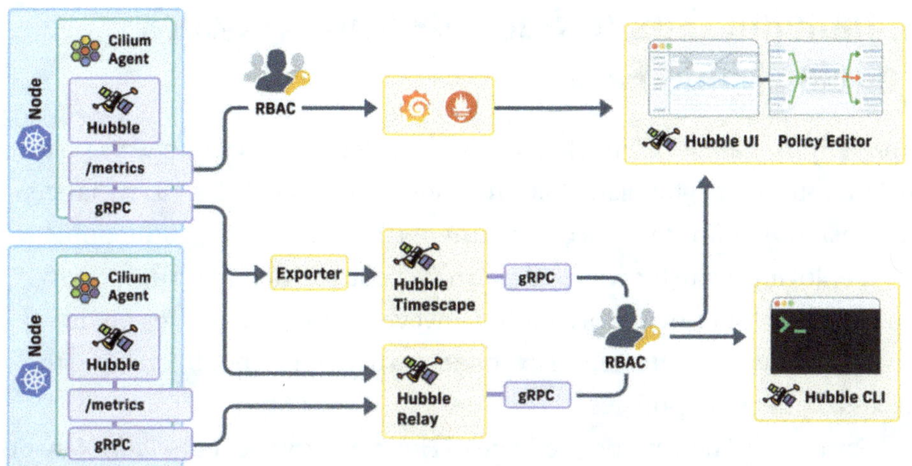

Figure 9-13. *Hubble Interfaces*

Is There Any Reason to Forgo Hubble?

While Hubble undoubtedly offers invaluable insights, there are a few considerations to bear in mind. Any tool collecting extensive observability data typically incurs minor performance costs, and Hubble is no exception, although its utilization of eBPF minimizes such overhead.

Presently, one limitation of Hubble is its inability to specify the data it collects – it's an all-or-nothing scenario. However, this will soon be addressed in an upcoming Cilium release, introducing filters to refine the type of events Hubble processes, thus offering users more control over data collection.

Another minor drawback concerns the latency introduced when enabling Layer 7 visibility. While this feature is disabled by default, activating it requires annotations or network policies. The latency arises from redirecting traffic to an embedded user-space Envoy proxy for Layer 7 parsing, albeit the increase is modest.

Enhancing Cluster Security with Network Policies Made Easy

A primary use case for Cilium lies in its support for Kubernetes network policies, including the more granular L7-aware Cilium Network Policies – a crucial step in transitioning Kubernetes environments from testing to production.

Deploying a cluster without internal traffic restrictions is a risk not worth taking for critical workloads. However, the challenge lies not in convincing users of the necessity for zero trust, but rather in creating the necessary network policies.

Fortunately, the Enterprise edition of Hubble helps with its built-in Network Policy editor. This editor provides a live view of your environment, allowing you to dynamically create policies based on captured flows, thereby permitting or denying specific traffic. The intuitive design simplifies policy creation, enabling users to select existing traffic flows or build policies from scratch with ease.

Furthermore, the Network Policy editor covers both standard Kubernetes network policies and the more robust Cilium Network Policies, which extend to include rulesets for Layer 7 network traffic. Transitioning to a zero-trust model is streamlined, with the ability to build policies from live network flows, define default ingress/egress rules, and specify selectors based on Kubernetes labels to identify relevant endpoints.

In modern CNA 1.0 operations, small SRE teams often prioritize empowering developers to investigate connectivity issues independently, reducing the need for support tickets.

While the Hubble UI CE version provides a namespace-based view of network connectivity, it lacks features for restricting views or user privileges. However, in the Cilium EE edition, multi-tenant self-service access is achievable through OpenID Connect (OIDC) integration, allowing integration with existing Identity and Authorization platforms such as Okta or Auth0.

Hubble EE employs policy-based authorization settings, enabling organizations to control access to resources and data, including flows and metrics, based on predefined policies.

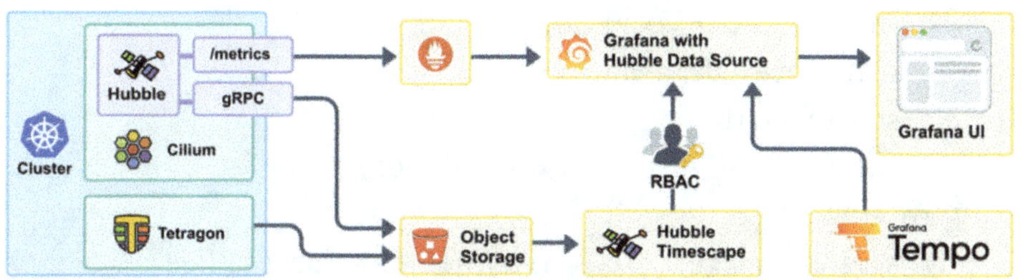

***Figure 9-14.** Grafana and Cilium Interconnection Architecture*

This sample Yaml configuration enables role-based access control (RBAC) with OIDC authentication for Cilium Hubble. by useing a ConfigMap to define access policies, mapping users to roles based on their email addresses via JWT claims. Two roles are defined: admin, which has unrestricted access to all data across all namespaces, and otel-demo-dev, which has read-only access (get actions) to flow and metric data, but only within the otel-demo namespace. This approch helps enforce fine-grained access control, supports multi-tenancy, and integrates securely with an identity provider using OIDC.

```
rbac:
  enabled: true
  observerProxy:
    authMode: oidc
    oidcURL: https://{oidcURL}
...
    oidcClientID: {oidcClientID}
    jwtScopeField: {jwtScopeField:}
  policy:
    mode: configMap
    configMap:
      bindings:
      - role: admin
        scope: email
```

```
    value: 'admin@example.com'
  - role: otel-demo-dev
    scope: email
    value: 'otel-demo-dev@example.com'
  roles:
  # admins can get flows from all namespaces.
  - name: admin
    rules:
      - actions:
          - "*"
        kind: "*"
        allowAllContexts: true
  # otel-demo- app team can get flows and metrics from the
  otel-demo namespace, but no other namespace.
  - name: otel-demo-dev
    rules:
      - actions:
          - get
        contexts:
          - field: namespace
            values:
              - otel-demo
        kind: flows
      - actions:
          - get
        contexts:
          - field: namespace
            values:
              - otel-demo
        kind: metrics
```

This feature extends throughout all the components of the Hubble architecture, including the UI and Timescape.

The platform administrator has access to all namespaces and views. When the "Otel-Demo" Developer logs in, they can access the service map within their namespace, but they are restricted from viewing other namespaces. Similarly, the "Tenant-Jobs" Developer has access only to their namespace's service map, which reveals a distinctly different application. Concluding with an overview of the RBAC Policies applied via Helm.

Assuming responsibility for troubleshooting not only empowers application owners but also cultivates a healthy and productive work environment. Active engagement in troubleshooting fosters collaboration and eliminates the blame game during post-mortems.

Post-mortems are inevitable, providing opportunities for conducting root cause analyses of incidents. This task is integral for both SREs and application owners as it facilitates proactive incident management, enhances system reliability, drives continuous improvement, promotes collaboration, and deepens understanding of the system.

While the Hubble Relay component offers real-time information, its utility diminishes over time. Hubble Timescape, however, allows users to rewind to the point where issues arose, providing comprehensive visibility into the network flow lifecycle for applications and associated services.

Delving into the architecture of Hubble Timescape, it is designed for deployment within the same cluster it monitors or, for larger environments, in a separate Kubernetes cluster. Hubble Enterprise is configured to export data to S3-compliant object storage or public cloud storage options such as Google Cloud Storage and Azure Blob Storage. Hubble Timescape leverages ClickHouse, an open source columnar database, which can be deployed in-cluster or externally, for instance, through ClickHouse Cloud. The optional Hubble Timescape Trimmer enforces predefined limits on ingested flows into the database. Hubble Timescape deploys an ingester to load flows and Tetragon process events into a ClickHouse Database. The Hubble Timescape server hosts the gRPC API, accessible via the Hubble UI or Hubble CLI.

Efficient visualization of this meaningful data within existing monitoring platforms is crucial. Recognizing that tool sprawl can be cumbersome, especially when tools lack interoperability, Cilium developers forged a strategic partnership with Grafana Labs. Through this collaboration, they developed the Hubble data source plug-in, aimed at providing deep insights into connectivity, security, and performance. This plug-in integrates with Hubble Timescape, Prometheus (for Hubble networking metrics), and Grafana Tempo (for traces correlated with different signals), offering a unified interface to reduce tool sprawl and enhance collaboration.

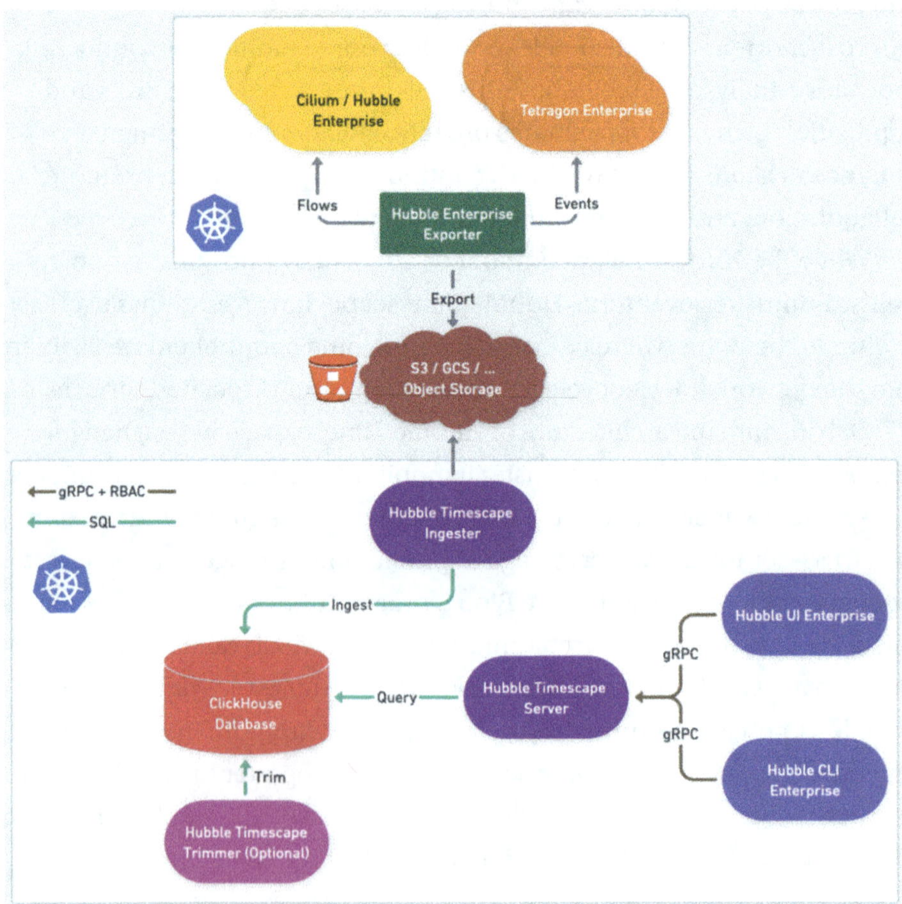

Figure 9-15. *Data Structure*

In the upcoming Grafana plug-in release, it will introduce a Tetragon dashboard, providing a process ancestry view similar to that in the Hubble Enterprise UI. This integration offers features such as the Network Policy editor for enhancing cluster security, role-based access control (RBAC) for delegated access, and Hubble Timescape for historical network flow analysis.

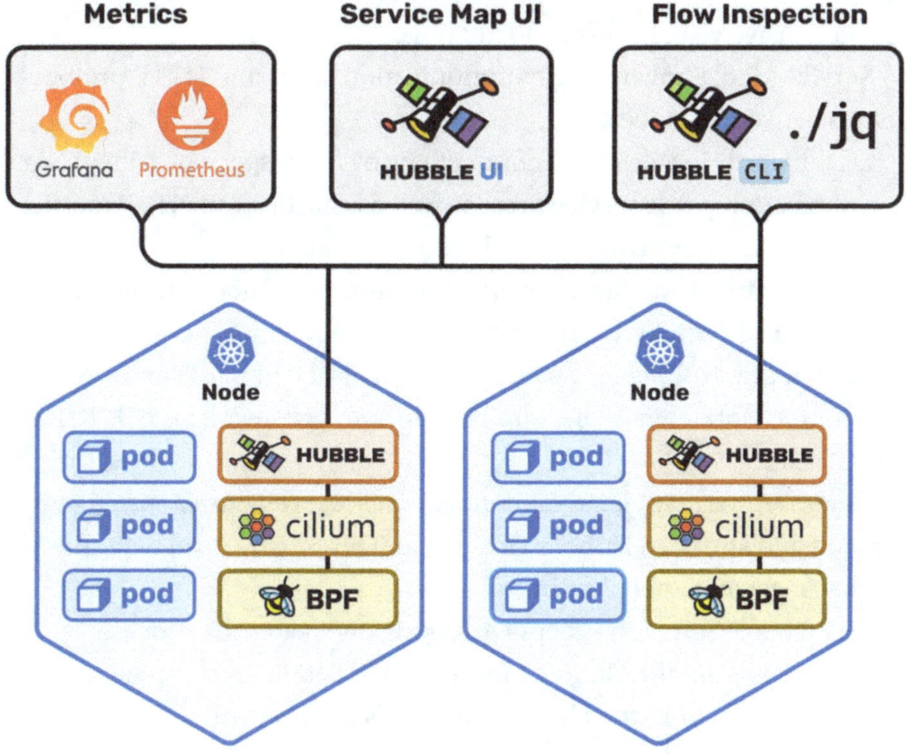

Figure 9-16. *Hubble Tracing*

Transitioning to the Cilium Hubble integration with Grafana, we'll explore real-world use cases, including identifying DNS-related issues in Kubernetes workloads and detecting potentially malicious activities in containers using Tetragon. These features promote improved security posture, delegated access, and efficient historical analysis of network flows.

The Hubble data source plug-in leverages Grafana plug-in development tools to integrate Hubble Timescape, Prometheus, and Grafana Tempo, along with Grafana Alloy, providing rich data alongside existing monitoring datasets without necessitating tooling changes or complex data joins. The plug-in supports three query types - Service Map, Flows, and Process Ancestry - accompanied by associated dashboards for comprehensive visualization and analysis.

Service Map: Showing the communication paths and HTTP protocol metrics between services.

Dashboard: Hubble HTTP connectivity by namespace provides a visual communication paths service map, as well as charting out HTTP metrics such as request rate, error rate, and request duration.

Flows: Retrieve the raw network flows stored in Hubble Timescape, which can also be linked to trace data with Tempo.

Dashboard: Hubble Flows by protocol. This dashboard shows all the flows for the workloads broken up by monitored protocols: HTTP, Kafka, TCP, UDP, ICMP.

Process Ancestry: Visual render of kernel-level events captured by Tetragon and stored in Hubble Timescape. This is to be used with the Process Ancestry panel plug-in.

Dashboard: Tetragon Process Ancestry. Replicates the Process Ancestry view from the Hubble Enterprise UI, detailing the process execution events from the chosen workloads in the cluster.

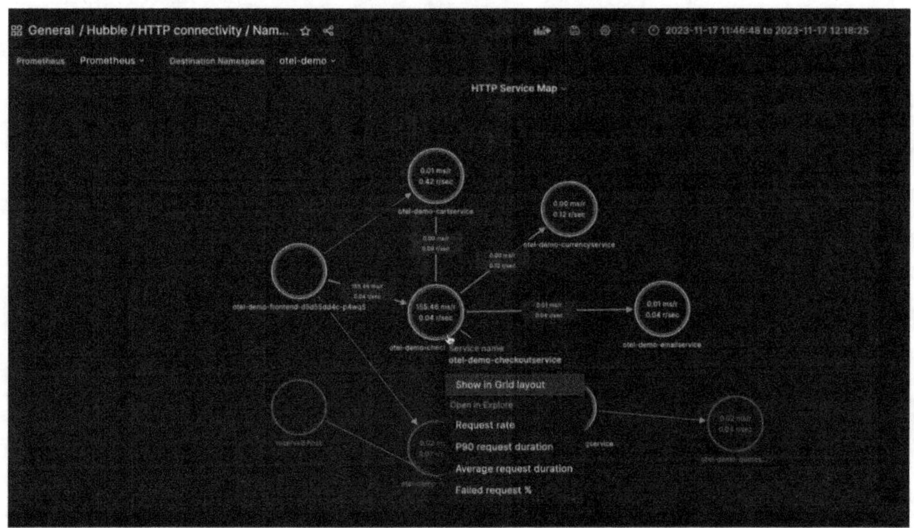

Figure 9-17. *Hubble Service Map*

To illustrate, the Service Map showcases communication paths and HTTP protocol metrics between services, while the Flows query retrieves raw network flows stored in Hubble Timescape, linked to trace data with Tempo. The Process Ancestry query offers a visual representation of kernel-level events captured by Tetragon. These capabilities, showcased in various dashboards, facilitate understanding and troubleshooting of application communication paths and metrics, without requiring additional instrumentation or modifications.

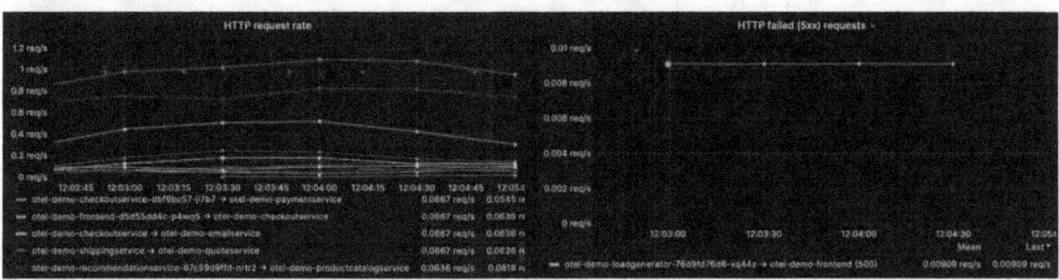

Figure 9-18. *HTTP Signals*

Utilize the "HTTP Connectivity" dashboard alongside the provided "Hubble L7 HTTP metrics By Workload" dashboard for a comprehensive breakdown of HTTP-related metrics, enabling deeper insights into workloads. These dashboards, available in both OSS and Enterprise configurations, offer flexibility and customization options to suit your environment's needs.

The data source implements three query types - Service Map, Flows, and Process Ancestry - and is supported by associated dashboards.

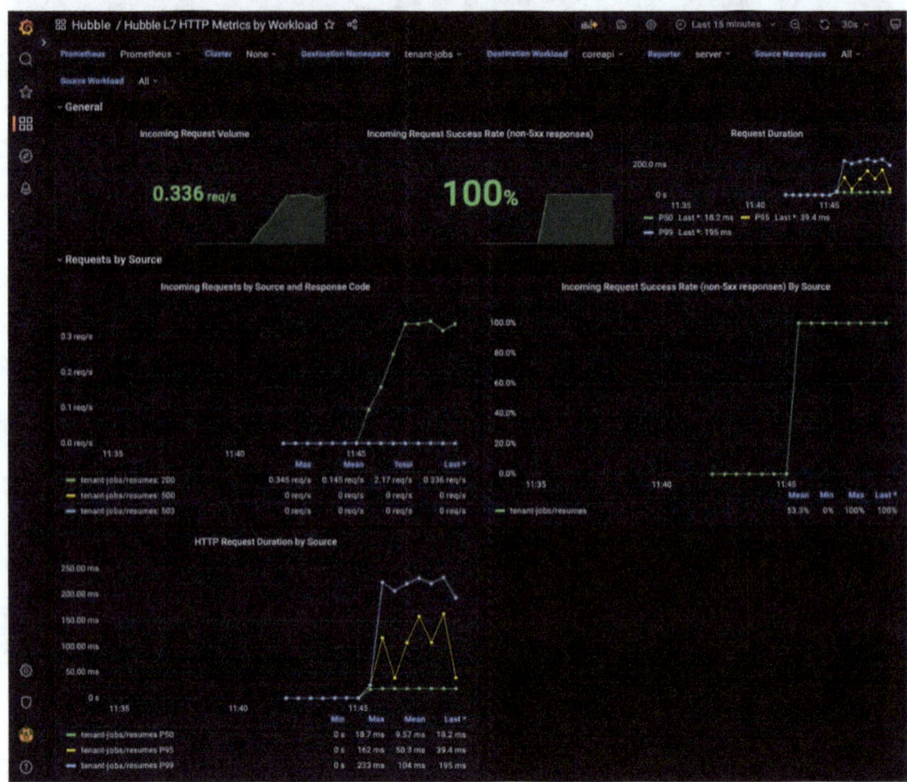

Figure 9-19. *Hubble HTTP Signals*

Next is an example of the Helm values used to configure Hubble Metrics and Dashboard (which can be loaded by the dashboards sidecar for Grafana).

```
hubble:
 metrics:
  enabled:
    - dns:query;ignoreAAAA
    - drop:sourceContext=identity;destinationContext=identity
    - tcp
    - flow
    - icmp
    - httpV2:exemplars=true;
labelsContext=source_ip,source_namespace,source_workload,
destination_ip,destination_namespace,destination_workload,
traffic_direction;
sourceContext=workload-name|reserved-identity;
destinationContext=workload-name|reserved-identity
  enableOpenMetrics: true
 dashboards:
  enabled: true
  namespace: monitoring
  annotations:
   grafana_folder: Hubble
```

When Tracing Comes to the Scene

Let's delve deeper into enriching our data by merging the insights from Hubble Metrics with application traces. This integration offers a comprehensive exploration of the inner workings and communication patterns within the application.

Enhanced support for tracing-enabled applications and Grafana Tempo integration and diagnosing issues within a distributed system is a multifaceted task. To pinpoint problems with precision, employing distributed tracing becomes imperative. Presently, a substantial number of application developers implement tracing within their applications, dispatching trace spans to their preferred tracing backend like Grafana Tempo. Furthermore, instrumentation can be automated, leveraging tools such as Grafana Beyla.

In recent Cilium versions, Hubble's Layer 7 HTTP visibility feature underwent further enhancement to autonomously extract existing, application-specific OpenTelemetry TraceContext headers from Layer 7 HTTP requests, incorporating them into a new field within Hubble flows. Notably, TraceContext, now widely adopted, can be configured in platforms like Datadog, Cribl Stream, and others. This integration facilitates correlating distributed traces with intricate network-level events. When traces are stored in Grafana Tempo, the Hubble data source plug-in seamlessly links Layer 7 flows to traces.

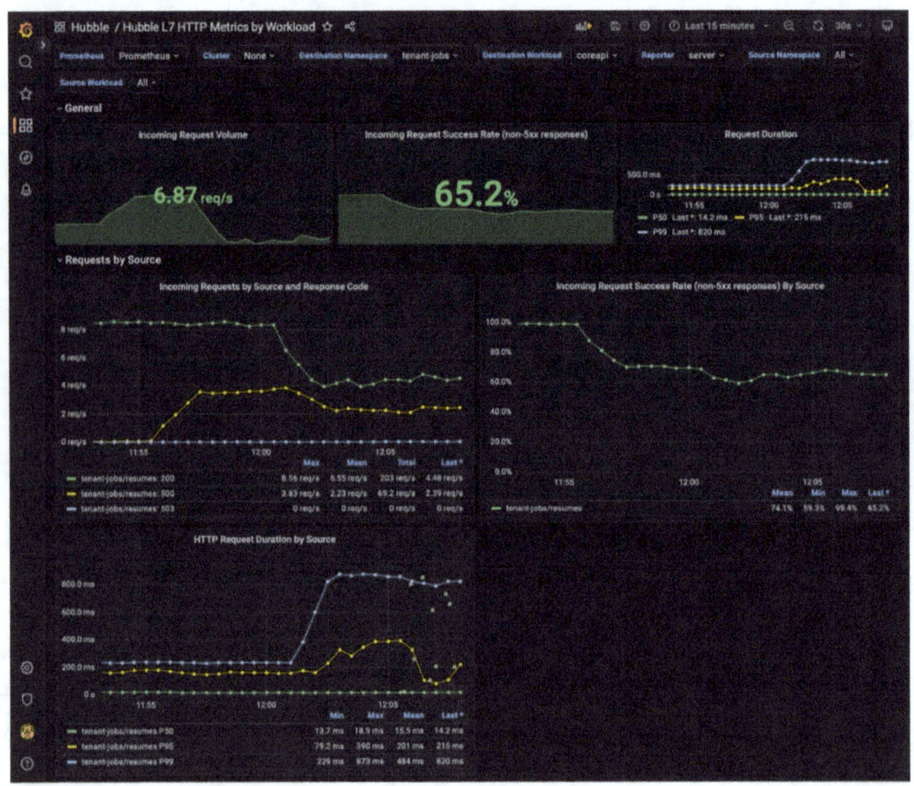

Figure 9-20. Sample of Hubble Dashboard

Additionally, the trace ID is embedded in Hubble metrics as OpenMetrics exemplars. This linkage between Hubble metrics and distributed traces empowers engineers to promptly investigate issues. For instance, engineers can define an alert based on high HTTP latency using Hubble metrics. Upon alert activation, engineers can utilize exemplars to navigate directly to a distributed trace, providing detailed insights into problematic requests.

In the following illustration, we observe a trace originating from a service named Crawler, establishing connections with the CoreAPI service via two intermediary services: Loader and Resumes. The trace data indicates multiple retries for this connection, suggesting a fault within the CoreAPI service.

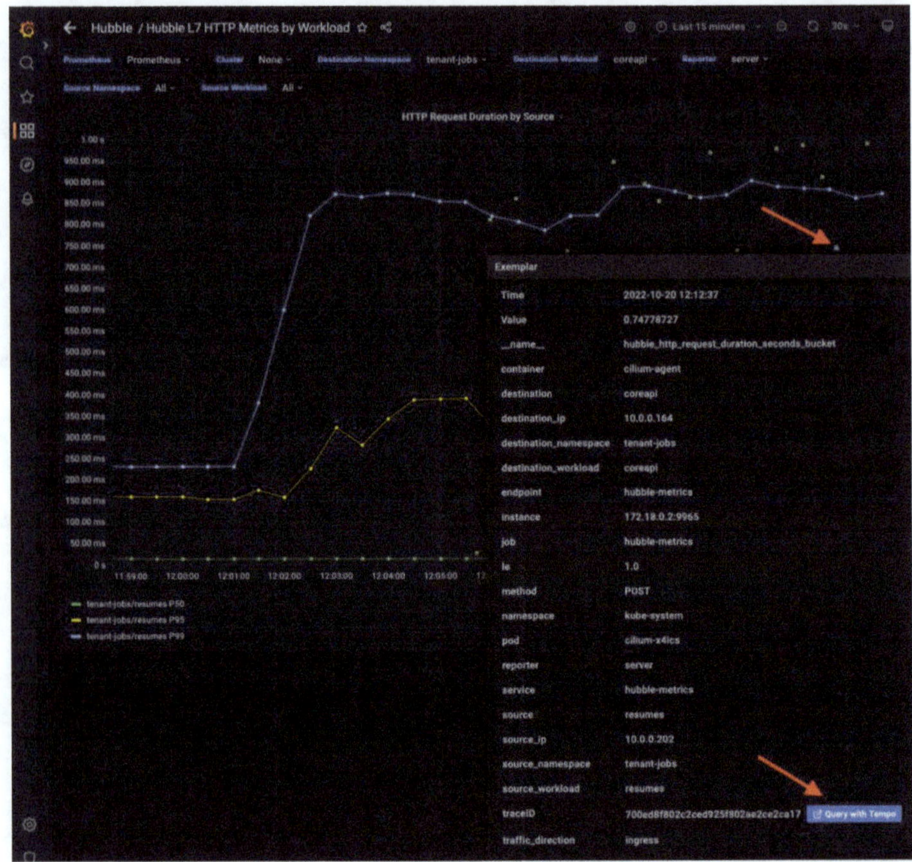

Figure 9-21. *Hubble HTTP Sample Dashboard view*

Analyze All Network Flows in Grafana

To examine all available network flows from Hubble Timescape in Grafana swiftly, utilize the Explore interface in Grafana. Simply select Hubble as the data source and specify the query type as Flows. Below, you'll find a list of table properties for each flow:

- Time
- Verdict

- Source
- Destination
- Trace ID
- Workloads
- Protocol
- IP
- IP Port
- L7 Protocol
- L7 Type
- HTTP Version
- Method
- URL
- Latency
- Status

Additionally, there are other properties relevant to various protocols, such as Kafka, that are not displayed in the screenshot but are captured for those specific types of traffic (e.g., Kafka version, API key, topic, correlation ID, etc.).

The Hubble Data Source offers the “Hubble/Flows by protocol” dashboard out of the box, providing a curated view across each protocol, which can be further refined with filters.

This serves as an excellent starting point to explore raw data. However, typically, you would customize these views and queries to suit your specific use cases and incorporate additional visualizations.

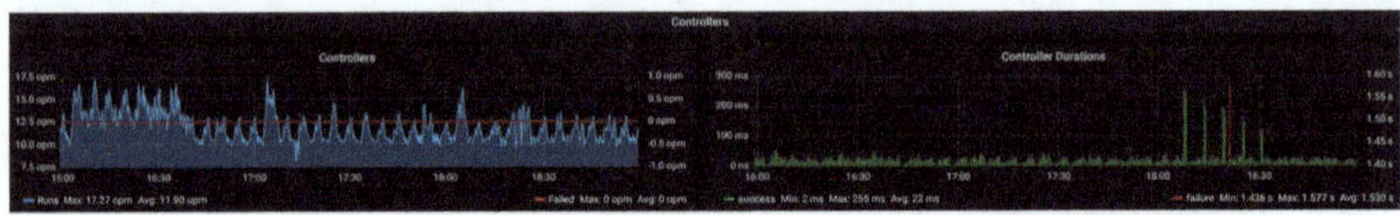

Figure 9-22. Level of details sample of Hubble DNS Dashboard

Troubleshoot a Specific Protocol Like DNS

We've all encountered situations where something isn't functioning correctly between our applications and services, often humorously attributed to DNS issues. But how can we substantiate whether DNS is genuinely at fault?

Thanks to Hubble Network flows, we can identify DNS protocol traffic and scrutinize the requests. With Cilium, we have access to the "Hubble/DNS Overview" Dashboard, which presents visualizations of DNS requests categorized by namespace. Crucially, it highlights missing DNS responses and DNS errors by reason. This overview serves as a valuable starting point to address the question "Is it DNS?"

From the data presented, we can infer that DNS is indeed causing some issues in our namespace. However, further investigation is warranted.

Monitor Process Executions Within Containers

The final aspect to focus on is security. Leveraging Hubble Timescape, a component of Cilium EE, to store process events from Tetragon provides a robust repository of data concerning process-level events within your platform.

Integrating this data directly into Grafana for your entire applications team to access seems like an obvious choice. However, simply parsing JSON files into tables might not suffice. This is where the Hubble Process Ancestry plug-in comes into play.

Process Ancestry amalgamates all process events into a coherent timeline against your Kubernetes workload. This facilitates the identification of late execution processes, which could indicate misconfigurations at an application level or potentially malicious activity, such as an attacker executing commands within an existing workload.

The "Pod Process Ancestry" dashboard not only offers a comprehensive visualization of the interlinked process events but also provides a detailed table output of the parsed JSON for each event captured within the Kubernetes workload.

Figure 9-23. *Level of detail Sample of Hubble Dashboard*

Below is an example illustrating a pod within the environment, with Tetragon recording process event information alongside TCP/HTTP requests and parsing them accordingly.

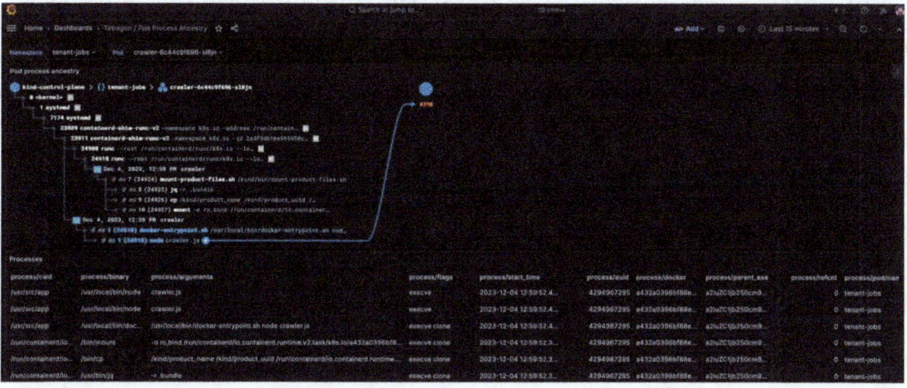

Figure 9-24. *Traffic Hunting*

Let's explore an instance where changes in our environment trigger suspicious behavior and delve into how visualization aids in detecting such activity!

Detecting Suspicious and Malicious Behaviors

Monitoring the events occurring during a container's startup in our environment is crucial. However, in cyber intrusions, attackers often aim for sustained access to platforms. This persistence, frequently established via a reverse shell, grants hackers remote access even after attempts to remediate the breach.

As we analyze an attack scenario, we anticipate that new processes will execute in the environment, a phenomenon termed "late running execution/process." Simply put, these are processes that run sometime after all the normal startup processes have executed.

In the screenshot below, you'll notice a new instance of my workload has been spun up, mirroring the previous one. The "nc" command facilitates network connections; here, we've utilized it to orchestrate a reverse shell attack on the container.

In the Pod Process Ancestry tree, these "late running executions" are now highlighted in yellow, enabling easy detection of changes in our workload. Additionally, with Tetragon, we've parsed and displayed the commands executed, along with the Fully Qualified Domain Names (FQDNs) and public IP addresses the container is currently connecting to. This information is further supported by comprehensive process event details in the table below the visualization.

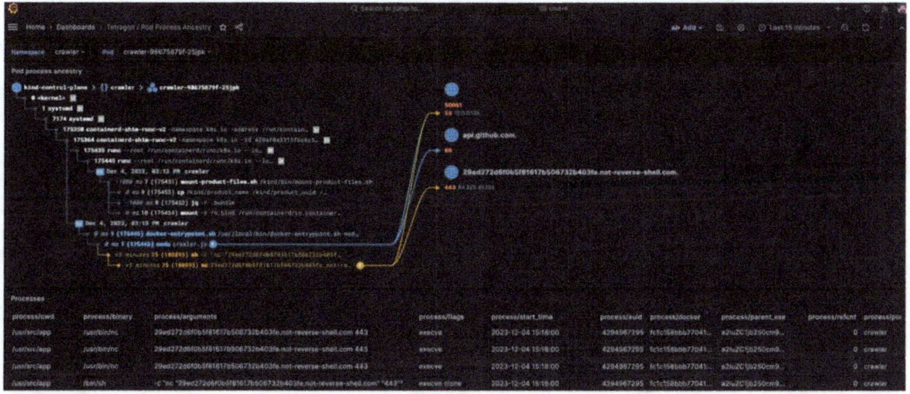

Figure 9-25. *Hubble Network Policy*

Immediately, we can act with Cilium EE. By utilizing the Network Policy editor feature in Hubble, we can create a new Cilium network policy to block any workload from contacting this malicious address while concurrently investigating and addressing the issue.

Hubble Plug-ins for Grafana

To begin, enable Hubble Metrics out of the box and configure Prometheus to scrape these metrics into the data store.

To fully leverage the integration of Hubble and Grafana, install both the Hubble plug-in and the Hubble Process Ancestry plug-in. As depicted in the following screenshot, if your Grafana instance has Internet access, you can install these plug-ins directly from the Plugins view.

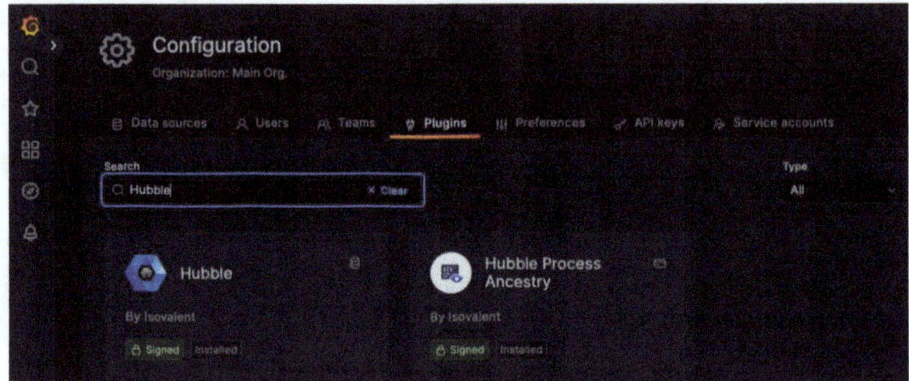

Figure 9-26. *Hubble Plug-in for Grafana*

Once the Hubble plug-in is installed, it will activate the Hubble Data Source configuration, enabling connectivity to both Hubble Timescape for comprehensive workload data such as network flows with protocol metrics, and Tetragon for security observability events.

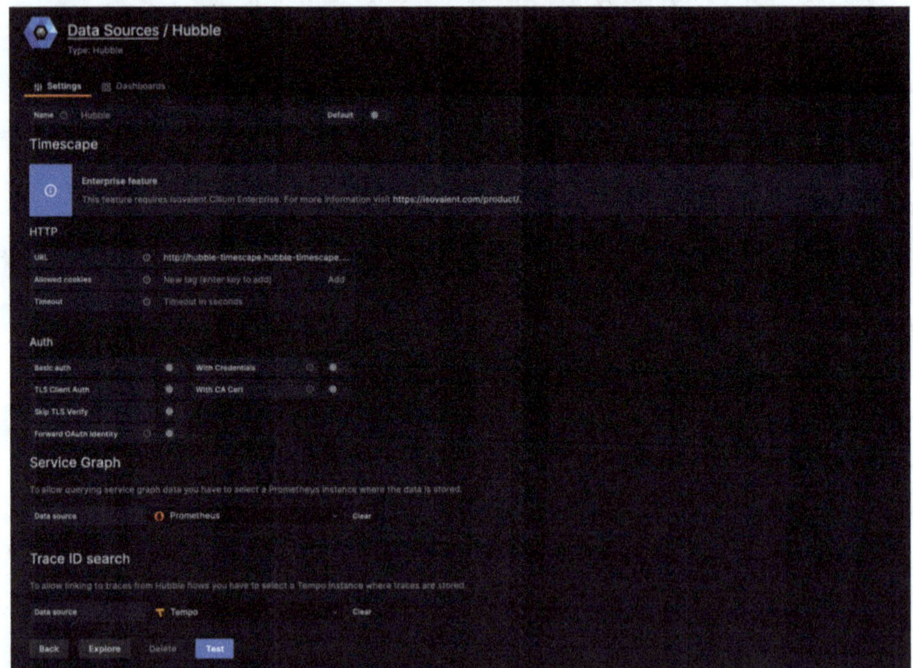

Figure 9-27. *Hubble Data Sources selection*

Accessing the dashboard tab allows you to install the associated dashboards for the Hubble plug-in covered in this chapter.

Note that the "Tetragon/Pod Process Ancestry" dashboard requires the installation of the Hubble Process Ancestry plug-in, but no further configuration is necessary once the connection to Hubble Timescape is established.

Figure 9-28. *Hubble Dashboards*

IMPORTANT NOTE

I firmly believe that the most comprehensive instructions and labs scenarios come from the creators and communities who rigorously build and test tools across diverse circumstances. Therefore, instead of simply duplicating content from others' Git repositories and presenting it as the best ultimate knowledge source, I have chosen to direct readers to the rich and meticulously tested lab scenarios and learning paths provided by Isovalent. You can find these resources directly at `https://isovalent.com/resource-library/labs/` (Isovalent Lab Scenarios) and `https://isovalent.com/learning-tracks/` (Learning Tracks), as well as `https://docs.cilium.io/en/stable/cheatsheet/` (the Cilium Cheatsheet).

By adopting this approach, I ensure that *Observability Engineering with Cilium* remains focused on delivering strategic and authoritative engineering insights rather than duplicating tool manuals.

Summary

This chapter focuses on achieving robust observability for CNA 1.0 applications using Cilium, Tetragon, Hubble, and Grafana. We discussed how these tools provide deep network observability from the kernel level, offering practical examples such as bandwidth, latency, and DNS monitoring.

The mechanics of Tetragon and Hubble are explored, highlighting the use of eBPF for deep kernel observability with minimal overhead. Tetragon offers a comprehensive understanding of network activities, decodes various protocols, and facilitates easy integration with existing observability solutions like Grafana and Splunk.

Hubble provides unparalleled visibility into network operations with minimal overhead, contextualizing network traffic within Kubernetes environments. It supports Layer 7 protocols and offers extensive data capture capabilities. The chapter covers Hubble's integration with existing tools and its role in enhancing cluster security with network policies and demonstrates real-world use cases for improved security and efficient historical analysis. Additionally, it discusses Hubble's utility in troubleshooting and improving system reliability through detailed network flow analysis.

CHAPTER 10

Cilium Outstanding, Yet Not Alone

A single melody can be beautiful, but a symphony is made of many.

Cloud-native applications, known as CNA 1.0 in this book, typically operate on well-architected platforms with decentralized management. However, they are precisely ruled by GitOps-enabled policies and manifests. Consider the performances of the Berlin Philharmonic in the Berlin Philharmonie Hall under the baton of Sir Simon Rattle. It's not uncommon for a few players to be absent on any given night, substituted seamlessly by others. Even section leaders, such as the principal violist or principal cellist, may change due to unforeseen circumstances like illness. As seasoned classical concert attendees, we rarely notice any decline in the quality of the performances. How is this possible? It's thanks to the orchestra's high operational excellence and maturity, as well as the loosely coupled nature of the repertoire and the musicians. As long as the concertmaster and the conductor are present, the show maintains the same high standard as the previous night. This mirrors the scenario with cloud-native applications and platforms. eBPF, instrumentation, and signals are just melodies, observability is the symphony. Microservices can be redeployed, upgraded, and transformed, yet the product and SLAs remain consistent with the promises made by the product manager and SRE team.

Dr. M. Ghane, *Observability Engineering with Cilium*,
https://doi.org/10.1007/979-8-8688-1258-3_10

Masterpieces are indeed timeless and immutable. With the advent of microservice and containerization technology, we've incorporated this concept into CNA 1.0 as well. When CNAs are deployed as immutable assets, our approach shifts from updating containers to patching and redeploying them. In urgent situations, we can swiftly implement an out-of-band change, temporarily treating immutable infrastructure as mutable.

These flexibilities are essential not only for CNAs but also for management and observability layers. Let's delve into alternative, yet robust solutions if Cilium stack proves impractical in a very specific scenario. Understanding these options is as crucial as recognizing the functionalities and advantages that Cilium offers thus far. In the last chapter, we will work on Pixie and Falco functionalities and mechanics as alternative eBPF-based observability toolsets.

Strategic Contingency Routes

In preceding chapters, we embarked on a journey through the evolution of modern information technology, beginning with an exploration of the pivotal role played by enterprise and corporate DataCenters. We traced the trajectory from traditional managed service providers to the emergence of cloud providers, highlighting the transition to multi-tenant DataCenters.

As technology progressed, so did the industrial and architectural paradigms, leading us from monolithic applications to the dynamic landscape of microservice event-driven applications. Throughout this transformation, a plethora of tools have emerged to aid in navigating this evolutionary path.

Consider **Monorepos**, helpful for managing dependencies within monolithic code bases, or API blueprints, indispensable for diagnosing and resolving network-blamed issues. Tools like **CallGraph** or **OmniSci** offer insights with generation of call graphs, providing visual representations of function calls within your code base. Meanwhile, **NDepend** and **Structure101** provide comprehensive analyses, generating dependency graphs to illuminate the intricacies of your code base.

Central to our discourse is the concept of observability, a cornerstone of continuous improvement and operational excellence. Delving into the realm of CNA 1.0, we delved into the foundational principles of observability engineering, tracing its roots through the rich history of mathematics and control theory and transformation to modern cloud-native architectures. We underscored the pillars of cloud-native observability: **M3PLT** or the modern telemetry data types. we have learned about distinctive nature of cloud-native observability and its significance in comparison to traditional software systems.

Furthermore, we examined the paradigm of truly native instrumentation, where the pursuit of semantically accurate instrumentation stands as the ultimate objective. Here, auto-instrumentation with **eBPF** emerged as a key strategy, enabling seamless integration and holistic monitoring of system performance.

The Berkeley Packet Filter (BPF) operates as an in-kernel virtual machine, executing programs provided from user space. Initially deployed on BSD systems and later on Linux, the “classic BPF” or cBPF mechanism was utilized alongside tools like tcpdump to filter packets within the kernel, thus avoiding unnecessary data copies to user space.

However, on March 20, 2014, the BPF infrastructure within the Linux kernel underwent a significant overhaul, giving rise to the “extended BPF” or eBPF. According to Kubernetes architecture, all pods on each host or node server share a single kernel, essentially having one kernel space per node with multiple separate user spaces. This Linux kernel manages communication with all user spaces. eBPF operates within this shared kernel space, enabling it to natively observe and manage the activities of all pods. This revamped framework introduced a plethora of new features, including verifier and termination checks, shared memory with BPF maps, just-in-time (JIT) compiling for programs, persistent maps, a standard library, and hardware offload support. As Linus Torvalds once said: “eBPF allows people to do specialized code that isn't enabled until asked for.”

Its natively an event-driven technology, by kprobes, uprobe, system calls, tracepoints, sockets, and others to provide **content-aware event streams**. eBPF has since become influential in a wide array of tasks, from processing packets at an ultra-low level (XDP) to tracing, observability platforms and events, and enforcing access control over cgroups. Its adoption brings forth enhanced performance, safety, observability, programmability, and flexibility.

Presently, eBPF has become the de facto standard in Kubernetes Container Network Interface (CNI), serving as the core of solutions like Cilium and Calico. Moreover, it has found widespread usage in numerous other solutions, including F5, Cisco, New Relic, VMware, Microsoft Windows, Elastic, and many more. Various products such as bpftrace, Pyroscope, Parca, Katran, Inspektor Gadget, and Grafana Beyla, as well as platforms like Cloudflare, Netflix, Meta, Apple, and Android, have integrated eBPF into their offerings.

Within the cloud-native observability and security landscape, eBPF plays a pivotal role, with tools like Pixie, Falco, KubeArmor, PWru, Tracee, OpenObserve, Netdata, and SkyWalking among the notable solutions.

AUTHENTIC EBPF

I intentionally avoid delving deeply into eBPF programming in this book to maintain focus. While I reference many eBPF functionalities, detailed technical exploration is beyond this book's scope. To learn more about this technology, I recommend visiting the eBPF website (`http://ebpf.io`); exploring *Buzzing Across Space*, the illustrated children's guide to eBPF, by Bill Mulligan; or reading Liz Rice's books on the subject. Enjoy your journey into eBPF!

In today's market, there's simply nothing that matches the comprehensive capabilities offered by the Cilium stack. Whether in the open source sphere or among commercial products, it stands unrivalled.

However, it's important to note that this isn't about establishing a monopoly. While competitors like Calico may shine in specific areas like CNI functionality, they often lack the robust observability features that define Cilium. Some mature product emerges as a strong contender, particularly when comparing Cilium Tetragon to Falco and Cilium Hubble to Pixie. Rather, it's akin to an orchestra where the concertmaster (principal observability engineer) and the conductor (CIO) guide the performance. Exploring alternatives such as Pixie and Falco enriches our capabilities and widens our range of options.

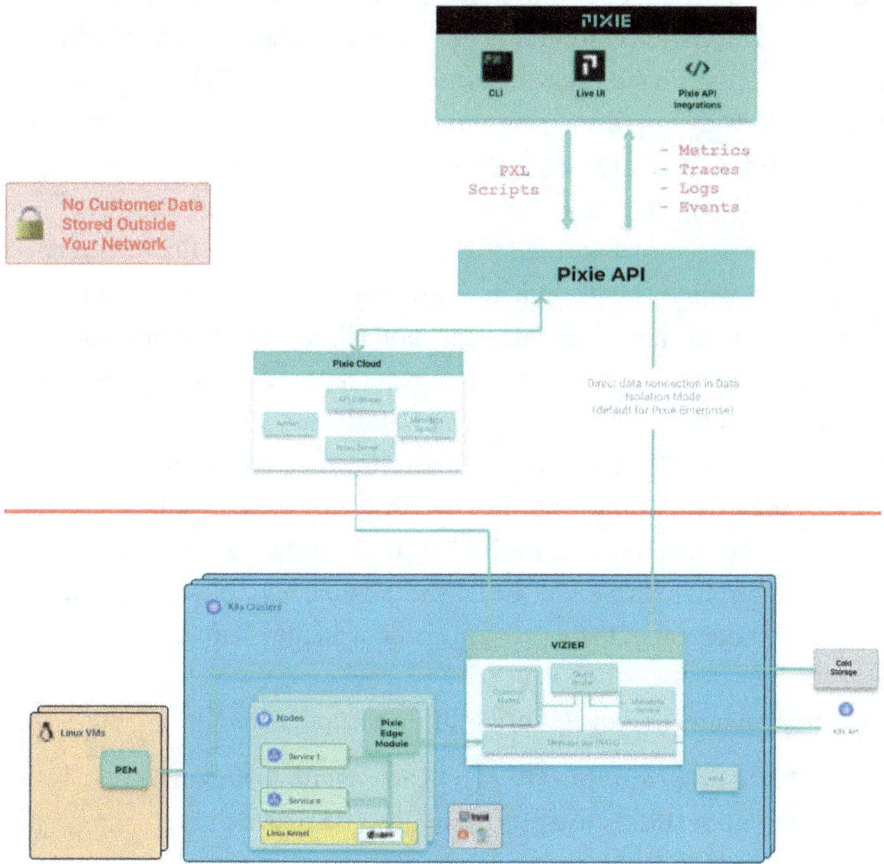

Figure 10-1. Architecture of PIXIE

The Mechanics of Pixie

Pixie is an open source auto-instrumentation observability tool designed specifically for Kubernetes applications. It was originally developed by the New Relic team and was donated to the Cloud-Native Computing Foundation (CNCF) and accepted as a sandbox project in June 2021. Pixie has a healthy development trend and userbase. You can effortlessly monitor the high-level state of their clusters, including service maps, cluster resources, and application traffic. Additionally, Pixie provides the capability to dive deeper into more detailed views such as pod states, flame graphs, and individual full-body application requests. By auto-instrumentation features, it gathers a wide array of telemetry data, including full-body requests, resource and network metrics, application profiles, and almost all of M3PLT. When configured properly, Pixie consumes less than 5% of the cluster's CPU, often using less than 2%.

Another interesting feature of Pixie is the scriptability. Pixie's query language, PxL, which is Pythonic in nature, can be utilized across Pixie's user interface, command-line interface, and client APIs. Furthermore, Pixie offers a collection of community scripts tailored for some use cases like Network Monitoring, Infrastructure Health, Service Performance, Database Query Profiling, Request Tracing, Continuous Application Profiling, and Kafka Monitoring. You can find very easy-to-follow hands-on experience tutorials for each of these use cases, written for someone unfamiliar with Pixie, and it should take less than five minutes each after installation of Pixie (`https://docs.px.dev/tutorials/pixie-101/`).

The Pixie platform consists of multiple components:

> **Pixie Edge Module (PEM):** Pixie's agent, installed per node. PEMs use eBPF to collect data, which is stored locally on the node.

Vizier: Pixie's collector, installed per cluster. Responsible for query execution and managing PEMs.

Pixie Cloud: Used for user management, authentication, and data proxying. Can be hosted or self-hosted.

Pixie CLI: Used to deploy Pixie. Can also be used to run queries and manage resources like API keys.

Pixie Client API: Used for programmatic access to Pixie (e.g., integrations, Slackbots, and custom user logic requiring Pixie data as an input).

PxL Language

Pixie Language (PxL) is a domain-specific language designed for handling machine data, utilizing a Python-based syntax. Drawing significant inspiration from the popular data processing library Pandas, PxL functions almost as a subset of it. The Pixie platform employs PxL to enable developers to construct high-performance data processing pipelines for monitoring, securing, and managing their applications and infrastructure.

As a declarative language, PxL allows programs to specify the desired outcomes, with the PxL engine performing evaluations by invoking functions with side effects (such as "px.display"). In PxL, all value types are immutable, meaning each assignment creates an implicit copy - rest assured, these are automatically optimized by our engine.

The fundamental unit of operation in PxL is the Dataframe, essentially a table of data accompanied by metadata operations. Operations performed on a Dataframe yield new Dataframes. Essentially, PxL delineates a sequence of data flows required to transform a set of Dataframes into the desired final output.

Similar to Python, PxL is implicitly and strongly typed, supporting high-level data types and functions. However, unlike Python, PxL is a data flow language that allows the Pixie platform to significantly optimize execution performance while preserving expressiveness in data processing. PxL programs are typically short-lived with no implicit side effects; hence, it does not support classes, exceptions, or other typical Python features.

PxL can be executed within the Pixie platform via a web-based UI, API, or CLI. It boasts a rich type system encompassing both concrete and semantic types. Semantic types serve several purposes:

- The query planner utilizes types to determine which PEM agents to retrieve data from.
- The UI leverages types to visualize data appropriately, such as displaying data of the ST_BYTES semantic type with corresponding labels (KB, MB, etc.).
- The Pixie execution engine supports a variety of semantic data types, including those related to
    - Kubernetes (e.g., pod name, node name, namespace name, pod status)
    - Infrastructure (e.g., IP address, port name, UPID)
    - Metrics (e.g., bytes, duration in nanoseconds, throughput per nanosecond)

A comprehensive list of semantic data types can be found in the Pixie GitHub repository.

The Pixie API serves as a handy tool for alerting integrations. For instance, it enables the creation of a Slackbot to monitor your Kubernetes cluster, leveraging data from Pixie's observability platform to provide real-time updates directly to Slack. With Pixie, even a basic Slackbot can furnish insights like the number of HTTP errors per service within your cluster, utilizing the wealth of data available through Pixie's capabilities.

Moreover, Pixie offers a versatile plug-in library, empowering users to enhance their data visualization and analysis. For instance, you can leverage data source plug-ins to seamlessly integrate Pixie data into platforms like Grafana. Additionally, Pixie's compatibility extends to OpenTelemetry, enabling the expansion of monitoring capabilities. By exporting Pixie data in the OpenTelemetry (OTel) format, users can employ an OTel collector deployed within their cluster to facilitate the transformation of Pixie DataFrames into OTel data. This process can be streamlined by either scripting PxL commands utilizing OTel methods or utilizing Pixie's API, complemented by the setup of the Pixie Plugin System to execute PxL scripts at predefined intervals.

But how do you get started? Fear not, the Pixie team has curated user-friendly tutorials and videos to guide you through the onboarding process effortlessly. Dive in, explore, and enjoy the journey of unlocking the full potential of Pixie's capabilities.

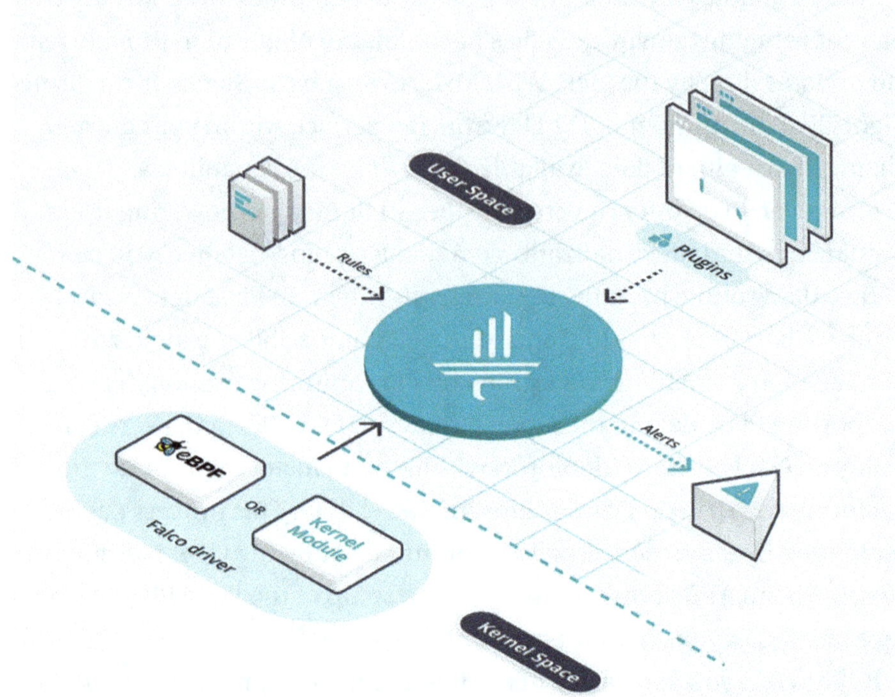

Figure 10-2. *Pixie API Architecture*

The Mechanics of Falco

Falco is a kernel monitoring and detection agent that observes events, such as syscalls, based on custom rules. It was originally developed by the Sysdig team and was donated to the Cloud-Native Computing Foundation (CNCF) as a sandbox project in October 2018 and graduated in February 2024. It is designed to detect and alert on abnormal behavior and potential security threats in real time. It can enhance these events by integrating metadata from the container runtime and Kubernetes. The collected events can be analyzed off-host in SIEM or observability platforms.

As we explore the use of Cilium Tetragon, it becomes clear that runtime security is not a replacement for any part of a multilayer defense system. Instead, it is a crucial operational component in CNA 1.0 security, enhancing the architecture and service observability.

Runtime security's effectiveness lies in its integration within the system and application resources. The closer we secure to the source, the better we can enforce security measures. This proximity allows us to scope and monitor the workloads within your workspace and their execution. Beyond filtering network traffic, we can act upon the comprehensive information available about a connection. We can detect and respond to suspicious software and unexpected file system changes. Moreover, we can identify and mitigate unauthorized privilege gains and unwanted binary executions. Runtime security, thus, provides a wide array of proactive measures.

Falco, a powerful runtime security tool, exemplifies these capabilities. It can detect when a file or directory is opened for read-write access, privilege escalation through privileged containers, and system binary drifts. Essentially, runtime security identifies threats, misbehaviors, and outages during runtime and takes appropriate actions.

Falco works by analyzing the current system behavior, comparing each activity against a predefined list of threat conditions, and triggering an alert if a match is found. Three core components define Falco's functionality: **events** introduced by Linux kernel intersections, a robust **rules engine** that processes the event stream, and an **alert** system that activates when a rule is violated.

Falco is composed of several main components:

Userspace Program: It is the CLI tool that you can use to interact with Falco. The userspace program handles signals, parses information from a Falco driver, and sends alerts.

Configuration: It defines how Falco is run, what rules to assert, and how to perform alerts.

Driver: It is a software that adheres to the Falco driver specification and sends a stream of kernel events. Currently, Falco supports the following drivers:

- (Default) Kernel module
- Modern eBPF Probe (CO-RE paradigm and more)
- Legacy eBPF probe built

Falco ingests events from various sources, including system calls, Kubernetes Audit Events, and Cloud Activity Logs. Using Falco plug-ins, it can also ingest events from AWS CloudTrail, for instance. For ingesting syscall events, different drivers are available.

It may not surprise you that I recommend the "Modern eBPF Probe," which utilizes the CO-RE (Compile Once, Run Everywhere) paradigm. This approach allows eBPF programs to be compiled once and run across different kernel versions. Below is a table summarizing the key characteristics and advantages of this driver:

Aspect	Details
Performance	High performance due to efficient execution within the kernel
Portability	Portable across different kernel versions, thanks to the CO-RE paradigm
Security	Safer due to the sandboxing environment provided by eBPF, reducing risks associated with system crashes and security vulnerabilities
Flexibility	Highly flexible, allowing for dynamic loading and unloading of eBPF programs without requiring a reboot or recompilation for different kernels
Development	Increasingly accessible development tools, such as libbpf, make it easier to develop and maintain eBPF programs

In short, the Modern eBPF Probe with CO-RE provides a robust, high-performance, and secure solution for syscall event ingestion, with the added benefit of portability and ease of development.

Plug-ins allow to extend the functionality of Falco by adding new event sources and new fields that can extract information from events. These plug-ins are shared libraries that adhere to a documented API, integrating seamlessly with Falco's core functionalities. They enable a variety of advanced features, including

Introducing New Event Sources: Plug-ins can add new event sources, allowing these events to be evaluated using filtering expressions and Falco rules.

Defining New Fields: Plug-ins can define new fields to extract specific information from events, enhancing the granularity and precision of event analysis.

Parsing Event Content: Plug-ins can parse the content of all events captured in a data stream, facilitating detailed and comprehensive analysis.

Injecting Events Asynchronously: Plug-ins can inject events asynchronously into a given data stream, ensuring that all relevant events are captured and processed in real time.

Falcoctl allows to easily install rules and plug-ins and perform administrative tasks with Falco. It is bundled together with Falco.

Falco Control (Falcoctl)

Working with Falcoctl (Falco Control) involves using a set of commands to manage Falco configurations, rules, plug-ins and deployments. Falcoctl simplifies the process of managing Falco instances and ensures you can efficiently interact with the runtime security tool. Here are some useful commands and a brief overview of how to use Falcoctl:

Task	Bash command	Description
Configuration	falcoctl config show	Displays the current Falco configuration
Set Configuration	falcoctl config set <key>=<value>	Sets a specific configuration key to the given value
Version Information	falcoctl version	Displays the version of Falcoctl and the Falco engine
List Rules	falcoctl rules list	Lists all the rules currently available in Falco
List Plug-ins	falcoctl plugins list	Lists all the plug-ins currently available
Show Logs	falcoctl logs	Displays the logs for the Falco instance
Observe Falco	falcoctl status	Checks the status of the Falco instance
Metrics	falcoctl metrics	Displays metrics related to the Falco instance performance
Run Diagnostics	falcoctl diagnose	Runs diagnostic checks on the Falco setup to ensure everything is functioning correctly
Backup Configuration	falcoctl backup -f <backup-file>	Creates a backup of the current Falco configuration
Restore Configuration	falcoctl restore -f <backup-file>	Restores the Falco configuration from a backup file

Automating repetitive tasks, such as rule updates and backups, can significantly streamline your workflow. Additionally, keeping your rules and plug-ins regularly updated ensures optimal security coverage. To maintain Falco's performance, it's important to consistently monitor logs and metrics, ensuring the system operates efficiently without negatively impacting performance.

Falco uses syscalls natively by eBPF from the kernel space at runtime and asserting the stream against a powerful rules engine and alerting when a rule is violated. Falco's observability capabilities are not limited to syscalls as it can be extended via plug-ins to ingest data from many more types of sources.

Falco ships with a default set of rules that check the kernel for unusual behavior such as privilege escalation using privileged containers; namespace changes using tools like setns; read/writes to well-known directories such as /etc, /usr/bin, /usr/sbin, etc.; creating symlinks; ownership and mode changes; unexpected network connections or socket mutations; spawned processes using execve; executing shell binaries such as sh, bash, csh, zsh, etc.; executing SSH binaries such as ssh, scp, sftp, etc.; mutating Linux coreutils executables; mutating login binaries; mutating shadowutil or passwd executables such as shadowconfig, pwck, chpasswd, getpasswd, change, useradd, etc.; and others.

Rules are the conditions under which an alert should be generated. A rule is accompanied by a descriptive output string sent with the alert. They are defined using YAML files and loaded by the Falco configuration file. For more information about writing, managing, and deploying rules, see Falco rules.

Alerts are configurable downstream actions that can be as simple as logging to stdout or as complex as delivering a gRPC call to a client. For more information about configuring, understanding, and developing alerts, see Falco alerts. Falco can send alerts to standard output, a predefined file, a Syslog backend, a spawned program, an HTTP[s] endpoint, or a client through the gRPC API.

Apart from the Falco core projects, the Falco organization also maintains and distributes ecosystem projects that help adopters get the most out of Falco. To learn more, visit the Falco Evolution repositories list. For example, the falcosidekick project makes it easier to output Falco events to many applications and channels; Falcoctl makes it easier to perform a number of administrative tasks for Falco, including installing and updating rules and plug-ins; and the falco-exporter tool is used to integrate Falco with Prometheus.

Summary

The Cilium stack is a standout in cloud-native networking, security, and observability. However, it's far from being the only mature eBPF-based solution on the market. There are strong competitors in each segment of Cilium's offerings. If, for any reason, we prefer to use another tool, the eBPF landscape offers over a hundred open source and commercial options.

The diversity of eBPF-based tools ensures that there are ample options to meet various needs and preferences. Additionally, the opportunity to participate in the Cilium developer's community, as well as other modern cloud-native open source observability products communities, means that building a new solution from scratch is often unnecessary. Leveraging these existing tools and communities allows us to benefit from collective expertise and innovation.

Among these alternatives, we introduced Pixie, an auto-instrumentation telemetry data provider, and Falco, a runtime security tool. Both Pixie and Falco integrate seamlessly with many other excellent toolsets, which we have discussed throughout this book.

Index

Dr. M. Ghane, *Observability Engineering with Cilium*,
https://doi.org/10.1007/979-8-8688-1258-3

D

E

F

I

J

K

L

M

N

P

Q

R

S

GPSR Compliance
The European Union's (EU) General Product Safety Regulation (GPSR) is a set of rules that requires consumer products to be safe and our obligations to ensure this.

If you have any concerns about our products, you can contact us on

ProductSafety@springernature.com

In case Publisher is established outside the EU, the EU authorized representative is:

Springer Nature Customer Service Center GmbH
Europaplatz 3
69115 Heidelberg, Germany

www.ingramcontent.com/pod-product-compliance
Lightning Source LLC
LaVergne TN
LVHW010336260326
834688LV00036B/730
9798868812576